My Traumatic Survival

Survival

I Am Okay!

My Traumatic Survival

I Am Okay!

SONIA DOMARASKY

CITI OF
BOOKS

CITIOFBOOKS, INC.
3736 Eubank NE Suite A1
Albuquerque, NM 87111-3579
www.citiofbooks.com
Hotline: 1 (877) 389-2759
Fax: 1 (505) 930-7244

Ordering Information:
Quantity sales. Special discounts are available on quantity purchases by corporations, associations, and others. For details, contact the publisher at the address above.

Printed in the United States of America.

ISBN-13:	Softcover	979-8-89391-256-2
	eBook	979-8-89391-257-9

Library of Congress Control Number: 2024916989

DEDICATION

Of all my accomplishments, my three wonderful, loving, kind, and intelligent children are my greatest. I dedicate this book as my legacy for them.

I want to thank them for their patience, understanding, and loving support as I worked through many hardships. In addition, I wrote my autobiography as a tribute to my loving mother, Soon Nam Lee, whom God so blessed me with, who sacrificed her life for me. Without whom, I wouldn't have survived.

ABOUT THE AUTHOR

I am a single mother of three exceptional adult children. I have two sons and one daughter. I also have two beautiful grandchildren. From the moment I became a mother and grandmother, I have always devoted my life to loving and providing happiness for my children.

I am a very family-oriented person that loves family traditions. I enjoy cooking, baking, gardening, working on my home, long walks, day trips, listening to music, going to festivals, vacations, and shopping.

I love to travel and have done so both domestically and internationally since I was a small child. I have lived in Maryland since very early childhood and as an adult.

I raised my children in Maryland. I have always been the type of person who likes to challenge myself and my body. I have gained and lost weight many times over the years.

I enjoy working out and trying to stay fit and healthy. I have completed a Marathon, half marathon, several 5K's, the Tough Mudder™, and Muddy Princess challenges. My mother was my rock, my role model, and my hero. She is why I am alive, and my strength comes from her.

When she passed away and my marriage ended several years back, I found myself lost. I had been a victim of circumstances from the moment I was born. Much of that continued through adulthood.

However, through my own resiliency, faith and determination, I choose not to think of myself as a victim but rather a fighter and survivor.

When my children were growing up and moving on with their own lives, I decided in 2018, that I needed a change of scenery. So, I moved to the Smoky Mountains in East Tennessee. It was time that I needed to dedicate a period of healing for myself.

It was what I needed to recover from the thought of being a victim to realizing that I am a survivor and that I am okay.

PREFACE

Each person experiences some type of trauma, and although ours may not be the same type or to the same degree, how they affect us and how we choose to handle it will define who we are and who we become.

Traumatic experiences will try to mold you into a fearful, angry, or bitter shell of yourself, but the shape it leaves you in is up to you.

My story will enlighten you on the traumatic experiences that I have lived through and how I coped with each of them. How I became tired of being a victim and feeling like a child afraid to speak up to a strong independent woman who can take on the world. How forgiving has set me free. Then I learned to reshape the shell and became a happy, healthy individual.

TABLE OF CONTENTS

PROLOGUE

A USUAL DAY IN LIFE

"*C*ome out here, both of you! Right this instant!*" My father's thunder-like voice bellowed from down the street and around Aunt Mary's pitch-black living room.

I peeked out the window, then closed my eyes and snuggled deeper into my mother's embrace. Her scent always had a calming effect on me, but even that wasn't helping this time.

I trembled, envisioning my heartless and mentally unstable father standing stark naked in the middle of the street with a loaded shotgun in his hand. This time, it felt like he was finally going to end it all. I trembled with fear, thinking how this summer night of 1972 was going to be our last.

Being just a five-year-old child, it was my time of playful laughter and silly pranks, with nothing to worry about. Carefree and careless should be the lifestyle of every child, but that wasn't the case for me. Today, too, had started as all the other days in our lives. It began as a regular day, yet we didn't know what catastrophe lay ahead.

The calamity always started with my father losing his mind on the most minor facts.

I don't remember what it was exactly, as always, as no one could ever pinpoint the root of his anger. One minute, everything would be fine,

1

and the next, our house would be a concoction of bad words and roaring anger. He would go blind with rage and throw whatever he could find lying around at mommy.

Only that day, it didn't stop, which was a sign that something was about to go seriously wrong. It wasn't until my father ran off to get his shotgun that my mother realized that if we didn't get out of the apartment right then, irreversible damage would occur.

I remember my mother picking me up in her arms and limping down each step from the second-story apartment we resided in. Once we got down to the street, mom put me down and held my hand tightly as we walked as fast as we could with mom's bad leg to get away from my father. We rushed down the street to Aunt Mary, our savior's home, our safe sanctuary.

Her trembling arms tightened around me as she frantically knocked on the door, waiting to be let in.

"*Open up!*" Mommy had almost cried.

The door had opened immediately, and Mary had sighed and hugged my mother, squishing me between them.

"*He is at it again. He is going to kill us!*" I heard mommy whisper.

"*Go hide.*" Mary had ordered us.

Mommy, with me by her side, frantically limped around the house, switching off all lights, surrounding us in pitch darkness.

"*They are not here! Go away!*" I had heard Aunt Mary yell from her window each time my father yelled for us to come out as mother moved the couch, and we hid behind it.

My eyes blurred as I let out quiet sniffles.

I would have sobbed if not for my mother's warning to keep quiet, after which I did my best to stifle any sounds.

"Kim! Sonia! Come down here!" Another boom from my father brought me back to the present.

"He is not going to leave, Kim. We need to call the cops." Aunt Mary whispered.

My mother's breath hitched slightly, but she didn't stop Mary as she ducked down below the window and crawled across the room reached for her phone resting on the lamp table beside the couch to call Frederick City Police. They assured her that the police had already been dispatched from the multiple calls made to 911 and were on their way.

My heart raced as my mother rocked me back and forth. I wanted to feel safe but couldn't for the life of me.

It seemed like forever, but then we heard the telltale signals of a police vehicle approaching. I moved my head away from the crook of my mother's neck to see red and blue flashing lights lighting up the dark living room.

Then, we heard the police yelling at my father to put the gun down. Anxious to see how things were rolling out onto the street, my mother, with me still clinging to her, got up from her position on the floor and, together with Mary, inched towards the living room window.

Looking down, my eyes met with my father's vengeful and malicious ones as he stood there naked with handcuffs on, and I immediately hid my face in the crook of Mother's neck, inhaling her sweet scent. Finally, we were able to breathe a sigh of relief, even if it was only temporary.

The Frederick City police knew my father as well as they did my mother and me from the numerous calls.

After the police car pulled off with him in it, another officer came to the door of Mary's apartment to ask if we were okay and took our statements. I closed my eyes and leaned against my mother's shoulder as the commotion occurred. Mary could have told us to leave and not get involved, but she was a good woman.

She did not have much, but she had a heart of gold. She was single and worked as a waitress in a downtown restaurant that her landlord owned. She lived a simple life but would do anything to help you. Mary was also suffering from the beginning stages of Parkinson's Disease. Time passed in a blur after that. I don't remember much until my mother picked me up and told me it was time to go home.

The police officer was kind enough to escort my mother and me back to our apartment, just four blocks down the street, and ensured we got inside safely. I still felt scared but tried putting on a brave face for mom.

After all, I was her brave girl. Mommy was always there for me, no matter what, and I also had to be there for her.

"Are you going to be okay?" The officer asked once my mother opened the door and stepped inside.

"Hope so." She answered and smiled at him. He smiled back and ruffled my hair.

"I'm going to send a patrol officer to check up on you guys every now and then." He assured me, and my mother nodded.

We talked to the officer about how much safer and better our lives would be if anyone could permanently put my father in jail or hospital for help.

He was in and out of jail and mental institutes for brief periods, but each time he was released, he became angrier and took out all his anger and frustration on both of us physically.

"Why don't you contact the Military or an attorney?" The officer suggested.

"I have tried that too. Anyway, thank you for your help today." My mother sighed and locked the door.

My mother had tried multiple times to have my father put in jail or put away for mental issues.

I am not sure why the process took so long or why he was constantly allowed to hurt us, but all I knew was that right now, with him not around, I felt safe.

He was in the US Army. According to my mother, it was the reason the Army and the Police weren't taking his actions against us seriously.

Mom and I knew we had to protect each other from my father. We were all we had, just the two of us, alone, fearful and yet fighting to live.

Our apartment was also on the second floor and above a dry cleaner business. To get to our apartment on the second floor, we had to go through the main door on the street level and walk a long dark hallway that ended with a set of wooden stairs going to the second and third floors. Our apartment had two doors.

The main door opened up to a hallway with the bathroom immediately on the left as you walked in and the living room at the end of the hallway.

Between the bathroom and living room was my mother's bedroom, which went around into a closet and then directly into my bedroom.

Directly across from my bedroom was the second door to our apartment, which led to the dining room, kitchen, and large walk-in kitchen pantry.

The kitchen had a door which led to the balcony. Both entry doors of our apartment had a brownish-orange thick frosted glass that went from the middle of the door to the top.

Oftentimes, I could see the outline and shadows of the people coming and going from the apartment above us. Once we were back in the apartment, we sat down on our worn-out couch.

"When will this all stop?" I looked up at my mother. "Why does he want to hurt us? Why can't he just go away and just leave us alone?"

"There is never a day that goes by that I don't try to make him stop, get him help, or do whatever it takes to protect you and me." My mother answered in a broken voice.

"Why can't we just go away then?" I cried.

"We have no place to go." She hugged me tightly.

"Why can't we go to Korea? That's far away, isn't it?"

I sobbed. "And what about my brother? Maybe he can help us, right?"

My mother stroked my hair, "My dear Sonia, we cannot go to Korea. I will do everything in my power to protect you. And why do you say you have a brother? You know you are an only child."

She wiped my tears and walked to the kitchen to get me an apple. My mother was great at hiding her tears and sadness, but I could tell she was sad. Unlike any other mother and daughter, my mother and I had such an incredibly strong bond. From when I was born until I was six years old, my mother and I were constantly saving each other's lives.

"It's all going to be alright." She assured me as she gave me the apple and successfully diverted my mind from the horrors we went through today.

Chapter One

Mixed Race

Iran, also called the misnomer Persia, and officially the Islamic Republic of Iran, is a country in West Asia. It borders to the west with Iraq and Turkey, to the northwest with Azerbaijan and Armenia, and with the Caspian Sea and Turkmenistan in the north.

Through Afghanistan and Pakistan, it borders in the east and through the Persian Gulf and the Gulf of Oman to the south.

It covers an area of 1,648,195 km², which makes it the fourth largest country in all of Asia and the second largest country in western Asia behind Saudi Arabia. Iran has eighty-five million inhabitants, making it the seventeenth most populous country in the world.

The historical and cultural usage of the word Iran is not limited to the actual modern state. "Greater Iran" refers to the areas of the Iranian cultural and language zones. In addition to modern Iran, it includes parts of the Caucasus, Anatolia, Mesopotamia, Afghanistan, and Central Asia.

Iran is a region and central power with a geopolitically strategic location on the Asiatic continent. Of the United Nations, ECO, OIC, and OPEC, it is a founding member. It has large reserves of fossil fuels, including the second-largest natural gas reserves and the fourth-largest proven oil reserves

Historically, Iran is a multi-ethnic country. Iran remains a pluralistic society made up of numerous ethnic, linguistic, and religious groups, the largest of them being Persians, Azeris, Kurds, Mazandaranis, and Lurs.

This country is now home to one of the oldest civilizations in the world, beginning with the founding of the Elamite kingdoms in the fourth millennium BC. It was mentioned first in the 7th century BC. United by the Medes and ancient Iranian people, it reached its territorial peak in the 6th century BC.

When Cyrus the Great founded the Persian Achaemenid Empire, this empire then grew to become one of the greatest empires in history and was described as the world's first influential superpower. The Achaemenid Empire fell before Alexander the Great in the 4th century BC and was later divided into several Hellenistic states.

Then, an Iranian uprising started in the 3rd century BC, and a significant war for power continued for the next four centuries.

Arab Muslims conquered the empire in the 7th century AD, leading to the Islamization of Iran. It subsequently became an important center of Islamic culture and learning, with its art, literature, philosophy, and architecture spreading throughout the Muslim world and beyond during the Islamic Golden Age. A number of native Iranian Muslim dynasties emerged over the next two centuries before the Seljuks and Mongols conquered the region. In the 15th century, the native Safavids restored a unified Iranian state and national identity and converted the country to Shia Islam.

Under the rule of Nader Shah in the 18th century, Iran once again converted into a significant world power. Although in the 19th century, a series of conflicts with the Russian Empire resulted in significant territorial losses. Then, the Persian constitutional revolution took place at the start of the 20th century. Efforts to nationalize their supply of fossil fuels from Western companies led to an Anglo-American coup in 1953, which led to further autocratic rule under Mohammad Reza Pahlavi and growing western political influence. He then initiated a series of far-reaching reforms in 1963.

After the Iranian Revolution in 1979, the current Islamic Republic was founded by Ruhollah Khomeini, who became the country's first supreme leader.

The Iranian government is an Islamic theocracy incorporating elements of presidential democracy, with the ultimate authority vested in an autocratic "Supreme Leader." It was a position held by Ali Khamenei

9

since Khomeini's death in 1989. The Iranian government is widely regarded as authoritarian. It has been widely criticized for its widespread restrictions and abuses of human rights and civil liberties, including various violent repressions of mass protests, unfair elections, and restricted rights for women and children.

It is also a flash point for Shia Islam in the Middle East, counteracting longstanding Arab and Sunni hegemony in the region. Since the Iranian revolution, the country has been widely regarded as the greatest enemy of both Israel and Saudi Arabia.

Iran is also considered a significant player in Middle Eastern affairs, and its government is directly and indirectly involved in most modern Middle Eastern conflicts.

But enough about all this. Let's go on with what this book is actually about. *Me.*

Now, being born to a Korean mother, Soon Nam Hutchinson, and an American father, Breeden George Hutchinson, I was a mixed-race baby. I was born in 1967 in Iran. Daddy was a soldier in the American army, and when I was born, he was already stationed in Iran. But just a few months after I was born, my small family moved back to America.

During the move, they faced resistance from the Iranian government. My parents were targeted and literally had to move heaven and hell to get out of there. But that, I will narrate later in the story. As daddy was in the army, so all through their married life, my parents had to move from place to place, being stationed in Korea, Germany, and Iran, and now back in the USA.

My mother was a Korean woman. She was just under five feet, relatively thin, and weighed around 115 lbs. But that was until she was in her late fifties. As time passed, she did put on weight and became about 135-140 lbs. She had short black hair and the softest skin. I remember snuggling closer to her as I loved the warmth she radiated and the feeling of safety her embrace bestowed me with. Her complexion was beautiful and flawless, and like all other Asian women, she, too, aged quite well. She always looked much younger than her age.

In contrast to mommy, Daddy was about 6'2. He was skinny and had long, lanky arms. He always had a buzz cut for his hair. I remember his face having scars on it, the typical side effect of severe acne, like pop marks from popping, squeezing, or picking at acne, maybe in his earlier years. His nose was crooked because it had been broken several times.

As my mother describes, when my parents first met, daddy was a very kind, generous, and respectful man. Always wanting to please my mother, he spoiled her with expensive flowers, clothes, jewelry, furniture, etc.

But from what I actually remember, he was a man who was always mean, angry, and hurtful. A man who was calm one minute and within seconds became a crazy man you didn't know. He would get so mad that, in seconds, he would fly off the handle. He would trick you with lies and deception. He would tell you one thing but do the opposite. For me, he was the true definition of a lying and manipulative man.

My parents met each other when daddy was stationed in Korea. My mother worked at the E-Club on the military base and used to serve food and drinks to the soldiers. At that time, she was dating a Korean guy, and they planned to marry. His name was Mr. Kim, so all her friends nicknamed her Kimmy.

But one day, mommy heard a rumor that Mr. Kim had cheated on her, so she called off the wedding. She fought through that depressing period like the warrior that she was and made it her life's mission to work hard and make money to help her family.

Her father had passed away when she was only nine years old, and as the oldest child in the family, she had to step up, help raise her siblings and bring home additional income. Her mother, brother, and sisters all depended on her.

She graduated from high school, and she had many friends. She worked on the Military base almost every day. Then, one day, this tall, thin, American man walked in and sat down in the diner. He ordered some food, and they engaged in small talk. She did not speak much English, but they managed to understand each other between her broken English and his broken Korean.

He continued to come into the E-Club any chance he got just to see her. He called her by her nickname "Kimmy." They then also started spending time together outside of the E-Club, and soon, he asked her to marry him.

She knew that meant leaving Korea to be his wife and traveling to any location where he would be stationed at.

My mother's family was not happy about the marriage. They wanted her to stay in Korea. As the eldest child of the family, she was expected to stay with her family. They all warned her that she was making a huge mistake.

However, my mother took a chance at love and married my father in 1959 in a small ceremony on a US military base in South Korea. They left Korea as husband and wife and traveled to his next station in Germany. There, they stayed for about three years, from 1960-1963. After that, daddy got stationed in the US for one year. My mother took a job at the Frederick Memorial Hospital in the nursery section of the maternity ward. She absolutely loved and adored children and wanted some of her own too.

My mother told me that in the beginning, when she and daddy met, it was great. They were smitten with each other. He was kind, caring, generous, and so sweet to her. He bought her a beautiful home in Frederick County, Maryland, with the nicest furniture, custom-made curtains, professional landscaping, the newest appliances, and even a new Jeep. After they got married, things were still good for about the first seven years, but then, she started noticing a change in him. She witnessed aggression, anger, split personality, psychotic episodes, etc.

Then in 1964, they were then sent to Iran for three years, and that was where my mother's dreams came true. She and daddy had been trying to have a baby forever but were unsuccessful. She even went through miscarriages, which shattered her.

Then, at the age of thirty-two, while in Iran, she finally got the daughter she always wanted, a.k.a. me. She named me *Sonia*.

In Korean, the pronunciation of my name means *Angel*. She said she was blessed with an Angel. This came at the perfect time, just months before daddy's tour would end in Iran so they could go back to the states to raise me.

My mother always made it a point to speak Korean when we were at home. One of the most memorable songs I remember my mother singing to me as a child was a Doris Day song called "Que Sera Sera." Sometimes she sang it in Korean and other times in English. The piece emphasized, "whatever will be, will be." It is about a little girl asking her mother what she will be when she grows up, and my mother always believed as well, "whatever will be, will be." Looking back now as an adult, I understand what she meant.

She wanted me to learn as much of the language as I could. She would ask me in Korean to go get something from the kitchen, or what time it was, what I was doing, etc., so I would learn and comprehend the language. She taught me to count in Korean and made me learn the alphabet.

I was always eager to learn the language because, as a child, I thought it was pretty cool to be able to listen to the conversations my mother had in Korean with her other friends and actually be able to understand what she was saying.

She would teach me the Korean language, and I would teach her the English language. My mother took English-speaking classes when she came to the US to help her obtain a job, but I enjoyed helping her learn.

It helped me connect. But her English was broken for many years. She did get much better as time went on. She had a cute accent when she spoke English that I just adored, and her pronunciation of certain words would make me giggle, putting a smile on my face.

Sometimes, we would encounter rude people who were racists and wanted to make nasty comments about her pronunciation of words and the fact that she was Asian. But that was in the 70's and 80's and there were very few Koreans living in our area so the negativity and hate was more prevalent then.

It would make me so angry. I would always jump in front of my mother and yell what she said in their face and ask them, *"Can you understand now?" Mom would always pull me back towards her and tell me to stop worrying about what other people say. It doesn't matter what other people think or say. Just let it go.*

But it did matter to me. I hated seeing anyone say or do hurtful things to my mother. Without even knowing it, I became my mother's protector at a very early age.

As my mother was Korean, she followed all the Korean cultures. We would celebrate all the Korean holidays and festivals. I was raised with all the traditional Korean customs. We always took our shoes off when we entered our or anyone's home. I always had to bow to my elders, I always called my mother's friend's aunt or uncle in Korean, I never spoke out of turn, and I had my own Korean traditional dress called the HANBOK, which I actually wore for my senior prom.

I had to respect the fact that children never spoke out of turn, that education was a priority, and that it was not acceptable to come home with anything less than a B in any class on my report card. Speaking out of line, procrastination or being disrespectful to your parents was something that was never tolerated either.

My mother always said there was no reason to wait to do something that could be done now. Those are wise words that I live by today.

My mother used to cook us Korean specialties and always made the most delicious Korean foods. We rarely ever ate any American foods in our home unless we ordered a sub or chicken or something from a restaurant.

Every meal we had at home was Korean. It has been and always will be my favorite type of food.

The spices, the aroma of the food when it's cooking, the tastiness of the spices, and the spiciness of it were magnificent. The different types of meats were cooked to such tenderness that they would melt in your mouth.

The sticky rice was the main staple, along with Kimchi, at every meal, and to this day, they are still my comfort foods.

My mother and I would make homemade Kimchi together. I would watch her soak the Napa cabbage in salt water and then cut it to size.

Then we would begin seasoning the cabbage with red pepper flakes, spring onions, shredded carrots, garlic, anchovy sauce, MSG (Monosodium Glutamate), etc.

We would use our hands and mix all the ingredients until they were well blended. Then we would pack them in large glass jars and place them in the refrigerator.

Sometimes, we made five jars, and other times, around eight to ten jars. It took several days, and sometimes even more, before the fermentation set in, and then we couldn't wait to start eating it.

15

There were various types of Kimchi that we made. Some were made with Daikon radishes which were cut into cubes. Others were made with cucumbers, bean sprouts, garlic roots, mustard leaves, scallions, and more. Each one was a delicious side dish that complimented the sticky rice. Kimchi was the main staple side dish that traditionally comes with each and every meal. Fish cakes, seasoned squid, tofu, bean sprouts, pickled radishes and dried seaweed squares were many other side dishes that made the table a colorful array of healthy vegetables and spices.

The Korean culture never really had a lot of sugary sweets. They used fresh fruits for their dessert or as a treat for the children. One sweet treat that many Koreans make, and my mother did as well for me all the time, was to make a dough out of rice that was boiled down, and then when the sticky rice was boiled down into a pasty dough form, she would let it cool down and then flatten it out into small round cookie sized servings.

Then we would gently fry them in the pan until they became a little crispy, and finally, mom would sprinkle a little sugar on them, and we would eat them warm.

It was amazing! It melted in my mouth, and it was equivalent, if not better, than any ice cream cone my friends would eat.

One of the Korean specialties called MANDU (Korean Eggroll) was our mother & daughter's tradition using my mother's recipe. We would spend hours shredding the vegetables and mixing all the ingredients and then filling all the eggroll skins, and then deep frying each of them. The smell of the eggrolls would linger in the house for days.

We would just make them for a special occasion like Christmas or birthdays. When I was young, we would just sit at the table, and I would listen to mom talk and tell me stories while we made the eggrolls.

These were, by far, some of the best quality times we spent together. My mother always spoke about her siblings and her mother, and she would tell me stories about her life in Korea.

She was born in Pusan, South Korea. She would often smile as she told me stories of her as a teenager and how she would go to Haeundae Beach and jump in the water and swim all day. I could often see the twinkle or maybe tear in her eyes as she told me stories of her teenage years.

I knew she missed those days and her life in Korea. She would tell me about how strong my grandmother was to take care of her and her siblings all alone after her father died. She loved her mother so much, and I knew it broke her heart to be so far away from her mother. They often spoke on the phone, and most of the time, I did get to speak with my grandmother. Although my grandmother didn't speak any English, just knowing that we were trying to communicate on the phone was satisfying.

I did not share any bond with my father. He was a lying, manipulative, and hurtful man. He would always hurt and abuse me and tell me to keep my mouth shut, or he would hurt my mother.

But contrary to my father, the bond I had with my mother was absolutely incredible. There is nothing in this world I wouldn't have done for my mother. I would cut off my arm or take a bullet for my mother. She was my protector, my cheerleader, and my supporter. She gave me unconditional love, and she taught me to be the best version of myself.

She always looked at me as though I was the perfect child. Whenever I had a tummy ache, my mother would rub my stomach in a circular motion and sing a Korean song. It wasn't a famous song.

It was just a little chant that she would say that basically said, "*Tummy, tummy, do not hurt. Tummy, tummy, feel better, Pain, Pain go away so Sonia can get up and play*"

Somehow, whenever she rubbed my stomach and sang, my tummy felt better.

No matter how hard her life was, never once did she consider placing me in foster care or an orphanage to pack up and go back to her family in Korea. There was nothing that we didn't talk about or do together. We were literally joined at the hip.

Even after I married, we only lived about five blocks apart and saw each other daily. Grocery shopping, yard sales, festivals, picking strawberries, mall shopping, dinners out, black Friday shopping campouts, vacations, international traveling, you name it, and we did it together.

I would talk to her and ask her for her advice on so many things because I always trusted her advice, and of course, she was always right. She represented so many things to me.

She was my mother, father, brother, sister, aunt, uncle, grandparent, best friend—my *everything*.

My mother was an extraordinary woman, and even if given a chance, I would never have it any other way than to be her daughter.

CHAPTER TWO

A MENTALLY UNSTABLE FATHER

As I already mentioned, I did not share a special bond with my father, unlike my mother. And it was all because of his unstable and psychotic mind. After seven years of marriage, my mother started noticing a change in my father. Aggression, anger, split personality, psychotic episodes, etc.

After we moved back to the US from Iran because he was stationed at Fort Detrick, Maryland, he bought her a beautiful home in Frederick County, Maryland, I believe at the end of 1968 or early part of 1969, with the nicest furniture, custom made curtains, professional landscaping, newest appliances, a new Jeep and he even bought two horses so they could ride together. Daddy always loved riding horses. However, all those things could not hide the fact that he was suffering from some kind of mental illness.

Things only got worse after that. Daddy always had a deep passion for horses. He absolutely loved them. He rode them as a child and found comfort in them, but as time flew by, he even became mean to the horses we had, almost abusive. It was like he just lost interest in them too. One day, he took a terrible fall off one of the horses. He broke his nose and suffered a severe concussion and head trauma, which my mother and the military doctors believed exacerbated his mental illness.

Daddy was never really one to have a gun in the house according to mommy. But that seemed to have changed over time. One day, when I was about twenty months old, mommy and I were out all day visiting her Korean friends.

That day, when we returned home, daddy was sitting on the couch waiting for us with a shotgun in his hands. He pointed it at my mother and me when we walked in the door, with mommy holding me in her arms. Then, he started yelling at her, wanting to know where she had been all day and who she was seeing.

His mental state made him think that mommy was cheating on him. She tried to tell him that we only visited her friends, but he refused to believe it.

He kept yelling at her that she was sneaking around with her ex-fiancé, Mr. Kim, who, by the way, was still in Korea.

"You have gone completely crazy!" Mommy responded in her English-Korean accent.

Suddenly, he grabbed her arm while she was still holding me and shook her wildly. She held onto me tightly and sheltered me with her body.

Even I felt like the world had started spinning.

"I better not catch you two together, or I will kill you both." He seethed in her face.

He never believed in saying curse words in front of a woman. However, now he started using those words frequently at mommy.

Then there were days when he just wouldn't show up at the base, and his Staff Sergeant would question him, and he would become very agitated with his Sergeant. He forgot what days he had to report to the base and what time, and even his job duties.

Sometimes, mommy would often hear him talking to himself, and it would spook her. She said he was talking as though he was angry at someone or something and wanted to hurt them.

She said there were nights when he sat up all night long in bed and just stared at the wall.

He could be so mean and hateful one minute, and then the next minute, he was just as sweet and kind as he used to be.

My mother couldn't figure out what was going on and why he was acting like this. His unpredictability made mommy restless and on edge.

Finally, the army ordered him to have a psychiatric evaluation, and then they determined that he needed to be placed on medical leave and put into a mental illness facility for a month so the doctors could determine what was going on. He went reluctantly.

But even after he was released and sent back to work duty on the army base, he still wasn't the same. He was like Dr. Jekyll and Mr. Hyde. He could turn on the charm to make my mommy's friends think he was perfectly fine, and then he would become a monster behind closed doors.

Some days he was kind and sweet to my mommy, and he would call me *"daddy's little girl."* He would take me to the park or to the ice cream shop. He even took me out to the horses, set me on a horse, held me so proudly, and said, *"Sonia, you are riding the horse."*

I didn't realize it then, but that was when the molestation started too. He would touch me in places that made me uncomfortable.

I knew mommy didn't touch me there, so I didn't know why my daddy did. I was too young to understand and never said anything about it.

Overtime, he became more and more erratic and abusive. He would yell a lot, and his appearance went from clean-cut to disheveled. He was often confused and agitated, and sometimes forgetful. He would take his anger and frustration out on my mother constantly.

With the constant uncertainty of his mental state, my mother was pulling away, and he could tell. Finally, my mother decided that she just couldn't take it anymore. It wasn't safe for either of us.

She asked her friend Mary, who worked with her at the sewing factory in Frederick, MD, if we could possibly stay at her apartment for a few weeks so mommy could figure out what to do, and Mary agreed. Not knowing the laws or government policies in the United States and having broken English my mommy was in need of help to figure out how to get us away from my daddy.

So, one day, when my father was out, mommy packed up some of our clothes, personal items, jewelry, and a very special necklace of the Virgin Mary. That necklace was mine, something that my mommy said I could never loose and had to hold on to it forever. Then we got in the Jeep and went to Mary's apartment. My father was infuriated when he got home. He looked everywhere for us.

He walked up and down the street in the neighborhood where our house was, just firing from his shotgun in the air and yelling, *"Kimmy, I will get you! You will not get away with this!"*

We knew this because the neighbors called the police, and he was arrested. But eventually, the military got him out and had him re-institutionalized for further evaluation.

Over the course of the next eighteen months, he was in and out of the mental health institution. Each time he was released back to the military for light duty, he would do okay for a brief period of time.

But it seemed that something always caused him to do crazy things and become deranged and abusive. He was uncontrollable.

Finally, the army came to the conclusion that due to multiple brain injuries, one that may have occurred prior to enlisting and one during his service, along with the fall he took from his horse, he was no longer capable of serving and continuing his responsibilities for the US Army and, therefore, discharged him.

This made my father extremely angry. He was hurt because he felt that the country he so loved and wanted to serve and defend had abandoned him.

Just like he felt my mommy and I did.

Mommy and I stayed with her friend Mary and also with some of her Korean friends over the course of time.

I think she just wanted us to move around with different people so daddy wouldn't be able to find us easily.

Then, mommy was referred to an attorney by some of her co-workers at the factory to discuss divorcing my daddy.

The attorney suggested that my mother get a small apartment to rent so she could show the judge and the court that she could provide a stable home for me.

Mary introduced mommy to Ms. Nellie Hurst, who was her landlord and owned several apartment buildings as well as restaurants in downtown Frederick, Maryland, and Hagerstown, Maryland.

We moved in with barely anything. Ms. Hurst, or Nellie, as everyone called her, was kind enough to give mommy and me a used couch in good condition, a bed, and some dishes and cookware to use. It was a blessing that my mother met Ms. Hurst. She helped my mother in many ways. She gave us an apartment to live in after my mother left my father, she helped us with food and provided information on resources so my mother could get additional help to get us safely away from daddy.

She even helped my mother with collecting the S&H Green Stamps. Back then, you had to collect those stamps and use them to buy furniture, dishes, toasters, etc.

Grandma or Ms. Nellie as she was called by others was a very savvy, and successful business lady. She was smart, compassionate, sweet and yet she was also a tough lady and not afraid of getting dirty from doing hard work. She owned a 300-acre cattle farm in Everett, PA. From the time I was three until I was thirteen, I spent each summer on her farm. Her granddaughter, Stacey Hahn, and grandson, Jason Hahn, and I became best friends from the time I was three years old.

Each summer, we all got to go to the farm. It was fun and adventurous. Spending those summers on the farm was my outlet. I could go and do things that I couldn't in the city.

I was with nature, the cows, chickens, wide open land, the fresh air, the relaxed atmosphere, and the humble lifestyle of farmers.

My time on the farm, the experiences and all the things I learned from working on the farm was something that that I would come to appreciate even more as each year passed. Even though grandma made us work our butts off, I loved it there. She taught us how to pick apples and peaches from the trees and ground, work in the garden picking beans, tomatoes, and other vegetables, and how to sit on the porch at night snapping the beans. She had us gathering eggs from the chicken coup in the mornings and cleaning out the cow manure from the barn in the evenings.

We rode on the tractors, helping the farmers load the hay bales, and then we had to help stack the hay bales in the loft of the barn. She would have us walk up the mountains of the farm on those hot summer days to see if the salt blocks for the cattle needed changing. If we ran out of things to do, she had us walk up the very long gravel driveway to check the mail and walk back.

Every day on the farm was hard work but adventurous. Our days started the minute the Rooster crowed in the morning, which always seemed to be around 5 am. Grandma never allowed us to complain. You did as you were told, and you worked hard. She didn't believe in slacking. She made sure we worked all day. But Stacey and I always found a few minutes to be mischievous or chase each other with the garden hose. We always found time to run over to the farmer's house and get a snack from them. Sometimes we'd get to eat lunch over there with them. I always remember how good the food always smelled and tasted on the farm. Maybe because everything was so fresh. But fresh also meant a lot more vegetables from the garden that we had to eat. We had to eat whatever food was placed on the table. Even if we didn't like it, we still had to eat it or go hungry.

And, of course, if you didn't eat your dinner, you couldn't have any of the homemade ice cream made in the evenings from the peaches we picked. When we complained we were hot and wanted to go into town to go swimming, she'd ask if our chores were done and if not, she said we could jump in the cow's trough to cool off. So, believe it or not, we did that quite a few times. When the carnival was in town, she did take us to that and of course like any grandparent, she did spoil us. Evenings on the farm were lots of fun once our chores were done. We would play board games or cards with the farmers and farm boys, chase each other around outside, play hide and seek, eat ice cream, catch fireflies in jars and so much more. Although I do remember on Sunday nights having to sit in the house to watch The Lawerence Welk Show which I found boring as a child. Yes, grandma was tough on us at times, but that's because she loved us so much that she wanted the three of us to grow up to be strong minded and not afraid of a hard day's work. She wanted to teach us that if you want things, you work hard for it. Don't take food, money or health for granted and to value and appreciate all that God gives us.

She was a very tough woman and a successful business lady. After all, she owned several very successful restaurants in Frederick and Hagerstown, Maryland, and several apartment buildings along with her 300-acre cattle farm. The cattle on her farm were raised and butchered for the meat in her restaurants and the eggs from the chickens were used in her restaurants as well.

Mommy and I seemed to be going on without Daddy just fine, but then tragedy struck.

One day, in the November of 1970, mommy was teaching one of her Korean friends from the sewing factory how to drive. Mommy was sitting on the passenger side of the car while her friend was driving, and I was sitting in the back seat. They were driving on Urbana Pike in Frederick when her friend lost control of the car. The car flipped and rolled into a cow pasture.

Her friend, who was driving, walked away unscathed, and I was battered and bruised but otherwise okay. I was ejected out of the back window of the car, but mommy got trapped in the car with both of her legs pinned under the dashboard.

The accident took the most toll on her. Her ribs were broken, her face busted, and she suffered a concussion and internal bleeding. Mommy had to stay in the hospital for six months, and the doctors didn't think she would make it. They were almost sure they would have to amputate her left leg as it was crushed, and her kneecap was gone.

She lay in the hospital bed, listening to the doctors tell her that she may never walk again. But still begged the doctor not to amputate her leg and save it because she planned on walking again.

"I have to walk again. I have to. For my daughter and for myself!" She sobbed.

They did everything they could, and Dr. Harvey became so impressed with my mommy's determination that he ordered multiple surgeries and then put her in a body cast from her neck to her toes so her bones could heal. Her face was broken as well, so they had to wire her jaws shut for a period of time while she was in the hospital.

Two of her Korean friends, Song and Kim, and their husbands came to the hospital on the day of the accident. Once I was cleared from the hospital, her friend Song took me back to her home. Song and Kim took me to the hospital every day to visit mommy. Once mommy was coherent enough to try to speak, she asked Song and Kim take Sonia home with you and say you are family members taking care of her.

She told them not to hand me over to my daddy. She was afraid if he got me, she might never see me again. She didn't have any money to give them to help them pay for food or clothes for me, so she offered her wedding ring.

But being the kind-hearted souls they were, they refused to take anything from her and offered to take care of me while she was in the hospital. I felt comfortable, and they loved and cared for me as their own. They brought me to the hospital every day so mommy and I could see each other. But, on several occasions, they did allow my daddy to take me for visitation because he threatened them, but he did bring me back to them each time.

Social Services and Child Welfare came to the hospital to tell my mother that they would need to take me and place me into foster care because my father was mentally unstable, and she was in the hospital, but my mother refused. She told them that her sisters were taking care of me. They checked with her friends and somehow verified that they were her 'sisters,' so I was allowed to stay with them.

After four months in the hospital, mommy was released to go home. We were able to go back to the apartment on N. Market Street.

They set up a hospital bed in the living room for her. She will still have her body cast on for an additional two months or more. There was still so much healing she still had to do from the accident. They told her when the cast would come off, they would have her do physical therapy.

Meanwhile, her friends and Ms. Hurst checked in on us daily and brought us food. The hospital also sent over a home nurse to help mom out during the day for a few hours. Ms. Hurst would bring mommy and me some groceries, like fruits, vegetables, beef, chicken and eggs. Ms. Hurst let us stay there and pay no rent until my mother healed from her car accident and got a job. My mom's Korean friends brought us Korean food and large 50 lb. bags of rice. Her friends would come after the nurse left in the mornings so that someone was with mommy and I during most of the day.

They would help bathe my mother and me. When they weren't there, it was I who took care of mommy and brought her anything she needed.

I remember when I was four years old, my mother and I were living in an apartment on Market Street owned by our landlord Ms. Hurst, grandma and we really had no money.

My mother was in the recovery stages from her accident. She had lost most of her teeth in the back of her mouth on both the upper and lower portions. So, she had difficulty chewing anything hard.

I remember, on several occasions, my mother saying to me that she was hungry for an apple. So, I would fetch one from the refrigerator to hand it to her.

"I can't bite it. Bite into it, chew it up softly, and then feed it to me." She would say to me.

Although that may seem odd to most people, this was our life. She was hungry and unable to do it for herself, so it was up to me to take care of her until she was able to take care of me again. This was the bond that my mother and I had.

No way was I going to let my mother want something and for myself not give it to her. I loved her more than I loved myself. I would try to snuggle as close to mommy as I could on that hospital bed that took up much of our living room space.

Sometimes, we would just lie in bed and stare out the window. The sound of my mother's heartbeat as I lay in that bed next to her was the most soothing and comforting sound in the world, and it made me feel the safest.

There were days, though, that daddy would come knocking on the door demanding we open it up so he could spend time with me. I never wanted to open the door, but mommy said we had to listen to the attorney and let him have visitation.

These visitations changed my world and sculpted my mental and physical strength, determination, and protective instinct. The never-back-down attitude, the OCD, and the need to always be in control. But most of all, it made me a survivor, and I carry that with me each and every day.

I remember the evenings, sitting on the kitchen floor for hours, hiding from my father, hoping he wouldn't come knocking on our door.

Our front door and side door to the apartment had gold-colored frosted glass, and anyone standing on the other side could see outlines of our bodies or lights on. But no one could see us if we were in the kitchen or pantry. So, those places became my hiding spots.

It was during this time, while mommy was recovering in that bed in our living room, that daddy would take me to his apartment. Because daddy was so angry at mommy for moving out and leaving him, he stopped making payments on the house, furniture, and the jeep.

Eventually, all of those things were repossessed, so he was forced to rent a small little apartment on 5th street in downtown Frederick, MD.

Now, this is when the worst of the molestation took place. Once inside our apartment, he would yell at my mother while she lay in bed. Blaming her for his misery. Blaming her for taking me away. She was basically helpless. Living on the second floor, there was a Dry Cleaner business just below us. That, too, was owned by Ms. Hurst. Sometimes, mommy would tell me to run downstairs and ask them to call the police for help.

Once, I witnessed my father yank my mother off the hospital bed shortly after her body cast was removed and slapped her across the face so hard she dropped to the floor.

I have seen him bust her lip, hit her in the stomach, and thrash her around on the floor. He sat on her, kicked her, and twisted her arm so badly he nearly broke it.

I screamed out repeatedly, *"Stop! You're hurting her!"*

One time I witnessed him grab the back of her hair hard, dragged her to the bathroom, and shoved her inside so she could watch him flush her medication down the toilet, then beating her head against the toilet. I felt helpless as I screamed and begged him to leave her alone. Crying profusely, I was terrified that she would die.

I will never forget watching him grab the back of her head as he smashed her face into the floor. I witnessed the blood pour out of her nose and her mouth and the red knots on her face and forehead from him doing that. I tried grabbing his leg to pull him away from her but he just shoved me away so hard. *"Please let mommy alone, please, please, please."* I cried uncontrollably.

Finally, he just walked out of the apartment and left. I ran downstairs to the Dry Cleaners and told Mr. Eyeler to call the police. Mommy told me to tell him to call her Korean friends too, and they came as quickly as they could. When the police arrived, they called the ambulance, and they took mommy back to the hospital and kept her there for several days.

The police took a full report and then arrested daddy for assault and battery. But somehow, he always managed to get out on bail. He has a sister in Dallas, TX, and family in Cincinnati, OH. He came from a wealthy family, so mommy was sure they bailed him out all the time.

Every time he would pick me up for his visitation from my mom's friend's house while she was in the hospital, he would tell me he had something special for me. I remember I would get so excited. But he would take me out to the park for ice cream and then to his apartment. He would touch me and kiss me, and it was a very uncomfortable feeling.

I told him I didn't like it. He touched my private parts and said we were just playing, and I wasn't to say anything to anyone.

He told me if I said anything, he would punish me, and I would never see mommy again. But now mommy was home in our apartment, still recovering from the accident. When he came for his visitations, I dreaded it, and I resisted as much as possible as I knew what was coming, or at least I thought I did, except now the molestation was worse.

He would take me to the corner convenience store just across from his apartment. Then he would tell me to pick out the most expensive candy bar. When I would take too long to pick one, he would just grab a plain Hershey® Bar and a drink and would head to the register to pay. From then on, it was always a Hershey® Bar that he made me get.

Then he would walk me over to his apartment but would not let me eat the candy bar until I completed something for him. I can still vividly remember exactly how the apartment smelled, looked, and felt. I completely recognize the layout of the apartment.

When you opened the door, you immediately walked into a somewhat studio-style layout.

The bed was against the furthest wall from the front door towards the left side. An old couch that smelled of beer and body odor sat in the center of the room, facing the window that had a view of the street, and a small TV sat on a table in front of the window.

Once you walked into the apartment, on the right side was the kitchen with a metal kitchen table and two chairs. The floors were dark and discolored. There were many spots that were worn out or buckled.

Then, just past the kitchen on the same right side was the bathroom. It has a very dark brownish-black door on it. It was long, narrow, rectangular shaped, and so very dingy. When you turned the light on in the bathroom, it gave off a yellow hue. It also had an old claw-style tub that sat on the right side, with a toilet at the top end of the tub against the corner by the wall. A small sink was to the left of the toilet at the end of the wall in the bathroom.

Still, to this day, I remember standing in that bathroom as though it were yesterday. I remember the fear and anxiety. He would tell me to go to the bathroom, get undressed, leave my clothes on the floor of the bathroom, get into the bed, and lie down next to him.

I remember telling him no, that I wanted to go back to mommy, that I did not want to do that. In return, he would squeeze my arm hard, shake me and threaten me.

He would say, *"If you do not do as I say, I will take you back to mommy so you can sit and watch me kill her in front of you."*

He would stand by the bathroom door and force me to go in. He would then shut the door. I remember standing in there, crying, not wanting to come out. I could hear him in the living room yelling for me to hurry up.

"If you take any longer, I will come in and undress you myself! I bet you will love that!" He would yell.

I would cry, and that would make him so angry. He would say, *"If you make too much noise crying and someone knocks on the door, I will punish you."*

I'd cry and cry and no matter how hard I tried to stop, I just couldn't. I manage to hold in the noise from crying but the tears just flowed down my face. I had no other option. I didn't want him to take me back to mommy to sit and watch him kill her. I knew he was capable because I had seen him beat her so many times and I just didn't want mommy to hurt anymore. So, I would just do whatever he said. I took off my clothes. When I would come out of the bathroom, he would already be in bed.

"Come here and get in the bed with me." He would say, with the sickest smile that would always make my insides crawl.

I tried everything to prolong the walk from the bathroom to the bed, but I knew what I had to do, and it was inevitable.

And so, I climbed onto the bed and lay beside his naked body. At first, I had to lay facing him so he could stroke my hair and face and then my body. Then he reached for a jar of Vaseline and put globs of it on my private parts. He would yell at me to stop crying or else. I tried, I really tried not to cry. But it was so difficult. He would make me turn my back to him, maybe because it irritated him that I cried. He pulled my tiny body up against his. And with my butt against him and his arms holding onto to me tight so that I cannot squirm.

He would rub his penis on my labia and try to penetrate me. I was never allowed to talk, I couldn't even yell that it was hurting me because he would cover my mouth with his hand and I was forced to listen to him call me by my mother's name and moan. It hurt me so bad, and I lay there with my eyes closed as the tears streamed down my cheeks, trying not to make a sound.

When he was done, he would tell me to get up, go to the bathroom, wipe off, and get dressed. When I would come out of the bathroom, I couldn't even look at him. I kept my head down and cried as he handed me the Hershey® Bar and patted my head.

"You are a good girl." He would say, utterly pleased.

But I did not want the candy bar. I only wanted to go back to my mommy.

So, he would force me to eat the Hersey bar before I could leave. Trying to eat the candy bar while sobbing and trembling was difficult. My nose was stuffy and I couldn't breathe so trying to swallow the candy was like another torture.

And when he walked me up to my mother, he would put his hand around the back of my neck and say, *"Don't forget our little secret. You do not want mommy to die, do you? If you tell her, I will kill her. Just remember that."*

I had already watched him beat my mother bloody, so I knew quite well what he was capable of. To keep my mother alive and to save her life, I never told her about it and just allowed him to continue to do anything he wanted to me.

I remember once when a police officer knocked on the door of the apartment, and my father told me to hurry up and get into the bathroom. He shut the door and made me put my clothes on, but I was not allowed to come out and absolutely not allowed to say a word. The officer said he was doing a well, routine check. He came into the apartment and inquired my father about where I was.

"She's in the bathroom. Her stomach hurts." My father answered.

The officer stood outside the bathroom door and asked me if I was okay. I didn't answer. Then he asked again.

"She's fine!" Came my father's agitated reply.

The officer asked me to come out of the bathroom, so I did. He knelt down and whispered, *"Are you okay?"*

I looked up at my father, and his eyes just stared at me. I could see him bawl up his hands, and I knew I just couldn't say anything.

"Yes," I whispered back.

"Are you sure? Your mommy wants to make sure you are okay." He again whispered.

"Yes," I whispered back again as I tried to contain my tears.

"Your eyes are red and I can tell you have been crying". The officer said.

"I told you she has a stomach ache and she has been crying over that", said my father to the officer.

"Is that true?" the officer asked.

I looked at my father and I saw that look in his face and I just nodded my head yes.

"Alright, then." The officer sighed, got up, checked the apartment, and left.

I was so sad, fell to my knees and cried when he left. I wanted to go with the officer so he could take me home.

Once when my father came to the apartment to pick me up, I said I didn't want to go. Mommy asked why I didn't want to go. I believe she could tell something was wrong with me because I was always sad and cried when I came back from visiting with him. But daddy always told mommy that I fell, or hit my toe, or had a tummy ache or whatever else he could think of to deflect the fact that I had been crying. And of course, I had to go along with it. During the time that mommy was confined to the hospital bed in our living room, she asked him about what was going on and why I didn't want to go visit him.

"Are you touching her?" She questioned him outright, and he lost his temper.

And, of course, that was bound to happen.

A criminal always bounces on the victim and accuser to hide the crime.

"Is he touching you or doing something, Sonia?" She asked me in front of him.

My eyes widened, and my heart raced. I wanted to tell her. I wanted to tell her everything so desperately so I wouldn't have to go with him. But I remembered his threat. The question angered him so badly that he grabbed a knife from his pocket, held it at her throat, and kept pressing it on her throat, threatening to kill her.

"Sonia, you are going to watch me slit her throat and die." He laughed evilly.

My mommy kept yelling for me to open the door and run downstairs to get out and get help and stay safe in the Dry Cleaners. I ran to the door and twisted the lock on the door and tried to open it, and just at that moment my daddy threw his knife at me, which missed me by a few inches and hit the door. I just froze, fell to the ground trembling, I screamed out *"NO, NO, NO please daddy don't kill mommy".* As he walked towards me to grab the knife, I crawled to my mother. We were both crying and screaming. He continued yelling obscenities at my mother and walked back to her to press the knife against her throat again. I was holding my mother's hand with one hand and put my other arm across her chest. Yelling *"No daddy no!"* While my mommy was telling me to get out and find safety. *"No, I am not leaving you."* I said.

I believe someone from the dry cleaner downstairs must have heard all the commotion and called the police. Upon hearing the sirens, daddy ran out of the building as quickly as he could, but they were able to catch him, and once again, he was placed in jail.

At one point, my father kidnapped me from school and drove me to Ocean City, MD, about three and a half hours away. My mother had to call the police, and they put out an *All-Points Bulletin* to locate me. Finally, they found us in Ocean City, arrested him, and returned me to my mother. He said he didn't kidnap me and that he only wanted to take me to the beach for our visitation.

His court hearing came, and the judge did sentence him to serve a few months, but that was nothing and a slap in the face for all he had done to my mother.

Once he was released from jail, he discovered he was evicted from the apartment he had on 5th street, so he rented a room in a large house just off South Market Street. It was a Victorian-style house with multiple bedrooms rented out to vagrants.

It seemed to be a run-down place. There were different people in each of the rooms. Most of the men looked disheveled and stood in their doorways drinking beer and smoking cigarettes. He sometimes took me to that room which was on the third floor.

I remember walking up all those exterior steps, through a screen door, and down the hall crying the whole way up. I think he rented that room to blend in with the other vagrants so that my mom and other people wouldn't find us there.

He knew my mother sent that officer to his apartment on 5th street because she suspected something.

I couldn't tell anyone that I was hurt. But I also couldn't make the visions and memories go away. It wasn't so bad during the day when my mom and I were busy doing things. But then, at night, when the lights were off, and it was quiet, and I had to close my eyes, I would tremble. I was so fearful that daddy would come in the middle of the night and kill my mother and take me that I just couldn't fall asleep.

When I cried, my mother would hear me and come into my room to ensure I was okay.

"Why are you crying?" She would ask me.

"You can tell me anything." She would say.

But of course, I couldn't tell her, as daddy would kill her if I did.

"My tummy hurts." I would say instead.

"Are you sure?" She asked. *"Sonia please tell me what's going on. Is your father doing something?"*

"No, I'm just sad that daddy is so mean to you and my tummy hurts, that's all." I replied.

She would then crawl into the bed next to me, tell me we are both going to be okay, rock me in her arms, and then she would sing to me the song by Doris Day called *"Que Sera, Sera – Whatever will be will be,"* as she rubbed my tummy to make it feel better.

And just like the verses in the song, I asked the same questions.

> *When I was just a little girl*
> *I asked my mother, what will I be*
> *Will I be pretty? Will I be rich?*
> *Here's what she said to me*

Then she sang the chorus to me,

> *Qué será, será*
> *Whatever will be will be*
> *The future's not ours to see*
> *Qué será, será*
> *What will be, will be*

Mommy placed her head against mine and said *"You are already pretty and always will be."* *"But will my hurt ever go away, mommy?"* I would whisper in the dark with drooping eyes.

In response, she would just sigh and rub my head and hair until I fell asleep.

But I couldn't cry every night, too, now, could I? I knew it would worry my mother, and she had to go to work. I couldn't keep her up every night. So, I told myself not to cry and to comfort myself the way my mother reassured me.

I rocked my entire body from side to side until I fell asleep each night. Sometimes, it took ten minutes, and sometimes, I would have to do it for thirty minutes or more. It was my own way of comforting myself. I guess because when my mother rocked me in her arms it was so comforting, reassuring and peaceful.

The molestation went on for several years until I was six years old. I am sure my mother suspected something. She would always question me about what my father and I did when he took me to his apartment. I would tell her that we watched TV, went to the park, or played with toys. I knew I couldn't tell her the truth. I had to protect her. I didn't want my father to kill her. I loved her so much and was terrified I would never see her again if I told her.

Also, I had to protect myself. Because in my mind, if he killed her, then where would I go? Would I have to go live with him or strangers?

He had so many criminal charges against him, from assault, battery, theft, public nudity, carrying a gun in public, attempted murder, and so on.

The military had discharged him, and he had become completely mentally unstable between losing his career, his wife, and his daughter. Eventually, my daddy was sentenced to jail time.

I am not sure for how long and who did it, it was either the military or the state of Maryland, but finally, he was committed to a mental institution.

My mother got a restraining order against him so that he could not come near her or me. She also signed court documents that she did not want any type of child support or spousal support ever. She was also granted full and sole custody of me. She just wanted him out of our lives forever. So, after that, we never saw him again. Although there was always that constant fear of looking over our shoulders.

Although I will never forget the pain, the events, and the locations where the molestation took place, and I can still vividly see and remember everything, I chose not to let it consume me. I watched my mother being beaten bloody and getting back up, and I watched her overcome the tragedy of her accident and prove to the doctors that she could walk again. She was considered handicapped, but she didn't lose her leg. She just walked with a limp because she had no kneecap and could not bend her leg, but she still walked. She was my hero, my inspiration.

Also, those long hot days of summer on the farm helped me in more ways than anyone could have ever known. It taught me that daily life could be hard, and sometimes you have to struggle to survive, but you don't give up. You push harder, you work harder, you strive harder. Nothing is easy, but you make the best of it anyway you can.

You can hurt your hands, your back, your entire body, but you have to go on. You do what you must do to live, survive, and take care of the ones you love.

I learned each summer on that farm I can be beaten down by long hours of work in the garden, with the animals, cleaning out the barns, the hot sun, you name it, but I wasn't going to allow myself to be broken. Each morning, I woke up was a fresh new day and I was ready to seize it. I became stronger, tougher, wiser, and more determined each year, and that strength throughout the years led me to become a *survivor*.

I learned at a very young age that you could survive anything if you choose to. The mind is so powerful that if you allow it to say you can't, then you won't. But if you believe in your heart, you can and have a purpose, you can use your strength, experience, and tragic events to help others.

CHAPTER THREE

AND THE TRAUMA CONTINUES...

Now, as my dad was out of the picture, life suddenly felt free. Free from the drama, stress and fear that he brought into it. We didn't even bother to track his whereabouts as we wanted nothing to do with him. He made our lives a living hell, and I believe whatever he was going through, he deserved it. But we did know that he was in jail, and that information replaced my restless nights with somewhat peaceful ones if one could say that.

I don't know how long he was incarcerated and where he went after he got out of jail. I just knew I was happy that it was just mommy and me now.

Now, we didn't have a car because the Jeep was repossessed, so we used the city transit bus to get to places, and sometimes, we took a taxi to go to the grocery store.

Mommy needed to get a job that would pay well so she could afford a living for us. She took typing classes and English Language Speaking classes to help her understand the language and speak it a little better.

When I was seven years old, she got a job at *State Farm Insurance Company* in Frederick, MD. Finally, we were able to buy our own groceries and some additional furniture and pay the rent of the apartment.

I could see how happy mommy was. It was exciting for us to go to the store and buy things that we needed with our own money. *Yes, our own money.* It felt surreal to even say that out loud. We didn't have to ask anyone for assistance or worry about how many S&H Green Stamps we had in our book to buy household items anymore. Mommy and I were very grateful for her friends and grandma who helped us so much with food, shelter, furniture and everything we needed in our time of despair.

Although I did think it was fun collecting those stamps, licking the back of each stamp, and sticking them onto the little booklets. S&H Green Stamps were a type of reward that retailers participated in.

They usually had large signs on their display windows that let the consumer know that they handed out the S&H stamps with purchases and/or bonus stamps were given out to new customers.

So basically, if you went into the grocery store and bought groceries, you earned the stamps. The number of stamps you earned depended on how much you spent on your groceries.

The denomination of the stamps came in one, ten, or fifty points. You could also collect the stamps from gas stations and other retailers.

Once you got the stamps, you would lick the adhesive on the back of each stamp and put them on the square spaces in the booklet. Each booklet had twenty-four pages, and each page had to have fifty points in stamps on it. It was so cool to look at the S&H catalog to see how many stamps you needed to purchase items within the catalog.

Mommy often scanned through the pages and picked out what we needed and wanted. It had everything in it, ranging from dishes, glasses, sheets, furniture, bathroom items, and so much more.

So, we would save our stamps, and once we had enough to buy the item, we turned in our stamps and purchased new items.

It really helped that Ms. Hurst, our landlord, a.k.a. grandma, and some of mommy's other friends gave us every stamp they collected to help us out. Mommy bought the kinds of food she needed to make her traditional Korean dishes. We splurged every once in a while, and ate dinner out.

Mommy was able to buy nice clothes from some regular stores for us rather than have to go to all the thrift stores. She liked to wear nice clothes. We would go to the store and try on different outfits and then model them in the dressing room for each other, and finally, we would pick out the best one we liked.

Mommy also made sure we had shoes to match our clothes. I told her we looked like movie stars.

She would laugh and say to me, *"Maybe, someday, Sonia, you will be a movie star. But if not, you will always be my star."*

She bought me some toys and an awesome doll house and Barbies to go with it. Slowly, when she could afford it bit by bit, mommy also bought some of the most beautiful Korean furniture. Her Korean friends would sell it to her very inexpensively when they were scheduled to be transferred to another army base overseas.

It was shiny black lacquer with the elegance of Mother of Pearl embossed in it.

Those Korean items included a coffee table, lamp tables, a dresser, nightstands, vases, a China cabinet, and some other items too. Even though we lived in the apartment over the dry cleaners, mommy made it feel like we lived like queens in a mansion.

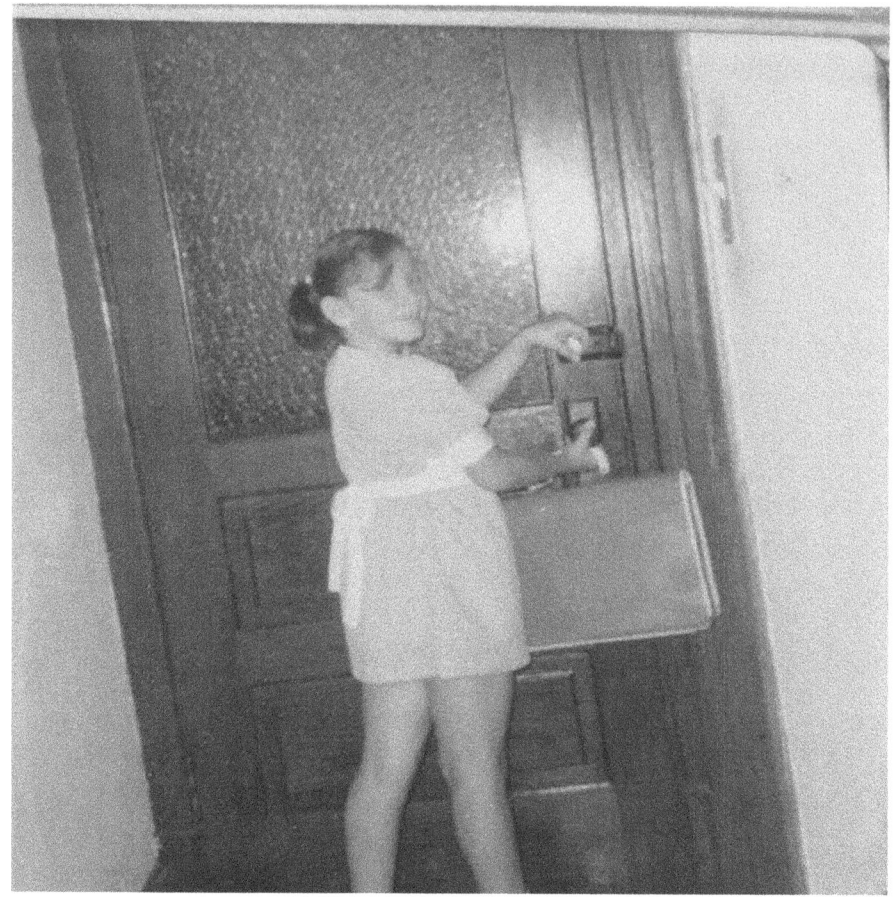

I could see how much it meant to my mother to finally feel that we were in control of our own lives. I really liked that feeling of us being in control.

That we were safe. Even when things were or did get a little out of control, she never wanted me to know. She did everything in her power to shelter me.

Occasionally, she would ask me if daddy ever did anything to me. I could feel a lump in my throat whenever she asked me that question.

"What do you mean?" I would ask her.

"I see anger and fear in your eyes. Sometimes, I hear you rocking yourself to sleep at night, whimpering." She wanted to know where it came from.

I thought about telling her a few times, but I couldn't. Her strength was amazing. She was my everything. She always said she wanted to give me a great life, and she meant it. It wasn't just about having money.

It was living comfortably, living healthy, living in peace, living safe, and most of all, living with her complete undying love and support. She was a tiny lady, but she could conquer the world. Over time mommy then bought a new blue Volkswagen Bug.

I was thrilled because it meant no more buses or taxis. Sometimes, we would go to McDonald's, grab some lunch, and sit at the park at the picnic table and eat. Other times, we went to Yellow Springs, ate at the picnic tables, parked the car in the creek, and washed it.

We would splash each other with the water and laugh. Sometimes, on Friday evenings, when mommy got paid, she would send me to *Snow White Grill* or *White Star Hotdogs* to pick up dinner for us. Ms. Hurst owned both of those restaurants.

The burgers at *Snow White* were the best, and they enticed the taste buds amazingly. The meat came from grandma's cows on her farm, and they were just tiny little burgers with fried onions and a pickle on little slider-type buns.

Eating three or more of them at a time was so easy. The French fries were so tasty too, and the milkshakes were out of the world. The hot dogs at *White Star* were grilled and topped with whatever toppings you liked from the menu.

Mommy always liked hers topped with ketchup, mustard, and onions. It was such a treat to go and get the food and come back and sit on the couch with Mommy as we sat in the most comfortable silence.

It was easy with mommy. The silence, I mean. There was no need for words. We could sit there for hours without a word, and I would still feel content. Also, that was the only time we were allowed to eat on the couch.

Any other time we ate, we had to eat at the kitchen table or at the sizeable Korean coffee table that is used in Korea as a dining table. We often sat on the floor at that coffee table with our legs crossed or straight out under the table and ate delicious, authentic Korean dishes that mommy made.

Although mommy and I always had fun, she was a woman with rules and discipline. She considered eating our meal on the couch while watching TV as a treat only to be done on occasion.

She felt that eating correctly at the table, whether it was at the dining room table or on the floor around the Korean coffee table, was proper etiquette. There were no distractions, we focused on our meal and communication, and I am sure it was mommy's way of ensuring I kept up with my chores, one of which was setting and clearing the table.

Mommy had lots of Korean friends, including Mary. Every now and then, we used to spend the weekends with them.

We would eat delicious Korean foods that mommy made. Her Korean friends would make some of the foods too, but in my mind and in my taste buds, no one could make the food taste as good as my mommy did.

I loved teaching mommy what I knew and learned in school. Sometimes, we would have our own English Language class at the kitchen table when mommy would ask me how to say certain things in English.

Ms. Hurst was so much like a mother to my mother, and they had such a great bond, so of course, she was always grandma to me.

As time went by, I started feeling like a normal kid. I had a nice bedroom in a nice apartment that we lived in, lots of toys and dolls, and most importantly, all of my mother's love and attention. It also felt like mommy was also at peace now, which, to be honest, was the greatest relief for me.

But still, I felt like something was missing. I could feel it, sense it in my bones and in my soul. Sometimes, I encountered some type of flashback or vision in my mind where I would see a little boy and girl holding a baby.

I felt like the baby was me and that the kids were my siblings.

So, I would ask my mommy, *"Where are my brother and sister?"*

I never got an answer, though. It seemed like she just brushed it off.

But it was okay because life was perfect, and it was just me and mommy and no one else.

One day, as we were driving to Silver Spring, Maryland, to the Korean grocery store in Volkswagen Bug, along with her friend. At the store, we ran into one of mom's friend's male friends, Mr. Lee. He was picking up a few groceries for himself. There, mommy's friend introduced the two of them.

She bragged about how he was in the Korean Military and held a high-ranking position, how he was a Black Belt Martial Artist, and that his hands were actually registered with the US government. They talked briefly, and then my mother walked away.

Finally, after we gathered all our groceries and left the store, mommy's friend suggested we stop by a Korean restaurant and get something to eat. Coincidentally, Mr. Lee just happened to stop by the same restaurant as well.

"How is it that Mr. Lee has shown up at the same restaurant that you suggested we go eat at?" Mommy asked her friend.

"I just thought, perhaps, it would be a good place for the two of you to sit and talk and get to know each other a bit. Mr. Lee is interested in getting to know you." Mommy's friend smiled.

Mr. Lee came to our table, sat down with us, and ordered food. Everyone was talking, and I just sat there sizing up this man that wanted to spend time talking with my mother. I had a very protective attitude. I wasn't going to let another man come into my mother's life and hurt her. I had made up my mind that I didn't like him, even though he was being very nice to me. I saw him and my mommy exchange phone numbers, and it made me sad.

Soon after, they started spending time together, and he started coming to our apartment and hanging out. He would take my mommy and me out for dinner, shopping, to the park, to amusement parks, drive-in theatres, day trips, picnics, and fishing.

He made sure to always include me in everything he planned with my mommy. I really loved it when we went fishing. I had never done that, and doing that was actually how I felt we bonded. He would bait my line and teach me how to throw the line in the water. When I had a bite, he would have me hold the rod while he reeled the fish in. Then he allowed me to hold the rod with the fish on it and praised me for catching the fish.

I remember Mr. Lee taking my mommy and me to *Kings Dominion amusement* park. It was an exciting day, and although the drive to get there was only about two hours, it seemed like it took forever. The anticipation of getting there and spending an entire day on rides and eating junk food felt like the joy you feel on Christmas morning, waiting to open your presents.

We walked around the entire park and got on every ride that would allow a child of my height. It was wonderful to see my mother smiling and laughing on the water rides as we got splashed and to feel the thrill as the animals passed by while riding on the monorail train.

One of the highest and lowest feelings of the day for me was when we all got on the roller coaster. I was so excited to have mommy and Mr. Lee get on it with me. I sat in the seat next to mommy, and Mr. Lee sat in the seat behind us.

My heart was throbbing as the coaster climbed to the top. Then, experiencing the raging descent down the tracks and the thrill of the rush, everyone screamed.

For some reason, everyone's scream almost became mute, and I was so focused on my mother screaming at that moment.

I started having flashbacks of my mother screaming as my father smashed her face into the floor of our apartment. I hated that those horrible memories would pop up sometimes.

When the ride was over and we got off the coaster, mommy and Mr. Lee were laughing and joking about how the old folks still like rollercoasters. I was happy that mommy was having so much fun, and of course, I was too. I just hated that I had to be haunted by those horrible memories.

Another exciting adventure we all went on was to *Niagara Falls.* We drove there and stayed for two days. We took lots of pictures. It was awesome!

The Falls were breathtaking. It was cold, but the beauty of it was definitely worth the visit. On our way back from Niagara Falls, we drove through Pittsburgh, PA. Mr. Lee wanted to stop and have dinner at a Japanese Steakhouse. The one where they cook on the table in front of you and do fun tricks with the onions and flipping of the spatula. It was my first time at that type of restaurant.

The show that the cook put on for our table was fascinating. I remember asking him what his name was, and he replied, *"George Washington."*

Then he asked me what my name was, and I said, *"Betsy Ross,"* and then everyone at the table started laughing.

The Japanese cook smiled at me and said, *"You are a smart young lady who is not afraid to speak up. Good quality."*

I smiled back and thanked him. But in reality, I was afraid to speak up. Afraid of the pain and anguish it would cause my mother if only she really knew what had happened to me and that I stayed quiet to save her life.

Mr. Lee definitely grew on me. I liked him, and so did all of my mommy's friends and co-workers. I was okay with having him around, but when he asked my mommy to marry him, I was not comfortable with that.

He told me that he would always protect my mommy and me no matter what. But it didn't matter to me because I didn't want a man in our lives who would be living with us. I felt like he was taking her away from me.

I was sad and mad as I felt I was going to lose the one-on-one connection that I had with mommy.

We were inseparable, and I was going to have to share her with him. I didn't care how nice he was and that he had grown on me. The fact that they were getting married was not okay with me. But eventually, the bond between the three of us became apparent, and we started feeling like a family already. Mommy loved him and saw how nice Mr. Lee was to me, and I guess that was one of the reasons she decided to marry him.

I was still not okay with it, but regardless of how I felt, the wedding date was set for August 28th.

Finally, mommy and Mr. Lee got married. I saw how happy he made my mommy and decided to give her happiness a chance.

Everything was beautiful. The flowers, the church setting, and especially my mother in her white wedding gown with the biggest smile on her face.

She kissed me on the head and said don't worry, *"You will always be my number one because you are my child."*

I was the flower girl, so I walked down the aisle in front of my mother and dropped the flower petals next to the ring bearer, who was walking beside me.

I smiled, but inside, I was still uneasy about at Mr. Lee and the wedding and somewhat frightened too. I just didn't want my mommy to marry him.

So, when the preacher asked if anyone had any objections to the marriage to speak up, I thought I should say something. I know I was only nine years old, but I did have an objection, so I had every right to speak up. So, I stood and spoke up. I stated that I objected.

"I don't want my mommy to get married because I don't want her to get hurt," I said.

Her friend, who I was sitting next to, politely told me to sit down.

Mommy looked at me and smiled, *"Sonia, it's okay. We will be fine."*

I sat down and kept quiet, and the wedding proceeded with the reception afterward. Mr. Lee didn't get upset that I stood up at the wedding and expressed my feelings.

He actually never spoke about it. I don't know if my mother ever told him about what we went through with my daddy. I never spoke about it to anyone. At the time of the wedding, I don't think either of us could truly see that, in fact, in the near future, she would get hurt again.

Not physically, but emotionally. But for me, it would be a repeat of the emotional and physical trauma inflicted before.

For several months after the wedding, things seemed to be great. Mommy and Mr. Lee were happy. Mr. Lee, or daddy, as I started calling him, was really good to mommy and me.

Once, when we went to Ocean City after they had gotten married, we let mommy sleep in the hotel room, and he and I went fishing, and that is when I caught an eel. I was so scared. I thought it was a snake.

But he assured me it wasn't and let me carry the bucket back to the hotel room to show mommy that I had caught an eel. He cleaned it, gutted it, and then we took it home and ate it for dinner one night.

He bought us things, took us places, and showed us off to everyone. He was so proud of his wife and daughter. He and mommy both worked, and I went to school during the days.

In the evenings, we would all eat dinner together at the dining room table. Daddy was a pretty good cook, so, oftentimes, he would already have dinner ready on the table by the time mommy got home from work. They seemed to be good for each other.

He even played with some of my toys with me. I remember complaining that I wanted a bike, but living in an apartment in downtown Frederick, there really was no place to go ride a bike. Then one day, he took me shopping, let me pick out a bike, and bought that bike for me. I was on cloud nine.

On the weekends, he would take mommy and me on trips, often camping, and usually, it was someplace where I could ride my bike or we could fish.

Sometimes, I would stand back and just watch as he would lay a blanket on the ground, have my mother lay on the blanket, warm up stones and place them on her back to warm her up, and then massage her back and her legs. I could see how caring he was with mommy and that he did love her very much.

So, finally, I let my guard down with him.

I felt like everything was going to be okay. Mommy was finally happy with a wonderful husband who treated her like a queen. She deserved happiness and I was happy for her.

Then, eight months into their marriage, mommy had to go to Korea to visit with her family because it had been so long since she had seen her family, her mother, and her siblings.

Now that she was married and felt safe leaving me with Mr. Lee, she felt like she could go and enjoy her time with her family and share the news of her marriage. So, she left for a month.

During her trip, she made sure to call once or twice a week to check in on us. Daddy said he wanted us to paint the apartment and surprise mommy when she was to get home. So, we worked hard every evening and, on the weekends, to get the apartment painted. He picked out the ugliest mustard yellow paint you could imagine. He said he liked it, and he was sure mommy would too, although I begged to differ with him. He even bought some new dishes and cookware for her.

We planned on making welcome home posters and getting flowers and balloons too. I couldn't wait for her to come home so we could pick her up at the airport and show her the surprise.

About two to three weeks into her visit to Korea, daddy and I were working on the apartment and playing around, and he was chasing me. We laughed and had so much fun. Then we both fell on the bed and talked about mommy and how much we both missed her.

But suddenly, out of nowhere, he said, *"Do you love me?"*

"Yes, I do," I answered.

I felt like I finally had a daddy that I could love.

Then he asked me, *"Can daddy have a kiss?"*

Immediately I looked at him strangely, feeling uncomfortable, like hot water was running through my body.

"What do you mean?" I questioned.

"Let me show you." He answered.

And there it was, the same thing happening again. He leaned over and kissed my lips. I felt his tongue inside my mouth and his hands running down my body.

I froze. I couldn't move, I couldn't speak, and I almost felt paralyzed. How could this be happening again? Why was this happening again? I felt so violated.

All the memories of what my own daddy did to me before came flooding back. But then, something clicked. I jumped up off the bed before anything more could happen. I ran into the bathroom and sat in the empty tub with my face buried in my knees, rocking myself. I was terrified and started crying.

He knocked on the door for what seemed like hours, apologizing and saying he was sorry. He said he didn't know why he did that. He said it was because he missed my mother so much.

Eventually, I came out of the bathroom and went into my bedroom. After that, I became distant from him. I didn't want to be around him anymore. He knew it. He knew what he had done, and he was trying to figure out how to fix it. He constantly begged me not to say anything to mommy. He said it was a mistake and he was very sorry. He said it would never happen again. He said it would crush her. I couldn't wait for her to come home because I was planning on telling her.

Finally, mommy was coming home from Korea and arrived at the airport. We went to pick her up with roses in our hands and beaming smiles on our faces. We had the apartment finished and had the welcome home banners up along with balloons. I hugged my mommy so hard I didn't want to let go.

I saw mommy hug daddy and kiss him. She was so excited to see him. They held onto each other so tightly and kept kissing as we walked to the car.

As we put her luggage into the trunk and got into the car, she asked, *"How was everything? What did you two do?"*

Daddy jumped in quickly and said, *"Let's go get something to eat so we don't have to worry about cooking tonight."*

I told her I would tell her tonight how everything was and what we did. I could see my daddy looking in the rear-view mirror at me, not in anger, but with a look of panic.

I could see how excited mommy was to tell him and me all about her trip to Korea and visiting her mother, siblings, cousins, aunts, uncles, and old friends.

She had brought back gifts for us and said we could have them when we got home.

At dinner, she sat so close to him, and I watched as they fed each other some of their food. On the car ride home, they held hands.

Once we were home, she saw our surprise. She gushed on the apartment we had painted, the banners, the balloons, and the new dishes and cookware. She was thrilled. Finally, mommy tucked me into bed. She shared with me how blessed she felt to have met and married Mr. Lee.

That he was a good man and a wonderful father and that she loves him and me so very much.

Then she asked me, *"So, do you want to tell me how everything was and what you two did besides paint and fix up the apartment?"*

I looked at her, and I saw the happiness shining in her eyes. After all, she had been through with the car accident and with her ex-husband, she deserved to be happy.

So, I couldn't. I just couldn't tell her. I could not and was not going to break her heart. I could not do that to her. Besides I had started distancing myself from daddy and I think he was on edge about whether or not I was going to tell her so I felt that maybe he wouldn't do it again.

So instead, I smiled at her.

"Everything was fine. We just stayed busy fixing up the apartment for you." I spoke.

She replied, *"It's beautiful, and I love it. Thank you for all your hard work."*

A month after her return from Korea, which was now ten months into mommy and daddy's marriage, Mr. Lee got a call from a family member that his oldest son in Korea was in the hospital and diagnosed with Tuberculous.

He told us he had to fly there immediately to see his son. He promised my mother that he would be back in a month.

A month went by, and now eleven months into their marriage, he said he was having second thoughts about coming back to the US.

In his defense, he did continuously call and checked on us. He said he was homesick for his country and that he needed to be there for his son and daughter.

Then he told my mother that, technically, he was still married in Korea and needed to sort things out.

I witnessed the pain in my mother's eyes as she hung up the phone. She had no idea he was still married in Korea. He never told her that. She started crying. She sat in her bed and bawled her eyes out.

I sat next to her, asking what happened, and as she explained what he said, all I wanted to do was take the hurt and pain away from her. After all, I felt like I was her protector and only I could make her feel better.

That day, she opened a bottle of liquor and poured some into a glass, and drank it. I just couldn't figure out what to say or do to make mommy stop crying and hurting.

It was about a week or so away from their one-year wedding anniversary when Mr. Lee called from Korea and said he wouldn't be back for their anniversary.

He said he wasn't sure when, or even if, he would be back.

My mother was crushed. It seemed like all the happiness she had because of him was now sucked out of her. She was depressed and sad every day. I was angry at him and also at myself because I felt like I was failing my mother because nothing I did seemed to take the sadness away from her.

She went to work and only cooked the basics that we needed to eat. She didn't have it in her to make all the elaborate Korean dishes. She made sure I was fed, clothed, made it to school, and had everything I needed but herself. She was emotionally dying on the inside.

She started smoking and continued to drink. She would just sit in her bed, smoking, crying, and drinking.

On the morning of her one-year anniversary, I took the top part of her wedding cake that they had saved to eat on their anniversary out of the freezer to thaw.

That evening, I brought the cake to her bed with two forks and said, *"Mommy, I will celebrate your anniversary with you. Let's eat it and cry or laugh together."*

I told her it didn't matter if Mr. Lee was here or ever came back because she always had me, and I wasn't going anywhere.

I think that was the first time I saw her smile in weeks. Mommy and I ate the cake, and *boy, oh boy, was it good!*

A few months went by, and mommy was still smoking and drinking. She didn't get drunk but I guess she just felt she needed a drink or two of alcohol to help numb her pain. I hated the smell of cigarettes and the smell of liquor on her breath when I snuggled next to her. I was so worried about mommy, and I was afraid she would die from drinking or smoking.

I just wanted my mommy back. I spent months telling her that our clothes stunk from cigarette smoke. I told her the smell was in our furniture and curtains too.

I hated Mr. Lee for what he had done to my mommy and what he did to me. In the back of my mind, I wondered if his reasoning for not coming back was partially because he couldn't face the fact of what he had done and was ashamed. Time went on, and he strung my mommy along for a period of two years, saying that he would eventually be back once he got things sorted out in Korea. He kept saying that he needed to be there for his son, daughter, and his wife and couldn't divorce his wife while his son was still sick. My mommy being her trusting self, still held out hope that he would come back.

Finally, one day, when I couldn't bear to see her like that anymore, all the emotions inside me were bottled up, and finally, I burst out!

"You have to stop smoking and drinking. You are the strongest person I know. You are my everything. I need you. If something happened to you, where would I go? What will happen to me? How would you feel if I started drinking and smoking when I got older because I learned it from you?"

Then, as we stood in front of her dresser and stared into the mirror, I said, *"Mommy, we have both sacrificed and suffered so much for each other because of the love we have for each other. But you smoking and drinking like this doesn't say that you love me. It makes me feel that you don't care about yourself or me enough to be here for me. I need you because I can't live without you."*

It was at that moment as tears ran down my mommy's face, she took the ashtray, threw it in the trash can, and poured out any liquor that was left in the house. Then we cried and held each other on the couch until we both fell asleep. It was then, that day, that I got my mommy back. A few months later, Mr. Lee called mommy from Korea and asked her to just pack everything we had and move to Korea with me.

She told him she couldn't do that.

"I can't do that to Sonia." She responded.

"The education and life here in the US would be better for Sonia, and she would not fit in with all the Korean children in school there because she is American." She continued.

She also told him that she couldn't give up her job at State Farm Insurance.

"My priority is Sonia and her happiness, her comfort." She concluded.

He continued to beg her, but the she continued to say no. *"The invitation will always be here should you ever change your mind."* Mr. Lee answered.

But as crazy as it sounds, I actually encouraged my mother to move us to Korea with Mr. Lee.

Not so much because of him but because I wanted her to be closer to her family and be with her mother. Because as much as I knew I needed my mother, I knew she needed hers as well. I already knew by this point in my life I could make any sacrifice I needed for the love, safety, and benefit of my mother. I even told her to put me in an orphanage or give me up for adoption if it meant she could be happy again.

Whatever it took, just as long as she was happy, I would be happy.

"I will never be happy in this world without you!" She cried in response. *"Me either"* I said.

But the amazing part is that no matter how much she loved him or would have liked to have been back in Korea closer to her family, she too sacrificed that love for the love, safety, and benefit of her only daughter, *me*.

CHAPTER FOUR

MY SAVIOR IN DISGUISE

Finally, 1978 started. Mom, done with all the sadness, decided that she wasn't going to go back to Korea with Mr. Lee. She became focused on saving as much money as possible because she wanted to get us out of the apartment and live in our own home.

I was eleven years old and often had a rough time in school. Even though my grades were always good, I usually got picked on for having an Asian mother and bullied because I developed my feminine features at an early age. My breasts were quite large for an eleven-year-old; to top it all off, my menstruation kicked in at the same age.

Mom did sign me up for Girl Scouts, and I did it for a couple of years and truly enjoyed it.

Having my best friend, Stacey Hahn, in my life from the time I was just three and throughout pre-teen was wonderful. We didn't go to the same school, but Stacey, her brother, and I were always inseparable. She and her brother Jason were Ms. Hurst, a.k.a. grandma's actual grandchildren.

We all got to hang out all the time. Stacey and I always enjoyed doing our girly things. We played dress up, tried and tested makeup on, and indulged in several other activities.

We could talk about anything and everything, our family lives, activities, school, the farm, our dreams for our future, what we wanted to do or become when we grew up, and our secrets—there were no reservations.

However, there were those one or two secrets that I just couldn't tell her. Even though we were best friends and could tell each other absolutely anything, those secrets of mine were something I just didn't want to share. I knew there was nothing she could do about it, and I didn't want her to feel bad about what happened to me, so I never talked about it with her.

We experienced farm life together every summer and worked our butts off. We learned about farm life, how to care for the animals, and how to grow and harvest our own food.

We also helped grandma with picking and canning apples and peaches from the trees and beans, tomatoes, and other vegetables from the garden. In the evenings, we had to sit on the porch, snap beans and hull peas, or peel the apples and peaches for pie, ice cream, and canning.

We had to get up when the rooster crowed and go to the chicken coop to pick fresh eggs for breakfast.

During the days, we had to help the farmers with cleaning out the barns of cattle and horse manure, bailing or stacking hay, brushing down the horses, walking over the mountainsides to check on the salt blocks and water troughs for the cattle, and more.

We learned that whatever grandma cooked and put on our plates for dinner was it.

There were no options and no concept of asking for something else to eat instead because we didn't like it.

Her motto was, *"Eat it or go Hungry. This isn't a cafeteria where you can order what you want."*

I can still envision her today, with that red lipstick she wore every day, standing there and shaking her finger at us.

Grandma never liked to waste food. She meant what she said. Several times, we went hungry because we refused to eat what she had put on the plate. But that also meant that we got no dessert either.

After a few times of that, we were on board with eating whatever she put on our plates.

No matter how long the days were and how hot, tired, and sweaty we felt, we always found time to laugh and joke, and of course, we always had each other's back. If one of us did a job or something that wasn't correct, we both took the blame. But, sometimes, though, we did try to blame it on her little brother Jason for giggles.

To this day, Stacey and I remain best friends and more so like sisters. We have an unbreakable friendship and sisterhood that I can say with surety will last through our lifetimes. Those summers on the farm helped mold me. They taught me discipline, hard work, teamwork, and more.

Around the age of 12, we would go to Fort Richie, a military base just outside of Waynesboro, PA, and spend the weekends with all of mom's Korean friends.

Their husbands were American, and they were stationed on the military base. So, for me, it was fun to live the somewhat military lifestyle on the weekends, going to the commissary, the military base bowling alley, the teen dance hall, and the movie theater.

Seeing all the military police and personnel in their suits always made me feel safe for some reason.

There was a lake on the base, and often, we would have picnics on the lakeside with all her friends and do paddle boating. There was also a Rod and Gun Club on the base, and we would go there for dances with our parents. I called all of my mom's Korean friends, aunts, and their husbands my uncles.

All of their children were close in age to me, so we all were great friends. And, of course, on occasions, we all did get into a little mischief.

Those weekends were a big part of my childhood life from the time I was ten until I was eighteen. Never at any point during those years with all of the Korean families did anyone ever make me feel as though I was different because I didn't have any Korean features that I should have had with a Korean mother.

But maybe, they knew something I didn't. I respected the culture and language, and, in some ways, I was more Korean than their children who had all the features.

My summers were quite different from the weekends on the military base with Mom's friends. Don't get me wrong, I loved the times we went there and the things we did, and I will always have fond memories of those times.

I got to see how husbands and wives and fathers and daughters got along and interacted, and it seemed perfect. Sometimes, I would even get angry and jealous. Because I felt like my mom and I were robbed of that. What was so wrong that we couldn't have had that? I knew I was never going to have a father-daughter relationship, and the first time one of her Korean friend's husbands handed me a Hershey® Bar at a bonfire so that all of us kids could make s'mores, a feeling of utter panic washed over me. I didn't want to eat the Hershey® Bar. I only wanted the marshmallows and graham crackers.

His daughter, I, and a few other friends were huddled in a circle waiting to make our s'mores. He patted his daughter's head and called her daddy's girl. I dropped the Hershey® Bar and wanted to run and hide. I wanted to disappear and not be seen. It was crazy that sometimes in the best of moments, something so simple could trigger that fear and nightmare.

Mom had to be at work by 8 am every morning, so she would drop me off at school, and then I had to walk home after school since she didn't get home until about 5 pm.

I remember the time when I was in the sixth grade at Parkway Elementary School. I thought I had a good friend, April.

We sat beside each other in classes and at lunch. Then one day, she came up to me in the hallway and said that someone had told her that I called her a name because she was a black girl. But color or race never mattered to me. I liked her for her. It just wasn't true, and I hadn't done anything I was being accused of, but I couldn't convince her of it.

So, after school the next day, as I walked through Baker Park on my way home with my book bag and purse, I was confronted by April and ten of her cousins and friends, all of which were teenagers and adults.

They had it all planned out and were already waiting on me. They hit me with sticks, beat me, yanked my hair, ripped my shirt and pulled my bra so hard it broke the clasps. Then they threw my book bag in the creek and broke raw eggs over my head.

When they were done attacking me, I got up and stumbled into the creek to recover my book bag and walked home to our apartment, crawled in the tub to wash off, and cried as hard as I could.

That day, when mom came home and saw me, I could see the pain in her eyes, she was heartbroken and angry. Her only child was beaten. My face was cut up, and I had whelps, cuts and bruises all over my back, legs, and arms. I had dried egg yolks in my hair and my head was pounding from being hit so many times in the head. She confronted the principal the next day, he said there was nothing he could do because it happened off of school property.

It was evident to mom and me that he didn't care because she was Korean, and it didn't matter to him what happened to my mother or me. He was more concerned about protecting those kids. Mom said she was going to file a police report and have them all locked up. I begged her not to do that because it would only make it worse for me at school and then they may try to beat me up again.

Because I had to walk home from school every day, I started feeling nervous and afraid. I never knew if they would be waiting for me in the park again. So, mom wrote a letter every day until the end of the school year that I had to leave school 15 minutes early. That gave me enough time to get out and run home as fast as I could before April or the others got out. Sometimes I ran home on some other side streets instead of going through the park. I had to stay in the apartment alone until mom came home. Yes, I was fearful for myself, but more so for my mother. I didn't want her to worry or have to come home again and see me like that. Everything in my life was about how it would affect my mother. I knew I was her protector.

Because I didn't want to be alone, sometimes, I would hang out in the dry cleaners below our apartment and chat with the staff until mom came home.

Sometimes, I would even walk around the corner where our landlord lived. A man's suit and tailor shop were next to the Snow-White Grill. The old man that owned it was probably about sixty-five years old. He was friends with Ms. Hurst, aka grandma, and knew my mother, especially since Mr. Lee did get a few suits from there.

I would hang out and tell them about my day at school or something fun that my mom and I did or had planned. He always gave me a soda pop from the machine in the back and a snack.

One day, the store owner asked me to come sit in the back with him. Being the naïve girl I was and that I was taught to respect my elders, I did so without thinking anything of it because they were like grandfathers to me. He asked me to sit on his lap and hugged me tightly. I did feel very uncomfortable. But I tried to tell myself that he must think of me as a granddaughter and that he was just expressing his love and care for me. After all, I was only twelve years old. Although, I always did look older than my age. At twelve, I looked like I was sixteen or seventeen.

However, after a few weeks of him doing that, one day, he said to give him a kiss, and he held my jaw sternly and kissed my lips.

He tried to force his tongue in my mouth and placed my hand in his private area. I was so shocked. I jumped up off his lap and grabbed my book bag. He was a very tall and thick-framed man who had large hands. Just as I stood up after grabbing my book bag, he reached for my hand and placed $2.00 in it.

"Go buy something for yourself with it." He said.

Still in shock, I had no idea what to say, so I quickly walked out of the back room, trying to keep my composure. I could feel myself trembling, and my heart was racing. As I walked past the co-owner, we locked eyes.

At that moment, I realized that his co-owner saw what had happened and yet, said nothing.

I went home, and again, I just couldn't tell my mother. I was afraid that maybe it was me. Was there something wrong with me? Why was I so vulnerable? Why did these men I trusted and should have protected me look towards me for their sexual gratification? Was it my aura?

Mom could tell something was wrong. I was angry and distant when she came home. She thought perhaps something had happened at school again.

I didn't want her to know, so I brushed it off as bullying at school. Afterall, I was bullied quite often at school for various reasons. She asked me what she could do to take the hurt and pain away or to make things better. But she didn't really know why I had so much hurt and pain, and perhaps, I didn't know hers either.

I know she hid her pain from me because she, too, didn't want me to worry. The amazing bond and relationship that my mother and I had for each other could allow each of us to endure our own pain without telling the other for the sake of love.

After that last incident, I was bitter toward those men that harmed me. I wondered if every man was like that. I questioned myself every day.

For some reason, I did continue to go back to that shop from time to time over the next two years. Perhaps it was the fear of being home alone until my mother got home from work. Or perhaps it was to finally have the strength to stare down at a man who can cause me pain, fear and anguish. I stayed in the front area, and I talked with the two owners. I guess I wanted to see what reason he had to do what he did to me. But he never mentioned it in front of his co-owner.

He continued to give me a soda and a snack each time I stopped by and continued to ask me to come in the back with him. *But what I really wanted was an answer.* Truth be told, I eventually ended up going back into the back room a few times. I did, so I could build up the strength from all the anger and fear that I had pent up. The last time he ever asked me to sit on his lap so he could fondle me was the start of my healing. I got up from his lap grabbed a coat hanger from the table hit him in the face with it as hard as I could and as he grabbed his face and started to stand up, I kicked him right in the nuts and said don't you ever touch me again. I was 14 years old then. As I walked out the store the co-owner nodded. That was the last time I ever stepped foot in that place. I truly wondered if I would never be able to trust any man.

It was time for middle school to start, and we all had to have our required physicals. For the girls, we were required to have a complete exam. This became a horrible experience for me, and I feared it would expose my secret to my mother.

When the nurse called me into the exam room, my mother was instructed to come with me. Once in the room, they said the doctor had to examine me and that I had to take off my bra to put on a gown so he could check me.

My heart was pounding, my palms were sweaty, and I started feeling nauseous. Once my breasts started developing, I wore a bra twenty-four hours a day. I never took it off, only to bathe. Wearing my bra all the time was a sense of security.

"No, I don't want to!" I cried.

The nurse and doctor told me again that I had to remove my bra, but I refused. I was now crying and rocking myself on the table in the exam room.

"It's going to be okay, baby." Mommy tried to assure me.

Finally, the doctor said he would just examine me with the bra on. But as soon as his hands touched my breasts, I panicked.

"Stop, stop, stop. I don't want to do this! I don't like it!" I screamed.

I jumped off the table and ran out of the room. When we got home, my mother asked me again, *"Did something happen to you? Did your father do something? Did he touch you? Did he hurt you?"*

I couldn't stop crying. I just said no and that I was okay. She told me that she had suspicions and needed to know what happened and that I needed to talk to her about it. I looked at her, and I saw fear in her eyes.

The fear that she thought she didn't protect me. I never wanted her to feel that. I wasn't going to crush her. It had nothing to do with her not protecting me. It was me who had to protect her.

So, I continue with my silence. I told her that if I wanted to talk about something, I would maybe, one day, talk with a counselor or psychiatrist. She held both my hands together and placed them up to her chest.

"My dear Sonia, you must be careful. I fear if you talk with a psychiatrist, someday, it may be held against you. Be careful. I am your mother. You can talk to me about anything, anytime. You know that, right?" She paused. I guess back in the late 70's that was taboo to talk to a physiatrist.

Then continued, *"You are young and may not understand the meaning of what I am saying, but as you get older, you will understand. I am working hard on saving money to buy us a house and get us out of downtown Frederick and into our own home so we can have a fresh new start."*

Finally, middle school started. I just wanted these two years to go by quickly. No one ever really likes 7th and 8th grade, apparently.

Middle school was just what it was, drama. Getting bullied was quite common for me. First, I was being teased about having a Korean mother, being a little overweight, having large breasts, and now, how the country I was born in was in danger.

The country of Iran was in upheaval as a revolution had begun. The religious leader Khomeini called for the Shah to be overthrown because he was westernizing the country. Riots were taking place in Tehran. Mom watched it unfold on the television. The Shah's regime was attacked and collapsed, forcing Shah to flee and then coming to the United States for health reasons, and a new leader, Khomeini, took over.

With the approval of Khomeini, militants stormed the US Embassy and took fifty-two American hostages in demand to have the US return Shah to Iran, and of course, the US refused. The hostages were held for four hundred and forty-four days.

I was being bullied because of the events that had unfolded in Iran and the fifty-two American hostages. I had always made it known to all my classmates throughout the years that I was born in Iran when my parents were in the military.

Now with what was going on in Iran, this gave my classmates more ammunition to bully me. I was shoved into lockers and told if I tried to escape, I would be beaten.

"How does it feel being a hostage? This is what your people are doing to us Americans." They chanted.

Some of the kids spit at me, and some tried to trip me in the hallways or down the stairs. In the bathrooms, the girls pulled my hair or punched me, calling me an Iranian pig. I guess that's what they heard from their parents.

I didn't want to tell mom too much about being bullied because I didn't want her to worry about me. I did, however, tell her about what the kids said about Iran and the American hostages and that they called me names.

She told me not to listen to them and just walk away. But, if only it were that easy. I was involved in a few fights.

Sometimes, I would stay after school, hiding, and leave when the teachers left, just to avoid walking home with all the kids. Sometimes, I would leave five minutes early and run as fast as I could to get as far away from the school before the bell rang and the kids were out. I didn't want them to see me.

At just twelve years of age, I was getting used to being beaten mentally and physically. I was beginning to build up a tolerance for pain. I kept thinking, *how can I protect my mother if I can't even stand up for myself?*

I thought about all the days on grandma's farm and how hard we had to work.

How there were days I thought I couldn't walk another step, pick up another bale of hay, lift another shovel of manure, and toss it out of the barn, getting pecked by another chicken for collecting their eggs, but I did. I pushed myself every day, learning to work through the long exhausting days and the pain. So, little by little, I started to stand up for myself and fight back. But it was scary. I was involved in a couple of fights, and although I may not have won, I didn't always lose either.

I figured if I was going to be beaten, I was going to be beaten putting up a fight. That was something I didn't do when my father molested me, beat my mother, or when my step-father, Mr. Lee, the owner of the men's clothing shop, touched me inappropriately.

Maybe it was the anger and frustration inside of me. By now, I had completely lost trust in men and had to figure out how to never let any man hurt my mother or me again. I was getting older, bigger, and bolder, and now these events had become a matter of fight or flight.

For me, I was done with the *flight*. I realized I could not back down for my own mental stability and that I must stand up for myself.

To help my mother save money for our new house, I asked grandma if I could wash dishes at the Snow White Grill and earn money. She agreed.

Nellie, a.k.a. grandma, and her deceased husband, Hansel, had opened the Snow White Grill in 1939. For many years, grandma kept the sign above the restaurant that they offered five-cent hamburgers. I knew firsthand that the hamburger came from the cattle on her farm. The farm on which I had the pleasure and opportunity to work for many summers.

So, at twelve years of age, I was washing dishes and had my own paper delivery route, which I did on my bike. In addition, I worked at the Frederick County Fair at a fudge stand in September for the week the fair was in town. Every dollar I made, I wanted to give to my mother.

By this time, my best friend Stacey had moved to Charlotte, NC, because her mother had remarried. Grandma started to have health issues. Eighth grade was coming to an end in about another month, and then I would be going to high school.

Then on May 1st, 1981, my mother said she would pick me up from an outing that I was on. She was supposed to pick me up at 3:00 pm. However, she showed up at 4:00 pm.

I was so worried and mad at the same time. When I got in the car, she said let's go get some dinner out and celebrate.

I was grouchy and said, *"I don't want to celebrate anything."*

She held my hand and said, *"Are you sure?"*

"Yes, what is there to celebrate? You picking me up late?" I answered somewhat sarcastically.

 Her response was absolute joy and pride. She said, *"Yes we can celebrate that."* I replied, *"I'm not in the mood the celebrate!"* Then she said, *"I am so sorry I was late picking you up. But I just signed all the paperwork for our brand-new home in Brunswick, so be happy."*

My head turned so quickly towards my mother and I said *"What!!!, Seriously?? You're not kidding?"* I screamed with excitement, leaned over, and hugged my mother as tightly as I could. It was the best news I had heard in a long time. She had all this planned and didn't tell me so she could surprise me.

I was so excited and yet so incredibly proud of my mother. Wow! What an accomplishment! A Korean lady, a single mother, with a language barrier and handicapped accomplished the American dream. I was so happy that my mother wouldn't have to put herself through walking up and down two flights of stairs everyday just to get in and out of our apartment. That we didn't have to fight for a place to park our car on the main street in downtown Frederick and that we didn't have to park three or four blocks away and have to carry groceries down the street and up the stairs anymore. Although, I always took care of bringing the groceries in because I wasn't going to allow my mother to do it and put a strain on her bad leg and have to limp since her left knee didn't bend. We both have a lot of good and bad memories in that apartment, and now it was time to start new ones in our brand new, just built home in Brunswick.

She coordinated with our church friends to have them help us move the very next morning. Grandma was sad to see us move out but so very proud of my mother, whom she felt was like a daughter to her.

When we arrived at our new home the next morning, it was on a dead-end cul-de-sac, and it was a brand-new house that mom had built for us. It wasn't a huge house, but it was ours.

It was a two-bedroom rancher with a full walkout basement and was built on a ¼ acre lot. It was absolutely perfect. We settled into our new home, and life became absolutely great!

I did have to finish eighth grade at my old school, but I sure was looking forward to starting high school in September in Brunswick. I made a few friends very quickly. I became friends with a girl that lived across the street on the connecting street named Karen.

We became best friends and did everything together. She was two years older than me and had a boyfriend named Michael.

I would say, for the most part, I was the typical teenager. In high school, I excelled. I took business classes and joined the FBLA. I was the VP of the FBLA (Future Business Leaders of America).

I was a Color Guard in the high school marching band, and in my Junior and Senior years of high school, I played Powder Puff Football. It's where the girls play flag football, and the boys are the cheerleaders. I got my driver's license at sixteen, and I also worked part-time jobs while in high school.

I was always involved with our Korean Baptist Church, but during my high school years, I took on the role of a Sunday school teacher for the kindergarten age group and really enjoyed it. I had lots of friends, and Brunswick was a great town to be a teenager in. It was a small town, and everyone knew everyone or was related to someone. It was just thirteen miles to Frederick, where almost everyone went to the malls and to grocery shops, the movie theatres, and roller or ice skating.

Brunswick didn't have much. We had our small-town stores and shops, a community pool, liquor stores, and bars. We did have a bowling alley where most of us loved to hang out at after school, in the evening, and on weekends.

That is where I met Donald, my first boyfriend, when I was fourteen years old.

One day, in December of 1981, Karen and I went bowling to meet up with her boyfriend, and he had his best friend, Donald, with him.

From the moment I met Donald, I was smitten with him. It was actually a nice feeling to look at a man and not feel so fearful. To actually have a feeling of wanting to have fun with him and do things together. He was five years older than me, but he was so kind and sweet. He had recently graduated from Brunswick High. I introduced him to my mother, and although she wasn't happy about the age gap, she did like him. He introduced me to his parents, and I adored them. They liked me as well.

We were in a relationship for five and a half years, and I was able to experience some wonderful moments during that time. He learned about the Korean culture and liked the food. We went to my junior and senior prom and did so many things together and with each other's parents as well.

We have the C&O Canal towpath that runs through Brunswick and alongside the Potomac River. The C&O Canal is 184.5 miles long, and people enjoy the towpath for walking, jogging, and riding bikes. It starts in Georgetown, Maryland, and runs to Cumberland, Maryland.

As a teenager, many of us hung out on the weekends underneath the Brunswick Bridge and beside the boat ramp to the Potomac River by the C&O Canal Towpath. Often, we would go to Shiley Acres in Inwood,

West Virginia, not far from Brunswick, for day-long rock concerts. It was a cornucopia of sex, drugs, and rock and roll.

Of course, we always found back roads as well to hang out, or we would just hang out at someone's house. We listened to classic rock music and drank beer and Boone's Farm Wine. Since my boyfriend Donald was nineteen when we met, most of the crowd of friends I had and hung out with were a few years older than me.

When I was seventeen years old, I wanted to surprise my mother with a nice and useful gift. We always drove about an hour to the Korean grocery store, and since we didn't have a deep freezer, it was hard to stock up on the Korean foods we needed.

We ate Korean food at each meal. The only time I really ever ate American food was at school lunches, at Donald's house, at a friend's house, or if we went out to eat.

We bought a 50 lb. bag of rice each time we went to the Korean grocery store, along with large packages of spices, meats, and other essential ingredients for the authentic Korean dishes that mom made each day.

So, that day, I bought my mother a deep freezer from the money that I had saved.

I had it delivered, and then I drove to the Korean grocery store and bought in excess of all of the foods we used so frequently and stocked them. Then I filled the deep freezer with all the food.

She was on an overnight church retreat, and when she came home the next day and I showed her the surprise, she broke down in tears. She was so shocked and so happy.

She told me she was blessed with the best daughter in the world. She said she couldn't believe I did that and that I should have saved my money for college. But I wanted to do anything and everything for my mother. When I turned eighteen, I got my first credit card, and I used it to have wall-to-wall carpet installed in our basement after mom had the bedroom, the bathroom, and the basement finished off as a large family room the previous year.

She had been using area carpets, but the concrete floor was cold, and I thought it would be much nicer to have padding and good-quality carpet down the stairs and throughout the basement.

I had that done one day when she was at work, and when she came home, she was blown away with gratitude and joy. I loved doing things like this for my mother. Not because I had to or because she asked. I did it out of love. I wanted to spoil her. She had always put me first, and everything she did, she did for me. So, I wanted to do everything for her.

Eventually, Donald and I broke up during my first year of college only because I felt like I wanted more. I knew he didn't want to have children someday, but I did. Also, I hadn't experienced the dating field, so we ended our relationship. However, I will always have fond memories of him.

The legal age to purchase alcohol was eighteen at the time. However, a few months before my eighteenth birthday, the state changed the legal age to twenty-one.

But it didn't matter as it was never a problem for anyone in our group to buy beer or wine. I never really was interested in drinking. I tried beer, but I hated the taste of it. Although, I did drink the Boone's Farm wine. We got the Strawberry Hill one, and honestly, it tasted like a combination of juice and Kool-Aid.

I drank it more to fit in rather than just purely having an interest in drinking it. Smoking pot back then was a big thing. Pretty much everybody was doing it.

At every party I went to, my friends and their friends were drinking, smoking a joint, or smoking it from a bong. Some also did cocaine.

In the beginning, someone would always try to pass a joint or the bong to me so I could partake in it. I always said no and just passed it on to someone else. I could never justify doing it, mostly because the smell of it was horrible. And also, because of seeing everyone coughing and putting their mouth on a bong, one person after another, was just gross to me. But more than anything, I put my mother first. I thought about when my mother smoked and how I begged and pleaded with her to stop. I didn't want her to smoke, so why would I?

Pot, weed, or a cigarette was the same in the end, smoking. Also, when I thought about how much my mother sacrificed in her life for me, there was no way I could disappoint her and smoke pot or drink much alcohol. She told me every day how much she loved me and how proud she was of me. So how could I disappoint her?

Mom was a small lady, but she could give me that look, and I knew I was in trouble. If she said something once, I had better listen to it. If she had to say it twice, I was in trouble. She was a firm believer in spanking and yes, I did have quite a few spankings growing up as a child of the '70s and '80s.

The spankings were a punishment when I did something wrong. And all I could think was, if my mother caught me smoking pot and spanked me, the spanking wouldn't hurt me as much as knowing I had disappointed her.

So, I chose not to partake in drugs. My friends understood my reasons, and none of them ever forced or pressured me. It never seemed to bother them. I was there to hang out and have a good time, just like them, but drug-free.

Occasionally, my mother and I would butt heads. Just like any teenager, I also tried to push the boundaries with my mom. It was usually over my curfew time or when I wanted to go out on a school night or somewhere with my friends, and mom said no, that was it. I knew I could never win an argument when it came to my mother. She raised me with love but also with the fear that if she said no, that meant no. If she said to do something, I better do it the first time. If she gave me an answer, I was not to question it. It was because she said so. You know the whole "do as I say and not as I do." It was called discipline and respect, and I am so grateful she raised me that way.

During my high school years, I believe during 9th grade; grandma passed away. I was told she suffered from Alzheimer's. It was hard on my mother when she passed. They were so close, and grandma had done so much to help my mother and me. In many ways, she was my mother's angel, always looking out for her. It was equally sad for me as well.

I missed those two-and-a-half-hour drives in her Cadillac to the farm with her beloved Chihuahua and spending those wonderful summers on the farm.

I would miss visiting her at her home and eating those delicious burgers and fries and slurping down those thick, sweet, freshly made milkshakes from the Snow White Grill. But all the lessons learned on the farm and the things she taught me will forever be in my heart. Finally, I graduated from Brunswick High School in 1985 and went to Hagerstown Business College, which was only a fifty-minute drive from home.

I didn't want to go far away to college and live in a dorm because the thought of being too far away from my mother was upsetting to me. I needed to be there with her. After all, I considered myself her protector. I couldn't leave her alone and just come back for visits or between semesters so I choose to stay close to home for college. My college years were good, I worked part time while attending school and saved as much money as I could. In 1988, I graduated from college with an AA Degree as a Paralegal.

My mother promised me that she would take me to Korea to meet my grandmother and my aunt, uncle, and cousins, and she kept that promise. Mom took us both to Seoul, Korea, for the 1988 Olympics as a graduation gift for me. She wanted me to meet my maternal side of the family. It was my first visit there.

We went to Korea for a month and had an amazing time. During our time there, we stayed in Seoul for two weeks, then in Pusan for ten days, and then we went to JaJudo Island for five days. While in Seoul, we also met up with her ex-husband, Mr. Lee, my stepfather.

Mr. Lee, whom my mother had married on August 28th, 1976, and the marriage dissolved a year later because he was homesick for Korea and had an ill child with Tuberculosis. He moved back to Korea, and my mother and I remained in the US, but they did remain friends.

When he found out we were coming to Seoul, he arranged for mom and I to have tickets for us to go to the Olympics. He was actually working as a crew member of the Olympics, so he got the tickets. It was incredible to actually sit in the stadium of the 1988 Seoul Olympics. The entire country was decorated with Olympic memorabilia and souvenirs.

It was odd to see him. He still looked the same, just a little aged. He and my mother embraced, and I could see they were happy to see each other. I know it took mom some time to get over him when he left and that she probably thought about him from time to time over the years, but I do believe she was happy that he was doing well and that she was over him and content now.

Getting to sit in the Olympic Stadium and watch the various events was the opportunity of a lifetime. I even got to meet Bryant Gumble and Jane Pauly from NBC News.

Mr. Lee commented on how much I had grown and what a beautiful young lady I had grown into.

Maybe, time had erased his memory but not mine. I was older now. I was twenty-one and wiser. I thanked him for giving my mother and me the opportunity to see the Olympics and for taking us out for dinner.

We even got to meet his children, all of which was quite nice. Even though I kept thinking I just wanted to say something about that day in the apartment all those years ago or how badly he hurt my mother and left her the way he did, made him an asshole in my eyes. I didn't. I stayed quiet.

This was a wonderful trip that my mother had planned for us, and I did not want to ruin it. It was a chance for me to meet my grandmother, my aunts and uncle, and so many cousins. I wasn't going to dampen the joy we had for a man that appeared to be nothing more than a brief moment in time for us.

While in Korea, we visited Pusan, which was where my mother was born and raised. There, I got to meet my grandmother for the first time, and it was bittersweet. We hugged and held hands, and although we really couldn't communicate because my Korean was not fluent, our eyes and hugs said all we needed to know was that we loved each other. My aunt and uncle and all my cousins were so kind, too, and made me feel quite welcomed.

I got to walk the streets that my mother walked as a teenager. One of the highlights of Pusan was when mom took us to Haeundae Beach.

The beach she spent so much of her childhood and teenage years at. The beach that was spoken of so often with that twinkle in her eyes.

She told me she and Mr. Kim would go swimming there all the time. The smile on my mother's face when we were standing on the beach was priceless. It was such a calming peace to me, and I saw the happiness she had felt at that moment shining in her eyes.

In conclusion, the awesome shopping, sightseeing, food, the guided tour in Jajudo I got to experience firsthand myself was a thrilling experience for me. To stand on the beach and on the sand, as my mother did so many years before, and to hold her hand while the tears ran down her face was very emotional for both of us. I wasn't sure if they were tears of joy or sadness or regret that ran down her face, but I knew that as long as I was standing there with her at that moment, we both had tears of joy.

But, as all things come to an end, our trip also came to an end. But hands down, the entire trip was one of the best experiences of my life till that age.

Once we got back from Korea, I started working. I actually had gotten a Federal Government job in Gaithersburg, MD, and worked there for a brief time. Then, I transferred to Fort Detrick in Frederick. What a coincidence it was, considering that was the military base that my parents were transferred to after leaving Iran. It was now partially used as a military base and partially for Cancer research.

I worked in the Leukemia and Lymphoma section, and within a year after being there, that department was moved to St. Jude's Children's Research Hospital in Memphis, TN.

So, I moved to an accounting job at an office furniture company. I took a liking to learning and doing bookkeeping work, and any job thereafter was in that field. All of my training in the bookkeeping/accounting field was job training experience with the exception of a few college courses.

I worked a few jobs, but the one I was at the longest was at an outdoor adventure company called River & Trail Outfitters, which did whitewater rafting, canoeing, kayaking, tubing, and more.

I was the office manager/bookkeeper. I worked there as a raft guide and shop girl for about four years during high school and college. Then after having my children, they offered me the office manager/bookkeeping job in April of 2000. I worked there until 2014.

It was while working at the office furniture place that I met my soon-to-be husband, Michael. I met him on March 9th, 1990, at a party that my friend Carla was having at her home.

It was a rather mild night for March, not too cold. The party was full of friends. There was lots of food and a bonfire outside. She told me she wanted to introduce me to a friend of hers named Michael. I wasn't really planning on going to the party. I helped her during the day to set up and get things prepped for the party but really hadn't planned on coming back for it that evening.

There was a police officer in town that I was interested in, and we talked and spent some time together. I was hoping that when he got off his shift that night that he and I might be able to hang out. She kept encouraging me to come back when the party started, so I could hang out with her and some other friends and meet this guy she kept talking about. So, I thought, *why not?*

I met Michael, '*Mike*,' at her party that evening. He was tall, six feet, and had dark brown/blackish hair. His physic was average build. He wasn't skinny and certainly wasn't overweight.

He was a good-looking guy, smart, funny, very sweet, had a good job, was independent, had his own home, and seemed to be a very responsible person. He was into Harley Davidson motorcycles and owned one that he was very proud of.

We spent that entire evening at the party by each other's side, chatting and getting to know each other. As we sat by the bonfire, I told him that my mother was Korean.

"You don't look Korean at all." He said.

"I have heard that a lot while I was growing up." I laughed. *"I look more American like my dad, I guess. But I do possess some of my mother's features."*

I don't know why, but I felt like I could trust him, so I continued. We talked about our families, how many brothers and sisters we had, how he was from Pennsylvania, close to Philadelphia, etc.

"I am an only child, but I am sure I have a brother and sister. I can feel it in my bones. Sometimes, I see a little boy and girl with a baby, and I think the baby is me."

I don't know how he didn't think I was crazy or strange or that I was pulling a joke on him. I mean, looking back on it now, if it was the other way around, I would have thought that and probably walked away.

But he didn't. Instead, he wanted to know more about me. He listened, and he cared. We left the party later that evening, stopped at a bar, shot some pool, had a few beers, and continued to get to know each other. Our relationship progressed quickly, and I moved in with him at the end of June 1990.

His house was just a little more than five blocks away from my mom's house. My mother wasn't too happy when I told her I wanted to move in with him. She was one of the Deacons of her Baptist Church and didn't believe it was right.

But I think she saw that we were in love with each other. He took me for rides on his motorcycle, and we went to a few biker events. It was definitely a new experience for me. I learned that sometimes, stereotypes aren't always true.

Most of the bikers I met and his biker friends were very nice and good-hearted. I got to learn a lot about his family and friends in Pennsylvania, and he got to learn about the Korean culture and food. We grew up differently, but we connected and fell in love. And to top it all off, he treated me so well.

She came to the house all the time. Mike was totally fine with Mom having a key to the house, and he told her that she was welcome in the house anytime.

Mike had a dry sense of humor and could spit out sarcasm on a dime. He was a jokester at times, but he was always a hard worker. He was a great handyman. He could fix almost anything in the house, the car, or his motorcycle.

Sometimes, without him knowing it, something would trigger flashbacks of the child molestation or the vision of the little boy and girl holding a baby that I so believe was me. During those times, I could become distant or very defensive. Sometimes, an overbearing need to protect myself occurred too. He never questioned it or me. He just always let me know that he was there for me, no matter what I was going through.

We visited his family often in PA. I really liked them and felt close to all of them immediately. And in return, they welcomed me with open arms.

That year was a whirlwind. We met in March of 1990, I moved in with him in June, and then on Christmas Eve, I found out I was pregnant. I started feeling sick in the mornings, and my body just didn't feel like itself.

On Christmas Eve, my employer let us off early, so I thought I would go to my OBGYN just to see if I could get a pregnancy test. I made it there about thirty minutes before they were closing up for Christmas. I did the test, and it came back positive. I was pregnant. I was thrilled but also frightened. I had to tell Mike, of course, but we weren't married, and I had to tell my mother too.

She worked so hard to raise me right, and I was worried because I knew in Korean culture, living together and not being married was one thing, but being *pregnant*, not being *married,* and *living together* was not acceptable at all! Not to mention, she was a Deacon of her Church.

I always felt that my goal in life was to make my mother proud and happy. And I was unsure how she would take the news of my pregnancy. Furthermore, I wasn't sure how Mike would take it.

I was only twenty-three years old. Would I have to be a single mom and move back with my mom to raise my baby?

That night, Christmas Eve, Mike and I decided to exchange one gift and do the rest in the morning with my mom when she came over. He gave me a large jewelry box that had several pull-out drawers and a pull-up lid with a mirror inside. He kept asking me to take it out of the box and open the drawers. I really didn't feel like it because my mind was on the pregnancy. I really liked what I saw on the box and appreciated it because I needed a jewelry box. But he was so insistent that I took it out of the box and opened each drawer to see if I really liked it. Finally, I caved it, took it out, and opened each drawer.

But, to my utter and complete surprise, there was a ring in one of the drawers. It wasn't a diamond, but rather a black onyx with a small diamond encased in the gold lining that went diagonally across the stone. I asked him what the ring meant. Was it an engagement ring?

"Are you saying you want to marry me?" I questioned, perplexed.

"No, it's just a ring to show you that I love you. I don't know if I am ready to get married just yet, but I do see us getting married in the future. So, it's kind of like a promise ring." He answered. *"A promise that you and I will get married one day. Because I love you, and an engagement ring is coming in the near future."* He finished.

I was happy, but I felt overwhelmed, and somewhat heartbroken too. I just found out I am pregnant, and he basically just told me he's not sure if he is ready to get married just yet. So what was his idea of the future? Two, five or ten years down the road?

I had so much to think about that I honestly took a week to think things through before I even told Mike. I just didn't want him to feel like he had to marry me because I was pregnant. But after thinking it through, I realized that he did tell me it was like a promise ring to marry me.

So, I knew he loved me and wanted to marry me before he even knew I was pregnant.

So finally, after much thinking, I told him on New Year's Eve in 1990. He was thrilled. He was twenty-nine years old and would be thirty by the time the baby arrived, so I guess he expected and wanted it all.

Mike and I went together on New Year's Day to tell my mother. She was actually very happy for us but also made it clear to Mike that if he loved me, then we should get married. We were going to be parents and should bring this child into the world with his parents married before he was born.

She explained if we decide to wait that, sometimes, it's difficult to plan a wedding because money and time are spent on the child or children, and it becomes difficult to plan and pay for the wedding.

So, she asked Mike, *"Do you love my daughter Sonia?"*

"Yes, I do." He answered.

Then she asked me, *"Do you love Mike?"*

"Yes, I do," I answered.

"So, then you guys are getting married, right?" She asked.

We looked at each other, grinned, and said yes.

We were very much in love, and we knew we would be getting married at some point in the next two years, so we figured, let's just do it now. My only regret was that he never got down on one knee and proposed or even asked me to marry him. That kind of broke my heart, as that's a girl's dream.

We made it special by picking March 9th, 1991, because it was exactly one year from the date that we met at our friend Carla's house party. Our anniversary.

We called his family and told them the news, and then the wedding planning began. We only had about two months to plan the entire wedding, including the catering, reception, bridal gown, best man, groomsmen, maid of honor, bride's maids, guest list, invitations, reception hall, and so much more.

Time flew by so fast for the planning of the wedding that I really didn't give myself time to think about anything other than making sure everything we arranged or scheduled would be perfect.

So, when the big day arrived, everything really turned out to be perfect. For early March, the weather was expected to be cold and snowy, but it was warm, and the sun was shining so bright.

My wedding was a beautiful event, even surreal. It was held at my Baptist Church. My mom, maid of honor, bridesmaid, and I decorated the church and the reception hall the night before the wedding. I chose the theme white and teal for my wedding.

The teal represented safety and renewal. For me, that was exactly what I thought I had found in my soon-to-be husband.

I had found safety in his arms, in the immense amount of love that he had for me, from what I could feel and witness when he looked into my eyes.

And it was also a renewal for me from the past on how I felt about men and how they treated me. We had about two hundred guests. Mike's family rented a charter bus from Pennsylvania and came to the wedding.

They brought so many delicious Slovakian and German cookies for the reception.

We had the reception at the Brunswick Eagles Club. The flowers, the ceremony, my hair, makeup, my dress, the songs at the wedding, our first dance as husband and wife, everything was just perfect, and we were ecstatic.

Our wedding day was perfect!

That day, as the night came to an end, I witnessed the laughter, the contentedness, and the happiness as I looked around at all the smiling and loving faces of all the friends and family that came to witness and celebrate the beginning of our lives as husband and wife.

That night, I finally decided to just be in the moment and forget everything. This was the start of my new life. Life as a wife and a mother. My mother expressed to me how happy and proud she was of me. How blessed she was to have gained a wonderful son-in-law and that soon she would be a grandmother.

Our once tiny family of just the two of us was now growing, and it was now going to be four of us, along with all my in-laws. I looked at Mike, my now husband, and yes, I did forget everything for a moment. I felt happy. I felt content. But most of all, I felt safe. Safe to love and *safe to have my happily ever after.*

CHAPTER FIVE

BECOMING A MOMMY

After the wedding, we took a mini honeymoon trip to Atlantic City, NJ, for three days. We didn't want to spend too much money, knowing we were expecting our baby in the next six months. Plus, we both had to get back to work.

The honeymoon was good, nothing spectacular, but we enjoyed it, and that was enough. But it was March and too chilly to lay on the beach, let alone get in the water. We did enjoy the casinos and a show or two, walking the boardwalk and having a romantic dinner. It was surreal to think I was a married woman.

I was then four months along. I was happy and excited to see what my marriage would behold. I kept staring down at my husband's and my hand, seeing our wedding rings, along with my growing baby bump, and it all made me feel so calm and safe.

I always felt safe and loved with my mom, but this was different. This was the love of my husband. I imagined a perfect life for us.

Mike was the man that I thought would change how I felt about men and that he would stand up for our children and me if we should need it or anytime in general. But that was what time would reveal.

From the time I was born, I had been hurt by the men in my life. Deep down, I thought I was born into a life of agony from men. But for now, everything was perfect. Life was perfect. My husband was perfect.

Over the course of the next six months, we spent all our free time preparing for our baby. We gutted out one of the bedrooms upstairs to make it a nursery. The house was over a hundred years old, and all the walls were plaster or paneling.

So, we rented a dumpster and began tearing out all the plaster in the bedroom. We smashed the plaster with hammers and threw it out the window, to the ground, or into the dumpster. It was oddly satisfying and gratifying.

For me, it was a release of frustration that had been built up inside me for many years. We finished the room within three weeks of the baby's arrival. The room was decorated with Mikey Mouse and the Clubhouse friends. We got everything we needed from the baby shower that was thrown for us.

My mom bought lots of things for the baby as well. Mike, me, and mom were eagerly waiting for the arrival of our baby. The pregnancy wasn't complicated; however, I did gain far too much weight. I gained 72 lbs, which was very unhealthy. My feet, hands, and face were always swollen, and sometimes, it was hard to walk or breathe.

I craved certain foods, and some foods or smells made me nauseous. I had no idea what to expect. I read some books, and of course, we took the birthing classes, but I don't think anything prepares you to be a mother or parent until you hold your child in your arms.

I continued to work at my job until my baby was due. My due date came and went, and still no baby. About a week later, mom and I spent the day going to yard sales, grocery shopping at the Korean grocery store, stopping for lunch, and just hanging out.

Later that evening, Mike and I sat on the floor, played a few games of Rummy, and snacked on cheese and crackers. I told him I felt such pressure all day, like the baby was trying to push out. I also told him I kept leaking, but neither of us thought anything of it. We went to bed, and early the following day, around 4 am, I started having cramps.

We called the doctor around 5 am, who advised us to go to the hospital immediately. We called my mom to let her know and finally arrived at the hospital at 6 am. Once I was admitted and hooked up to the monitors, they said I was about two centimeters long. The doctor asked me when my water broke, and I told him it didn't. He said there was no water, and when I told him I thought I had been leaking urine all day yesterday, he said it was the water.

Mom arrived at the hospital by 7 am, wearing her Sunday best as it was church day for her. She hoped the baby would be born before church so she could make the announcement. Within hours, the labor pains increased, and it all became unbearably painful for me. The doctor told my mother to go ahead and go to church because it was unlikely that the baby would be delivered until later that evening.

She didn't want to leave my side, but I encouraged her to go. I told her I would be fine and to say a prayer for me. Reluctantly, she left. She attended the service but did not stay for the fellowship and rushed back to me.

Mike was wonderful. He held my hand and rubbed my head and face. By now, the dilation had barely increased each time the doctor came in to check.

The pain was getting much worse, and my blood pressure was rising. They had the fetal monitor on my belly, listening to the baby's heartbeat. Then, the pain got so bad that I could hardly breathe. I was exhausted and just wanted the baby to come out.

Finally, I was four centimeters dilated. It was going so slowly, and I was drained. I hadn't eaten anything since we snacked on the cheese and crackers the night before, and I felt pretty weak. My mother was crying. I saw an odd fear in her eyes when she looked at me.

She kept saying she was terrified something wrong would happen to me. I couldn't pinpoint what or where that fear was coming from, but I told her I would be fine and that she shouldn't worry. She called for the doctor and nurses and told them to just take me down and do a C-section and that I had labored long enough.

Mike told her that his mother was in labor for much longer and that I would be fine staying in labor for several more hours, which made my mother lose her cool.

She jumped up and got in his face, *"I don't care how long your mother was in labor! This isn't about your mother. It's about **my** daughter."*

They both argued with each other, and I begged them to stop. Shortly after that, the fetal monitor showed signs that the baby was in distress.

The baby was pushing so hard to come out, and yet I just couldn't dilate. The doctor waited a bit longer, but then the pain got worse, and they rushed in, saying that the baby's lung had collapsed and they now needed to prep me for an emergency C-section.

My mother was so thankful that they were going to do the C-section and put an end to the pain. As they were ready to stroll me down for surgery, they told Mike he could go in with me and took him to get suited up in sterile clothing. My mother leaned over me just before they took me out of the room.

She cradled my face, kissed my cheek, and whispered, *"I am worried. I can't lose you. I love you so much. You are my world; you just don't know."*

I felt her tear run down the side of my cheek, and I smiled.

"I love you too, mom," I whispered back.

It was an odd, unsettling fear that she had. I felt it, but I couldn't understand why she was so panicked.

It wasn't then that I realized why my mother had such a tremendous amount of fear for my life and giving birth, but a few years later, I sure did.

Finally, he arrived. Our firstborn, our son Brandon, was born September of 1991. He was 9 lbs. 3 oz. I was only able to touch him for a brief second. They let Mike hold him and then rushed him into an incubator and inserted a tube into his lung to help him breathe. Then they took him to the NICU, where he had to stay for over a week. I was heartbroken.

I felt like I wasn't a complete woman because I couldn't deliver my child naturally. I thought in the back of my head if perhaps something with the molestation may have caused this to happen.

Once they took me back to the room to recover, I asked my mother why she was so stressed, and she said all mothers worry about their children, and then she changed the subject.

This was my baby, and yet I couldn't hold him. I was in the hospital for five days, and then they released me. It was difficult to leave the hospital without my child, but I had to. Finally, we were able to bring him home on day seven.

I didn't have a job to go back to. I had planned on taking ten weeks off to stay home with Brandon and then go back. However, the owner of the company stopped by to visit me after Brandon was born to bring me flowers, a gift and to see the baby, and also to tell me that he was closing the business in six weeks and because of that, I had no job to come back to. He brought me a check for the ten weeks of maternity leave. I wasn't upset. I was excited because that meant that I could spend all of my time with Brandon.

My mother was elated to be a grandmother. She was a very proud grandmother. To honor my mother, I gave Brandon his middle name, after my mother. I will say that it was a little terrifying being a mother at first. Everything was so new, and I wasn't sure I even knew what to

105

do. However, I had comfort in knowing I had my mother by my side to help guide me.

Brandon was the perfect baby and so precious. I was afraid I was doing everything wrong. He was so tiny and fragile that I worried that I would hurt him just by putting clothes on him. A few months later, the doctors cleared him and said his lungs would be fine. He would grow up to be a strong boy, and that once-collapsed lung would not bring him any trouble in the future if he wanted to play any kind of sport.

Me, Mike, and my mother were overjoyed. We quickly learned how to be parents. And not to mention, my mom was a huge help.

She came over every evening after work and on the weekends to spend time with Brandon and me. I loved being a mother. Growing up, for me, being an only child was lonely at times. I often envied other kids who had siblings. Although I didn't physically have siblings, in my mind, I felt I had siblings. With the constant flashes, I knew there had to be a reason I had them.

Regardless, I knew I wanted six children. I wanted a house full of wonderful kids. When Brandon was six months old, I told Mike I wanted to try for another baby. I wanted a girl. He agreed and was ready as well.

So, the plan was set in motion. By the time Brandon was nine months old, we had found out we were expecting our second child. I took a home pregnancy test, and it was positive. I was pregnant again, and Mike and I were thrilled.

I still hadn't gone back to work. I was a stay-at-home mom, enjoying my life as a wife and mother. I was so blessed to get to spend all my days at home with Brandon. He was a wonderful baby, so happy all the time. His smile would make any day perfect. I cooked meals from scratch, made my own crafts, curtains, and throw pillows, gardened, and kept the house neat and clean.

Now, I was preparing for our second child. My mother was happy to hear that we were expecting baby number two, but sometimes, during my pregnancy, I could see the same unsettling fear in her eyes that I saw in the hospital while I was in labor with Brandon. My married life was great. Mom watched Brandon when we wanted a night out to ourselves. The four of us did all kinds of things together. We went shopping together, dined out, went to festivals and vacations, and even visited Mike's family in Pennsylvania quite often.

My mom was my best friend, my biggest fan and supporter, and I knew she would do anything in the world for me. There wasn't a day that we didn't chat or see each other. I also had a wonderful marriage. My husband and I could talk about anything and everything. The finances were good. Mike had a great job. We had a nice home, one child and another on the way.

I had a perfect life. A life people dreamt of having. What could possibly go wrong?

Being pregnant with our second child was a little easier. Now, I felt like I knew what to expect. Although I tried not to gain as much weight this time as I did with Brandon, I still gained sixty-three pounds.

My mother was worried about my weight because I never really had enough time to lose the extra weight I had gained while pregnant with Brandon.

This pregnancy was just like my first one. The first three months, I was nauseous, then, of course, I had certain cravings for foods, and some foods or smells just made me sick.

My hands, feet, and face swelled again, the heartburn was unbearable at times, and of course, sometimes, pregnancy has a few other discreet symptoms that can be annoying, but I loved being pregnant. I didn't mind it at all.

One day in October, while Brandon was taking a nap and I was just a little over three months pregnant with our second child, I decided to clean out my jewelry box and get rid of some of the old, cheap costume jewelry.

While doing so, I came across the set of dog tags that belonged to my father. I was never quite sure why my mother held on to them or if she even knew they were mixed in with her jewelry when she packed up our things to leave my dad and the house on Chestnut Grove Rd in Frederick all those years ago. She gave them to me when I was around seven or eight years old as a trinket to play with.

I thought it was pretty cool, so I held on to it all those years and just kept it in my jewelry box like mom. I kept that jewelry box in our bedroom on the side of the bed.

I had a large standing jewelry box that had multiple pull-out drawers, sides that opened up, and a top that opened with a mirror inside it. The jewelry box stood about three feet high with legs under it.

I held those dog tags in my hand. It was the only thing I had that belonged to my father. I sat on my bed and stared at it. Then, I began to read the engraving on it. I read his name, his military ID number, his religious preference, and then, an *O*…

O? What could that mean? It must have stood for an officer, I thought to myself. I knew from all my mom's friends at Fort Ritchie that all military staff was given identification tags, also known as dog tags, to identify them. So, if they needed any medical attention, the dog tags listed their blood type. I didn't see his blood type listed on his tags.

Certainly, the *O* couldn't have meant it was his blood type. I knew I was type *A*, and my mother was type *O*. So, my father had to be type *A* because I had to have gotten type A blood from one of my parents, no?

I sat there, full of curiosity. I thought about how the military could make such a mistake as to leave his blood type off of the dog tags.

I picked up the phone and called an Army Recruiting Office. I spoke to a recruiting officer about the identification tags.

"My father's tag says O on it. What does that mean?" I asked.

He replied, *"O means his blood type."*

"Are you sure? Does it not mean officer?" I questioned.

He assured me that the tags do not list the ranking of the enlisted personnel but rather their name, identification number, religious preference, and blood type only.

My heart sank as I hung up the phone. I was so confused. Perhaps my dad gave the Army the wrong blood type. My own thought didn't even make sense to me.

I couldn't understand what was going on. I could hear Brandon waking up from his nap, so I put the tags back in the jewelry box. I got him out of his crib, and we went downstairs to play with his toys, but in the back of my mind lingered my confusion about the blood type.

It was very confusing for me. I did not want to accept the fact that my mind was screaming at me to acknowledge it.

I glanced at Brandon, placed my hand on my growing belly, closed my eyes, and exhaled. I tried to let go of the thought. This was more important for now. *My present. My babies. My happy family.*

That day, when Mike came home from work, I was agitated. Not at him, but just because I was frustrated with not being able to comprehend what the *O* on the dog tag meant. I told him what I had discovered on my father's dog tag and that I had called the recruiting office for an explanation.

"Something is not right. This isn't making any sense." I said to him.

He really didn't know what to say, but he was there and listened. The next day, after Mike went to work, I called a lab company that tested blood for various reasons.

I asked them if they knew whether two adults with type *O* blood could produce a child with type A blood. They told me that could not happen. That one adult would have to have type *A*.

Still not satisfied, I called my OBGYN and asked to speak with my doctor. He was busy with a patient, but he did call me back. And when I asked him the same question, he said it was absolutely impossible for two adults with type *O* blood to have a child that has type *A*.

I hung up the phone and stood there with a huge lump in my throat. I tried to make sense of this. All kinds of things were running through my mind. But then I thought, my mother must have had an affair and didn't tell my father, so my real father must have type *A* blood because my mother certainly was my biological mother.

I was somewhat happy at that moment to think that the monster that I thought was my father, who molested me, most likely wasn't my father. And maybe, that explained why he was so crazy and could beat and hurt my mother and me.

My mother was a very private woman and didn't talk much about her past. She never brought up the pain she suffered from my father, or rather, the man that I assumed was my father.

Most Koreans are very private, and they don't discuss their personal business. I needed to figure out how to bring this up with my mother.

A few days went by, and I thought, what better way to find out than in the divorce records? Perhaps, it would say who my real father was.

I called the Frederick County Courthouse and requested a copy of my parent's divorce record. They told me that it was in the archive, but they could pull it. It would take up to ten weeks, but once they got it, they would give me a call, and I could pick it up.

So, I waited for that call. I never mentioned anything to my mother about the dog tag, the blood type, or requesting the divorce records. I wanted to wait until I knew more. During that time, my pregnancy with my second child progressed well. Halloween and Thanksgiving came and went. Christmas was just a few weeks away. Wednesday, December 9th, 1992, I had just come back home from a doctor's appointment when I got a call from the Frederick County Courthouse.

They had my mother's divorce records, and I could come to pick them up. I didn't want to drive back to Frederick since I had just had a minor procedure done on my foot. It was a little painful, and I didn't want to put my shoes back on.

I asked if my husband could pick it up, and they said yes. I called Mike at work and asked him to swing by the court house after work and pick up the papers.

Then, I waited for him to come home. He usually got home by 4:45 pm, but I knew it would probably be by around 5:30 pm since he had to stop on his way home to pick up the papers. Soon, it was 6 pm, and then 7 pm, when he finally walked in the door.

My heart was racing. I was aggravated that he took so long but also filled with anticipation and couldn't wait to read every single page of the divorce papers. We put Brandon to bed for the night and then sat on the couch.

Finally, I opened the manila envelope and started reading each page. By the time I got to the last page, I was elated.

I yelled out with joy, *"Thank God! See, everyone was wrong for thinking I wasn't half Korean! Nowhere in the divorce papers does it say that they are not my parents or that I am adopted! My mom didn't have an affair. I*

am half Korean, and I don't have a different biological father somewhere."
Although that part of it would have been nice.

That night, when we went to bed, I asked Mike what took him so long to get home. He said he stopped by the Rite Aid to pick up some things and saw Beth, my mother's neighbor who was the manager there. She was working, and they chatted for a few minutes.

"Okay," I said and brushed it off.

That night, I slept soundly for the first time since I discovered the *O* on my father's dog tags. Now, it was all behind me. I was a peace with it. Whatever that *O* was supposed to mean, it didn't change anything for me. My mother was my mother, and I was half-Korean.

The next day, Brandon and I stopped by my mom's house for a bit after she got home from work just to hang out. She was going to be off the next day, so it was okay if we stayed a little late. I wasn't going to mention anything about the dog tags or the divorce papers. What was the point now? Everything was fine.

While I was there, I spoke with her neighbor, Beth, as we were outside. The whole neighborhood was close as friends. We chatted for about ten minutes.

"Mike told me that he saw you at work last night," I said to her.

She looked a bit confused. She said she wasn't at work last night and, in fact, she hadn't been in the Rite Aid at all for the past two days. I didn't know what to say, so I brushed it off as it must have been a miscommunication between Mike and me.

I enjoyed my visit at mom's, and then Brandon and I went home. I told her I would be back tomorrow to spend the day with her since she was off work. That evening, when Mike and I were sitting on the couch, I started interrogating him about where he was and what took him longer than it should have to come home with the divorce papers. I knew he didn't see Beth, and he didn't talk to her. What I couldn't figure out was why he lied and what he was up to.

As Mike and I lay in bed, snuggled to each other, I told him again how happy I was to have put the doubts about my parents to rest. All I really cared about was that my mother was and will always be my mother. As far as I was concerned, whether the O on the dog tag meant officer, blood type, or something else, I would further investigate in the near future.

For now, my mind shifted to figuring out what Mike was hiding.

"What was it again that took you so long to get home last night with the papers?" I questioned him one last time before we fell asleep.

He replied, *"Traffic was bad. I think there was an accident that backed up traffic."*

"Okay," I responded. *"Then you stopped at Rite Aid?"*

"Yes." He answered.

"What did you go in there to buy?" I questioned.

"I just picked up a few things I needed." He answered.

But oddly, he never walked into the house with a bag from Rite Aid.

"So, what did you and Beth talk about?" I continued my interrogation.

"It wasn't much, just the usual. 'Hi, how are you? How are things going?'" He said nonchalantly.

"Good night," I said and rolled over.

My mind was spinning. I needed to know what was going on, and I was determined to get to the bottom of it. I am sure Mike could sense my suspicions. After all, he was my husband, and he knew me. He knew that I didn't let anything go.

The next morning, Mike went off to work, and after breakfast, Brandon and I headed over to spend the day with my mother. I told my mother that Mike was a little late getting home that night and that I thought he might be cheating on me. She asked me why I thought that, and I told her his excuse for coming home late was that he stopped at Rite Aid to buy a few things and ran into Beth while he was there. I told her that Beth wasn't at Rite Aid, didn't talk to him, and he came home with no bag from Rite Aid.

She assured me that it was probably my hormones out of whack from being pregnant. She told me that Mike loved me very much and that I was worrying for nothing and to just let it go.

Mike and I had plans to go out for a Chinese dinner in Charles Town, WV that evening, which was only twelve miles from our home in Brunswick. We could be in Virginia or West Virginia within five minutes of our home in Brunswick, MD. It was crazy, yet pretty cool, that we could drive from our home in Maryland to Virginia and West Virginia, both in a matter of only five minutes. Mom had planned on having Brandon spend the night with her so Mike and I could have a date night.

It was a cold chilly night, December 11th, 1992, when Mike and I went out for dinner. I was a bit quiet and a little distant.

"If I was hiding something from you, would you want to know?" I asked.

"It depends on the secret." He responded.

"What if I were hiding something, and you knew it? Would it make you mad?" I further probed.

"Again, it depends on what is being hidden." He answered.

I knew he was up to something. Now I was hurt and getting mad. Dinner was good, the food there was always delicious. It was his favorite Chinese restaurant. When we walked out of the restaurant, it was snowing. and the road and sidewalks were already lightly covered. He held my hand and my arm as we walked out to make sure I wouldn't slip. I knew he loved me because he was so caring, or maybe it was because I was five months along, carrying our second child, but I needed an answer, and I needed it now.

As we started driving slowly back to Brunswick, I told him I had spoken with Beth, so I knew he didn't see her or talk to her. I told him I wasn't stupid. I knew he didn't walk into the house with a bag from Rite Aid.

"So, tell me why you were so late coming back home?" I blurted.

I saw his Adam's apple go up and down as he took a big swallow. He brushed it off as heavy traffic, looking a bit nervous.

"Just stop!" I shouted. *"Just tell me the truth! Are you cheating on me?"*

"No, I am not." He replied.

I told him he was lying and I didn't believe him, and that I wasn't going to stay with a cheater. He reached over to hold my hand as we navigated through the snow to get home. I brushed his hand away from mine.

"If you can't be honest with me, then we are done. I will raise our babies just fine without you." You are a cheater! A Cheater and a liar!! I yelled.

At that moment, as we were approaching the top of the hill at Harper's Ferry, WV, on Interstate 340, he pulled the car over onto the shoulder of the highway.

"Why are we stopping?" I questioned.

He looked at me and said, *"I am not cheating on you. The reason I came home late with the divorce papers wasn't because of traffic or stopping by Rite Aid, but because I stopped by your mother's house to talk with her about the divorce papers and that you had requested them."* He explained.

I looked at him with anger, *"Why would you do that? I didn't want her to know I pulled the divorce records! That was supposed to be something that only you and I knew about. What were you thinking?"* I yelled at him.

"You don't care about me! I can't trust you. I can't tell you things and think you have my back! What is wrong with you?" I continued to yell.

Then he reached into his pocket, pulled out his wallet, and pulled out a piece of paper that had been folded down to fit in the wallet.

As he held that paper in his hand, he looked into my eyes, took a big sigh, and said, *"I stopped by to speak with your mother after I had picked up her divorce records. When I got the papers, I sat in my car and read through each page, and when I got to this page,"* he held the folded piece of paper up.

"I pulled it out. I went to your mother to show her the papers, and specifically this page, and to tell her that she needs to talk to you and tell you herself before you find out on your own. I told her that I would pull this page out before I handed you the envelope so you wouldn't see it. But I told her that I know you, and you will not give up searching for answers, and it would be best if she told you the truth, but that she should wait until after you have the baby. I did it to protect you, Sonia, not to hurt you. I did it to protect you and your mother." He finished.

"You should wait until we get home to read it." He sighed.

We were only about ten minutes away, but with the snowfall, it was most likely going to take us about twenty minutes. I couldn't wait. I needed to read it now. What was on this page that I needed protecting from? What truth did I need to know from my mother?

He handed me the folded paper. I switched the dome light of the car on and began to read from the very first line of the page.

And there, in the middle of the page, in black and white, were the words that would change my life. It said Sonia Hutchinson, the **adopted child**

of both Breeden George Hutchinson and Soon Nam Hutchinson, would remain in the full and sole custody of the adoptive mother, Soon Nam Hutchinson.

I folded the paper and put it in my purse as my eyes welled up with tears. I felt I couldn't breathe or even get words to come out of my mouth. Mike leaned over to hold me, but I didn't want him to touch me. I just wanted to go home.

He kept asking me if I was okay. He kept saying he just wanted my mother to tell me after I had the baby. He didn't want me to find out this way, especially while pregnant. He didn't want me to deal with the stress of it all. I couldn't speak. I was in shock. I just stared at the windshield, watching the snow fall as Mike drove us home.

Once we got home, I went upstairs to change my clothes. I sat on the edge of my bed and opened the drawer of the jewelry box. I retrieved the dog tag and stared at it again; I was so overloaded with emotions.

I felt like a zombie. I was empty. I felt lost. I didn't know who I was or where I came from. For the first time in my life, I realized that I was not Korean. I thought about all the people who lied to my face, her friends, my grandmother, my Korean aunts, and my uncles.

I thought about all of my friends, teachers, classmates, and acquaintances that questioned or doubted that I was or looked Korean, and I assured them I was Korean. How stupid was I?

My tears ran down my face, and I sobbed so hard. Mike came into the bedroom to console me, but I just wanted to be left alone. I told him I would be downstairs in a minute and to just go.

After he walked out of the room, I walked down to the bathroom, climbed in the cold tub, and just sat in the tub and cried. I sat in the tub for quite a while, bawling my eyes out, trying to make sense of it all.

How could someone I love more than my own life, someone I sacrificed so much for and did whatever it took to protect her and her life, lie to me about who I was? Why would my mom do that to me? I felt truly empty and lost.

Mike came back upstairs looking for me. I had the bathroom door locked. He banged on the door, begging me to come out. Pleading with me that I needed to come out because I was pregnant and needed to think about the baby.

He didn't want me to stress about this situation. I wouldn't call it stress. It was more anxiety and panic because I now didn't know anything about myself.

Who was I? Where was I from? Who were my biological parents? Where were they? Were the boy and girl I always saw holding an infant my siblings? Where were they? Why was I given up for adoption? Did my biological parents not want me? Did they not love me?

Questions after questions scurried around in my head. Mike was still banging on the bathroom door, begging me to come out, so finally, I did. We went downstairs and sat on the couch. He tried talking to me, but honestly, it was like I couldn't hear him. My mind was in another place. I sat on the couch, numb, staring at the paneled walls or out the window. Nothing made sense. I worked so hard for my life to be happy and now it was shattered again.

Later, when Mike said we should head to bed to get some rest, I couldn't budge. I just wanted to sit on the couch all night and figure out the past twenty-four years. Why couldn't I see the fact that I wasn't Korean?

More than anything, I just couldn't understand what the reasoning was for hiding it from me that I was adopted.

Finally, Mike went upstairs to bed, and I decided to sit on the couch with only a dimly lit lamp in the corner. As I sat there, I was tormented by the memories of what my father did to me, the molestation, and the mental anguish he put me through by telling me he would kill my mother if I told her what he was doing to me.

The disgust I felt at times when even my own husband wanted to touch me. The shame I felt. The helplessness of having to watch my father beat and torture my mother.

The glimpses of seeing that baby in the arms of a little boy and girl, believing in my soul that it was me and they were my siblings. The agony of keeping it all bottled up inside and not telling anyone.

Then I was overcome with a tingling sensation. I could feel my heart beating faster as it became hard to breathe. My chest felt tight, and I felt so dizzy that I thought I was having a heart attack. It lasted about fifteen minutes and then subsided.

'What is happening to me?' I thought.

I was shaking so badly. I lay on the couch and curled up the best I could. Being five months pregnant, draped a blanket over myself and eventually cried myself to sleep.

Morning came, and mom called. She wanted to see if I wanted to come over to her house for a bit, and then perhaps, she, myself, and Brandon could go out for the day Christmas shopping. I told her I wasn't feeling well, and she offered to make me some Korean soup, bring it over with Brandon, and nurse me to health.

I told her I would feel better if I just stayed home alone and rested. I told her Mike could come to pick up Brandon, but she insisted on keeping him to help me if I wasn't feeling well. I muddled around the house for a bit in the morning, and then I sat at the kitchen table, looking at photos and thinking back.

Were there clues that I missed? I wanted answers. No—*I needed answers.*

CHAPTER SIX

MY BEAUTIFUL WORLD SHATTERED

Mike cooked breakfast, but I wasn't hungry. I knew I needed to eat for the baby, but the thought of food made me nauseous. I sat there trying to figure out how to approach my mother about my adoption. I knew it wasn't going to be easy. My mother was very private. If she didn't want to talk about something, she didn't. And since she hadn't told me in all these years about my adoption, I figured she wasn't about to now.

I loved her very much. No matter what, she was still my mother. Nothing was going to change that. But I needed to know. I had the right to know. I had one child and one on the way. I needed to know my medical history. I wanted to know about my biological family.

Later that afternoon, mom stopped by to bring Brandon back home. She made a pot of Miyeok-Guk, a Korean seaweed soup, for me. This delicious traditional soup is heart-healthy and is eaten to promote good health. It is consumed often, but as a tradition in Korea, women have the soup several times a day after childbirth to cleanse their blood, heal their bodies and help produce milk for the child.

Because I was pregnant, mom made it for me so I would have it for my health and the baby. We sat at the table, and I enjoyed a large bowl of it.

She asked me what was wrong and if I had a cold, stomach bug, a headache, or what. I told her I was just feeling very tired and drained, probably from being pregnant. I asked her if she ever felt like that when she was carrying me. Her answer was that she couldn't remember.

I didn't say anything else as I just needed a little more time to gather my thoughts and figure out how to approach her. She stayed at the house, and we all sat in the living room watching TV. Mom sat next to me, rubbing my back and my head. I held back the tears because I just didn't want her to know quite yet that I knew. Around 7 pm, mom headed home to get ready for church the next day.

We hugged and kissed each other and said, '*I love you*' to each other.

We always told each other '*I Love You*' every day, any time we hugged goodbye and at the end of any phone conversation. It didn't matter what mood we were in, the situation, or the conversation. We made it a point to always say *I love you*. We always wanted each other to know that if something happened, you knew the last words spoken, and the feelings to each other were *"I love you."*

The next day, I called mom after she got home from church and asked if I could stop by.

"Of course, this is your home. You can come by anytime," she said.

I headed over to her house around 4 pm. Mike kept Brandon with him so I could talk with mom. We sat at the kitchen table, chatting for a few minutes as she was preparing dinner. I still wasn't sure how to exactly bring up the topic of my adoption, so I just started with how I was cleaning out my jewelry box, saw dad's dog tags, and noticed they had an *O* on them. I told her I thought that meant officer but that I did some research and found out that it actually meant his blood type.

I told her I knew she had type *O* blood because she had had several surgeries over the years and needed blood, and I wasn't a match since I was *A* and she was *O*.

She sat there, silent. I could see she was caught off guard.

"Am I adopted?" I asked her.

She replied, *"You are my daughter."*

I said, *"Yes, yes, I am. And always will be. But am I adopted?"*

She didn't answer. I waited a few minutes, hoping that she just needed a moment before telling me. But she remained silent.

"Mom, I know. I know." I said in a small voice and a lump in my throat. *"I requested a copy of the divorce records from the courthouse, so I know I am adopted. Please tell me about it."*

She got up from the table and went to the stove to check on the food she was cooking. Then she walked around the house doing a few things, gathering laundry, etc. I knew, in part, it was to deflect from the topic.

When she returned to the kitchen, I asked her again to please tell me something.

"Did you know my family? Why did they give me up for adoption? Did they not want me?" I probed further. Begging her to tell me something.

She calmly looked at me and said, *"I don't know anything. You were dropped off on my doorstep, and when I opened the door, there you were, wrapped in a pink blanket in a basket. No note or anything. I brought you inside, and we contacted the military to inform them. Then, when no one claimed you, your father and I adopted you. End of story."* She narrated.

"So that's it? That's the whole story?" I asked.

"Yes." She answered.

"So why didn't you just tell me years ago," I questioned.

"There was nothing to tell." She concluded.

I could tell my mother was agitated with me. She wasn't comfortable with our conversation. I sat there for a few minutes silent while she finished cooking and set the food on the table for us to eat.

"Okay." I finally sighed.

"Do you remember anything at all about the adoption? If the military tried to locate my parents or family? If the military knew anything? Does my father know anything?" I ranted.

She stayed firm and said, "No."

"I love you very much. You are my mother, always were and always will be. You are my world. Nothing will ever change any of that. Please, I beg you, tell me anything that you remember or know." I almost cried.

She shrugged her shoulders and reiterated that she didn't know anything. We both sat in silence not saying a word as we ate the delicious food that mom just prepared. It broke my heart to see my mother uncomfortable with our conversation. I knew it pained her. The last thing I ever wanted to do was cause any pain for my mother, but all I wanted were answers to my questions. I tried to make small talk as we cleared the table and cleaned the kitchen, but she said very little back. A few minutes went by, and there was complete silence in the house as neither of us said anything. I realized at that moment that if I wanted answers, I had to find them on my own.

Mom then told me it was time for me to go. She was tired and had to get ready for work the next day. I knew she was done with our conversation, and to avoid continuing the topic, it was best for her to have me leave. I kissed her, hugged her, told her I loved her, and went home. That evening at home, I had another episode where my heart pounded so hard and fast, I couldn't breathe. I felt dizzy, my hands and arms were tingling, and I thought I was going to have a heart attack.

The next morning, Mike left for work, and Brandon and I were home alone. I started thinking of how I could get some answers. I thought perhaps, her Korean friends, Song and Kim, the two ladies who had taken care of me when mom was in the hospital from the car accident in 1970, might know about my adoption. They were still friends with mom. Maybe mom told them about my adoption. It was worth a try to give them a call.

So, I called them both and told them I had just found out about my adoption. I begged them to tell me if they knew anything. I told them that I wouldn't tell my mom that I called them and asked them not to tell her either. They both wanted to know what she had told me about it.

So, I told them her story about how I was left on her doorstep, wrapped in a pink blanket in a basket. They both said that because of their loyalty of the friendship to my mother, they weren't comfortable telling me much. But they felt I should know something at least. They said the doorstep story wasn't true. They said that my mother did tell them a little about me. Not much, and not because she wanted to, but basically because they could tell I wasn't biologically her daughter and because they were caring for me when I was three years old while she was in the hospital.

They questioned her, and she offered just a little background. She did tell them that I did have a brother and sister. That I was the youngest of five children and that my biological mother died. What did I just hear? I couldn't believe she just said that I do have a brother and sister. Chills ran down my back. Is that the vision of the little boy and girl I see so often holding a baby? My heart skipped a beat.

They said they really couldn't give me more information and that I should talk with my mother because she knows more than she is telling me. I thanked them for their honesty.

Over the next several days, I tried to figure out ways to get more information on my adoption. I looked at my Social Security Card, my birth certificate, and my passport, but I couldn't think of anything or how they could help me. Mom and I didn't talk too much over the course of that week. I think we both needed some time to absorb what was happening.

Christmas was a week away, and mom and I still had last-minute shopping to do. I decided it was best to put it on the back burner until after Christmas and New Year's.

We all wanted to enjoy the holidays, and we wanted it to be special for Brandon. He was fifteen months old. Mom and I didn't discuss the adoption and acted like nothing was ever discovered. I was still having these crazy episodes of rapid heart beating, tingling arms and hands, shortness of breath, and a feeling of dying. I wasn't sure if it had something to do with the pregnancy because I had never experienced it before, and certainly not when I was pregnant with Brandon, either.

Christmas and New Year were great. It was now January 1993, and our baby was going to be arriving in just four months. I tried to reason with mom during those four months that I just wanted to know about my adoption. I tried so hard to convince her to tell me. But I felt like she was beating around the bush. I told her what if I were to die giving birth to my second child. I would die not knowing anything, or at least what she knew. I asked her to at least explain to me why she didn't tell me. Perhaps, I said something in this conversation that persuaded my mother to reveal the secret she had kept from me all these years.

So finally, with tears running down her face, she said she was ready to tell me everything. She explained that I was born in Iran, a country that I probably would not be able to go back to. More than likely, that meant that I would never see any of my biological family anyways. She also explained that in her heart, she never thought of me as an adopted child but solely as her own child. She said she knew in her heart that I was her child from the moment she saw me and held me. She knew God sent her there to be my mother. She loved me more than she could ever love anyone or anything, and she feared if I knew about the adoption or what a piece of paper said, then perhaps, I wouldn't love her as much.

I cried and told her that was simply not true. *"Of course, you are my mother. My world, my heart, and my soul. You have raised me, taken such great care of me, and provided me with everything a child could need. You are such a strong woman, my role model, and my hero. God gave me to you and you to me, and no one and no piece of paper can ever change that. We are mother and daughter for all of eternity."*

I hugged her so tightly because I wanted her to feel the love I had for her then and always will. Just as we were hugging, the baby kicked, and my mom felt it.

I jokingly told her, *"The baby kicked you for thinking otherwise. See how smart the baby is already?"*

We laughed and wiped each other's tears.

As much as I felt like I was the victim in this situation with my mom keeping my adoption a secret, I focused on the fact that it was hurting her. My whole life, I did everything I could to protect her from anyone who tried to hurt her, and I dedicated myself to never wanting to hurt or cause pain for my mother. And yet, in that moment, I felt like I was the one hurting her. She was an angel who took care of me. She didn't deserve to be badgered by me.

I figured, in time, when she was ready, she would tell me everything. But until that time, I had to do all the leg work on finding out the whole story on my own. Those days of sitting back and being silent with no voice to speak up or fight back are gone. I realized at that moment that I was a survivor of life's circumstances. So that made me a fighter.

My mother taught me that you could do anything you put your mind to. After all, she did it time and time again. Now, I was a mother, and I needed to know for myself and for the protection of my own children about myself. I was going to get the answers. I was going to move mountains. There was absolutely nothing that was going to get in my way.

So, I spent the next several months calling some of mom's various other Korean friends, asking them if they had any information. I think because of their loyalty to my mother's friendship, and because Koreans are private people, and if their friend tells them something, they also keep it private, I was always going to hit a dead end. Or perhaps, they just really didn't know anything about it at all. As frustrating as it was, I did admire the loyalty that mom and her friends had for each other.

Then, my search for answers came to a stop for a few weeks when our beautiful baby girl, Shelby, arrived in April of 1993. She was seven pounds. I chose the name Shelby because I wanted to make a tradition of keeping the S as the first initial for the girls. Soon, Sonia and Shelby, and also because I really like the name. I was so elated and overjoyed. I needed to focus on being a mother of two now and getting a routine down. I wanted to nurse Brandon and Shelby both, and I did try with Brandon for about three weeks. I had to stop, though, because of the circumstances with my father and the molestation. I found it extremely uncomfortable nursing my children even though I knew it was a very natural thing. I just couldn't do it. The things that man robbed me of were horrible. I will bear each of those scars for the rest of my life.

I had scheduled a C-section in advance for the birth of my second child. Knowing Brandon's lung had collapsed during labor, I didn't want to take any chances with our second child. Also, after spending the last four months of this pregnancy discovering secrets, not knowing my own identity, feeling lost, and having an influx of so many emotions, scheduling the C-section was the right thing for me to do.

Having two children was wonderful. Shelby, too, was a good baby. There were some nights when she wanted to grace us for the entire night with the sound of her voice crying, and it seemed as though there was nothing we could do to calm her. She had colic, and those nights that she cried made me feel so helpless.

Shelby was like a real-life baby doll. She was so adorable, and I just wanted to dress her in the cutest clothes and put bows in her hair. One of the cutest things about Shelby was her unwillingness to want to crawl or walk. She would sit on her butt and bounce up and down as she scooted herself from one side of the room to the other or from room to room. It was absolutely adorable.

She was born with a severe stigmatism which made her eyes cross. At just six months old, we had her first surgery done to help correct the issue. She did have several more surgeries over the years, which corrected the muscle in her eyes.

About Brandon, he was the doting brother. He and Shelby were nineteen months apart. He loved his little sister and would bring her toys or her bottle to her. He played with her all the time and always asked us to hold her. I would make him sit on the couch and place Shelby in his lap, and watch him as he rubbed her head. I don't know why, but it would trigger those flashbacks of a little boy and girl holding a baby and feeding her. Now, I just knew in my heart that *that baby was me.*

There was something about Brandon that resembled that little boy that I felt was my brother.

My mother was thrilled to have two grandchildren. She spoiled them so much.

Me, I adjusted very well to having two children. It was like I was meant to be a mom. The joy I felt from being a mother was amazing. I took them with me anytime I had to go to the store, the mall, or grocery shopping. I wanted my children with me all the time, everywhere I went. Mike and I would walk in the evenings and push the children in their strollers.

We even got a little trailer to attach to his bike that we put the kids in and rode on the C & O Canal Towpath. Our family life was great.

When mom wasn't working, she was at our house, or I was at hers with the children.

The episodes of heart palpations, dizziness, tingling arms and hands, erratic breathing, and fear of dying were progressing more often and in public places. It started happening in the grocery store when Mike and I would go out to eat and even while shopping in the mall.

Each time it happened in a public place, I had to leave immediately. I would leave the shopping cart full of groceries and race out to my car. If we were at dinner, sometimes, I would leave the restaurant even before our food was brought out so I could race to the car to suffer the episode alone and then go home. I thought if I was going to die, I didn't want to do it in a public place for everyone to see.

Mike was working rotating night shifts, and it seemed each night he had to work, I had a severe case of it. It would usually hit me at night when the kids were in bed. Sometimes, I would run outside onto the porch just to feel like I could breathe. The more determined I was to find the answers, the more visions I started having of the little boy and girl that I assumed are my brother and sister.

Sometimes, I dreamt of a little boy crying as he ran down a dirt road. Other times, the overwhelming sense or memory of a man looking down at me with such resentment would shake the hell out of me.

Sometimes, I would be someplace, and I would smell a scent that immediately took me back to the apartment that my father had. Often times, just seeing a Hershey® Bar or a jar of Vaseline on a shelf in a store would trigger those horrible memories.

I wasn't sure if I was losing my mind or losing control of myself. There wasn't a day that I didn't question who I was, where I came from, how many siblings did I really have, why I had been given up for adoption, or what my birth name actually was. I wanted answers.

As much as it pained and frightened me, I thought if I could locate my adoptive father, then perhaps, he could give me the information. I mean, after all, he was there when I was adopted, and he owed it to me. After everything he did to me, that man owed it to me to tell me everything. Even if I had to beat it out of him.

I never wanted anything from him, and I sure as heck never wanted to see him again.

But this was different. I found myself needing answers so severely that I was willing to stand face-to-face with my horrible and mentally ill adoptive father. I hoped he had some sort of memory of being in Iran or even of him and my mother adopting me. The frightening aspect of locating him was that perhaps he would try to come back into our lives. Mom and I never had any desire to want to see him again, but this was necessary.

Now, not only did I have to worry about what he could do to my mother or myself, but also to my children and husband. Mom and I knew he was mentally ill, but we had no idea what he would be capable of now. Unquestionably, now that he was in his sixties, I couldn't imagine he could do much. I was older, stronger, wiser, and most importantly, I refused to ever allow him to hurt us again.

I had no idea how to locate my adoptive father. I knew he wasn't in the Army anymore, but where did he relocate to? I remember my mom saying that he had family in Cincinnati, OH, and in Dallas, TX. I started searching on the computer for any Hutchinson I could find in those areas. I narrowed my search to George and Breeden but didn't have any luck.

I spent my time while the kids were napping, making random calls to every Hutchinson I could find on the computer, asking them if they knew or were related to George Hutchinson.

Every call I made, I was given the same answer. *No.*

I asked if they had other family members who might know him since he was an older man. But each time, again, I was told *no.*

Some people were quick to hang up the phone afterward, and yet some asked me who he was and why I was looking for him. I told them that he was my father and that I was looking for him because I hadn't seen him since I was a little girl. I did so in hopes that it would pull on their heartstrings, and if they did know him, they would tell me. But it was to no avail, as each call ended without information.

I started circling back, calling my mom's friends again. Hoping that maybe, they knew where he relocated to. Any information they could offer would be some help. If they could give me a city or a state, just somewhere that I could search. Again, none of them really knew where he was, or due to their friendship-loyalty, they revealed nothing.

One day, while mom was at work, I stopped by her house to drop off some lasagna that I had made the night before for dinner and put it in her fridge.

As I stood there, staring down the hall to her bedroom, I contemplated going through a suitcase that she kept in the back of her closet with all her important documents. I hated what my obsession with the answers and truth was doing to me. I tiptoed down the hallway, trying not to make a sound, entered her bedroom, and gently opened the closet door. I don't know why I tiptoed into her room so quietly like a criminal when I knew she wasn't home, but I did.

I reached in, grabbed the suitcase, and laid it on her bed. There was no lock on it. I stared at it for a few seconds. The answers I was looking for could very well be in there. I just needed to open it.

But at the last moment, I hesitated. I couldn't do it. That suitcase and whatever personal items she had inside were just that, her personal items. Rummaging through that would be an invasion and violation of her privacy. I always prided myself on how dedicated I was to protecting my mother and never allowing anyone to violate her in any way, so how could I do that to her myself?

Tears ran down my face when I picked the suitcase up and placed it back in her closet, unopened. I walked out of the house, determined to find the answers that I was looking for on my own, with any help that was handed to me along the way graciously accepted.

The months ticked by. Shelby is now just over seven months old, and it was December. It was just about a year ago that I found out that I was adopted. I was still dealing with heart palpitations, shortness of breath, dizziness, and the feeling that I was going to die. It was odd how they could come on at random times of the day or evening.

Sometimes, I would have one or two episodes a week, and other times, it could be three or four. Quite often, I drove myself to the Emergency Room, or when Mike was home, I would have him take me. Every time we were at the ER, they ran tests but always said they couldn't find anything wrong. They said my heart was just fine. But I wasn't convinced. I felt there was something that they just weren't catching.

I thought maybe I could find out where my father was or relocated to from the military. That perhaps, they had a last known address for him. I called the Army recruiting office again, and this time, I asked if they keep records of their personnel from years ago and, perhaps, a last known address or forwarding address for the discharged personnel.

The gentleman I spoke with on the phone didn't seem very willing to offer any help. He brushed me off and basically said they did not give out that information. Well, I thought, he just gave me a bit of information without even realizing it.

What he said was, *"We don't give out that information."*

He didn't say they don't keep that kind of information.

So, I had a thought. All those years mom and I spent going back and forth, visiting her friends at Fort Ritchie, and building a very close friendship with them gave me an idea. My mom's closest Korean friend on that base was Chung Soon Ye. Everyone called her Pak. Her husband, Smitty, was now retired from the Army, and he and his wife, Pak, and their two sons had moved to Hampton, VA, when he was transferred to Fort Eustis at Newport News, VA, years ago.

Smitty was somewhat like a godfather to me. Mom and I went many times to visit them in Hampton, VA. Smitty and Pak opened up a restaurant and bar after he retired, but he still had very close connections with friends on the Army base. I called Smitty to ask a favor of him. I told him that I was trying to locate my father. I needed to find him to ask him questions about my adoption. I told him my mother wasn't comfortable discussing my adoption, so I couldn't get any information from her.

Having a Korean wife, he knew what that meant. I explained that I needed to know if the Army knew his last known address, a forwarding address, or where he was so I could contact him. I wanted to know if they had a phone number or something or if there was any way I could get in touch with him. He said he would help me. He had friends on the base who could do some digging. He said it might take a bit since they have to be very discreet about it, but if he found anything, he would let me know. I told him my father's name, and I gave him the identification number from his dog tags. I prayed he would find something or some information.

Daily life with Brandon and Shelby was wonderful. My babies were growing and flourishing well. Married life was great, and mom and I were busy going Christmas shopping, wrapping presents, and buying all the ingredients we needed to make her Korean eggrolls which she gave out to all the neighbors and her friends for Christmas.

Christmas was wonderful, and 1994 was about to begin. I had hoped the new year would bring the answers I so desperately wanted and the terrifying episodes of heart palpitations and the constant memories of the molestation would end.

One evening, towards the end of January, I received a call from Smitty. I was excited to hear from him. I figured that meant he had found some information about my father's whereabouts. The conversation started off with cordials, asking how the holidays went and how our families were doing.

Then he said, *"Well, I have some news. My buddy was able to get his last known address."*

I felt excited and nervous at the same time. Before he could get another word in, I thanked him for doing this for me and told him that hopefully, when I talk with my father, he will be able to give me more information about my adoption and that with that information, hopefully, I would be able to locate my biological family.

Then Smitty said to me, *"The news isn't what you were expecting. I'm so sorry, Sonia, but he passed away about ten months ago in a Veteran's Administration Hospital in Louisiana. I have the phone number and address of the VA hospital if you'd like that info. Maybe they can give you some information about him."*

I was heartbroken. Not because he was dead. He deserved to be dead after what he did to my mother and me. I was heartbroken because if he did have any information, that was now gone to the grave with him, and that put me back on a dead-end road again. I did take the name and number of the VA Hospital, thanked him again for his help, and we hung up. That night, I went to bed angry at the world. And feeling somewhat sorry for myself because it always seems like I have to

135

jump hurdles and maneuver obstacles in life. I went to bed, praying for strength and wisdom.

The next morning, as I sat at the kitchen table feeding the children, I kept looking at the phone number of the VA Hospital that I had written on a piece of paper. I wondered why the hospital didn't call me to tell me he had passed away. Shouldn't I have been the next of kin? So that made me think if they didn't call me, then they must have called another family member as a next of kin.

I talked to Mike about it when he came home and mentioned that I'd like to call the hospital and ask them who he had listed as a next of kin. If they would give me the name and phone number of that person, wouldn't that help me?

Mike was skeptical and didn't think they would do that. But he knew me. If I mentioned something or had my mind set on something, I was going to do it.

I waited a few days before calling, preparing myself in case this, too, would end up as a dead end.

The next day, while Shelby was taking her nap and Brandon was occupied with his favorite cartoon show, I called the hospital in Louisiana. A very nice lady answered the phone.

I told her I was calling about George Hutchinson and that I was his daughter and I had just found out that he had passed away. I told her that I hadn't seen him in years and didn't know he was there.

I asked her if she could tell me a little bit about him and who he listed as the next of kin.

To my surprise, this lovely lady did tell me about him. She explained that he was a nice guy, polite, mostly kept to himself, occasionally participated in activities, enjoyed his cigarettes, and that he died alone from Emphysema. Nice and polite were not words I expected to describe him.

She said he only had a few visitors every now and then, that the only things he owned when he passed were a few sets of clothes, a TV, and some pictures; all she gave to the next of kin and that the next of kin donated the TV to the hospital.

I asked her if it was possible that she could give me the name and contact information of that next of kin he listed. In utter disbelief, she did tell me it was Mac McNabb of Kentwood. Kentwood is in Tangipahoa Parish and not too far from the hospital.

She said the Hutchinsons and McNabbs were good folks and well-known around there. She didn't give me a phone number, but she did at least give me a name.

I waited for the weekend when Mike was home and could watch the children. Then, I spent the day making calls in search of Mac McNabb.

I had already looked on the computer and found quite a few McNabb's listed in the Kentwood and Tangipahoa Parish area and was eager to make the calls.

The first few calls, I got nothing. The people said they didn't know Mac, but I kept going down my list.

The next call was to Bobby McNabb. I asked the lady on the phone if she knew of a Mac McNabb.

She said, *"Are you asking about Edgar McNabb? That's who everyone calls Mac."*

"Yes," I replied, *"I am looking to speak with him, please."* Not knowing if Edgar and Mac were the same person.

She told me her name was Carolyn and that Mac was her brother-in-law. He lived across from her, and she gave me his phone number. I called the number immediately, and a lady answered.

I told her, *"I would like to speak with Edgar Mac McNabb, please."*

She told me she was his daughter and asked what it was in reference to. I explained that I needed to talk with him about my father, George Hutchinson.

There were a few seconds of silence, and then a man picked up the phone and said, *"This is Mac. How can I help you?"*

"Hello, Mr. McNabb. My name is Sonia, and I am calling about my father, George Hutchinson. I know he passed away, but I am hoping you could help me." I spoke.

Then I heard a click and a dial tone.

I wasn't sure what had happened. Did we accidentally get disconnected? I called right back, and he picked up the phone.

I proceeded to repeat who I was and why I was calling when he interrupted me and said, *"I don't know who you think you are and what kind of prank you are pulling, but you are not his daughter Sonia. His wife and daughter passed away many years ago. You should be ashamed of yourself."*

What! I was shocked.

"Wait! Please, don't hang up, please!" I begged.

What did he just say? I was caught off guard. He thinks my mother and I passed away? That was shocking to hear, and why would he think that?

I begged him to just give me a few minutes of his time.

"I can prove to you that I am his daughter and that my mother and I are alive," I begged, desperation clear in my voice.

He was very skeptical of me but allowed me to continue and explain. I told him what I knew about my father and being in the Army.

That he married my mother in Korea and that I am their only child. I told him that I knew he had family in Cincinnati and that his sister lives in Dallas.

I told him the name of his mother, my grandmother.

Then I heard him say, *"Oh, my God, you are his daughter Sonia!"*

We spoke on the phone for about ten to fifteen minutes, getting acquainted with each other. He told me a little about my father and that he was buried on the property.

Then he told me that every year in April, the family holds the Hutchinson family reunion.

He invited my family and me, and of course, my mother, to come for the reunion. He then handed the phone to his daughter Peggy, and we chatted a bit.

I told her I had to figure out if I would be able to come for the reunion and that we would touch base within a few weeks. I was excited and wanted to go.

I couldn't believe I had found my adoptive father's family. In some ways, it was bittersweet.

There was a comfort in knowing my father had passed, so my mother and I never had to see or fear him again.

But that also meant that I would never know what he could have told me.

There was also the joy of actually finding my adoptive family members, knowing I have more family, and hoping that maybe my father revealed to some of them the story of my adoption and biological family.

Mike and I talked about going to the reunion; we both wanted to go. We didn't want to take the children.

They were too small, and this was a trip for me to see if I could get answers about my adoption. To find out more about the monster, I called my father.

And even though Mr. McNabb and his daughter were very compassionate and nice, Mike and I didn't know them and felt it was better if we didn't take the children.

We knew we could always take them in the future if we decided to go back to visit again.

Now came the hard part. I had to go to my mother and let her know that I had been searching for my father to get the answers about my adoption. I had to tell her that I had found him, he had passed away, and to let her know that I then found his side of the family in Louisiana and that we all were invited to the Hutchinson family reunion in April.

I went to my mother's home that evening with the kids in tow. Anytime we went to grandma's house, they were always two steps ahead of me. Brandon was putting on his shoes, and Shelby was scooting and bouncing her way to the door because they wanted their grandma.

After about half an hour or so at mom's, I told her I needed to talk to her and tell her something. I proceeded to tell her how I located my father without telling her that I had some help from Smitty and his family.

I told her that he had passed away in a VA Hospital in Louisiana about ten months ago.

Then I told her that I spoke with his family members there and we had been invited to the Hutchinson family reunion in April.

I really wanted to go and asked if she minded keeping the children for a week while Mike and I went. To my surprise, my mother was very calm about everything.

I waited a few seconds, and she didn't get angry, or yell at me, which sometimes she did in both English and Korean, or even cry.

She was awfully calm about it. She said she was happy that I found his family and that she would love to watch the children so Mike and I could go.

Perhaps, in her heart, she knew it was time for me to know the truth about who I was and where I came from.

But more than anything, she knew by now *there was no stopping me.*

Chapter Seven

Love Conquered All

In April of 1994, Mike and I headed to Kentwood, Louisiana, to meet Mr. McNabb or Uncle Mac, as he told me to call him, which is what everyone called him. Katherine, his wife, invited Mike and me to stay in their home for our visit. Every member of the family I met was the kindest and sweetest country folk I had ever met.

My cousin, Peggy, Uncle Mac's daughter, lived just across the road and stopped by every day to visit with us. We all spent some time visiting New Orleans, which was great. We walked on Bourbon Street, stopped at Café Du Monde in the French Quarter for the Beignets, rode a horse and carriage, enjoyed authentic Crawfish Etouffee at a local eatery, learned about Mardi Gras and the famous King Cakes, and visited all the shops downtown.

Back in Kentwood, at Uncle Mac's, I visited the Hutchinson cemetery, located on "Hutchinson Hill," as they called it because the entire land was owned by the Hutchinsons and then subdivided for the children and family members to build their own homes on. To this day, it is still only family members who live on any part of that land. We all walked to the back side of the land where the cemetery was to pay respect to all our family members.

Uncle Mac told me that my father was buried in the family cemetery, but seeing that tombstone there with his name on it, it felt surreal. For years, all I could think about was how badly I wanted him to die. I wanted him to die a slow, miserable death as a punishment for what he did to my mother and me. And now, as I stared at the tombstone with his name on it, I didn't feel happy.

Flashbacks of the horrible things he did ran through my mind. I wanted to spit on his grave, but all I could do was cry. Cry for the little girl that was forced to fight for her own life and her mother's. Cry for the little girl that was forced to lay naked in a bed while her father pleasured himself in her private parts. Cry for the little girl who couldn't cry then, who held it all in to protect herself and her mother. For the little girl who couldn't sleep at night, who rocked herself to sleep every night until she was eighteen. And for the little girl that became a woman who still hides the rocking by rocking her legs side to side at night for comfort to fall asleep.

For the little girl that didn't have a father to protect her. For making this little girl feel ashamed of her own body, who slept in her bra and fully clothed until she met her husband. For the anger that was inside me and that had built up over the years. For the compulsive need to be in control and for everything to be perfect.

With all these emotions flooding my mind, at that moment, staring at his tombstone a feeling of peace came over me. His death solidified the end of fearing that he was out there somewhere, lurking and watching us and knowing he couldn't hurt us anymore. I also knew I couldn't get the satisfaction of confronting him about what he did to me and my mother and for a brief moment that aggravated me.

Did he win? What punishment did he get for hurting us?

He moved on to live his life even if it was in a VA hospital, and then he died before I could find him to even ask what information he could offer about my adoption. I wondered if he was looking at me laughing or with remorse. Damn, this flood of emotions!

He did that to me! And most likely, those things were going to remain inside me forever. I needed closure, but I realized maybe that was something not in the cards for me. Now, at that very moment, in time I needed to breathe, so I walked away.

Each evening at Uncle Mac's, we'd gather around the kitchen table and enjoy one of Aunt Katherine's delicious homemade pies or cake and chat about life. I asked Uncle Mac if my father had ever mentioned anything about my adoption.

"No, never. I didn't even know you were adopted. Your father mentioned only that you and your mother were killed in a car accident." He answered.

I wondered why he would have said that. Was it to gain sympathy, or in his mentally ill mind, was the car accident the last thing he remembered? And since he wasn't allowed to see my mother and me, did he associate the accident with death?

Or did he make up that story to hide from telling the family the awful things he did that caused my mother to divorce him, lose custody of me, and get discharged from the Army? No one will ever know.

However, what I wanted to know now was what kind of man he was before he became ill. What was he like before he was admitted to the VA Hospital?

Uncle Mac, his wife, his two brothers, and their wives, Peggy and her husband, along with Mike and I, all sat around the table one evening as they told me stories of the wonderful man my father used to be. How kind and respectful he was. That he was a good man who wanted to serve his country. About how much he loved my mother and me, how he would have done anything for us, and how sweet he was to his nieces and nephews.

They narrated how when he came back from Maryland, he told them about the death of his wife and daughter. He stayed there with them, got along incredibly, and helped out, but on a few occasions, they noticed that something was off. They said he was ill and admitted to the VA Hospital and developed Emphysema, and then passed away. I was happy to hear that my adoptive father wasn't born evil and that, maybe, just maybe, his actions were a result of multiple brain injuries.

Finally, on the day of the reunion, many relatives came to Hutchinson Hill. It was an extraordinary gathering, and everyone took lots of pictures. I loved their southern accent, and boy oh boy, between the Cajun and country cooking, and old fashion baked deserts, the food the family members made for the reunion was absolutely mouthwatering. They also did a Civil War reenactment with everyone dressed in replicated Civil War clothing which was great to watch. The entire family made Mike and me feel so welcomed.

We returned home, and I was so happy to see my mom and my babies. I told my mother all about the trip and how wonderful the Hutchinson side of the family is. I told her they didn't know I was adopted. I am not sure if my mother breathed a sigh of relief or if she felt bad for me.

But I again decided that I was not going to give up. I was going to keep chiseling away at this mountain until I got it moved.

The following year, I spent it trying to figure out if my biological family was another American family stationed in Iran or if I was born to an Iranian family and given up for adoption. The unresolved questions and thoughts I had caused me so much anxiety that it led to so many episodes with my heart palpitations and going back and forth to the Emergency Room and my primary care doctors.

Eventually, it was diagnosed that I had panic attacks. I had them so often that I felt like a prisoner of my own home. My weight picked up because I was so depressed.

My doctor prescribed Prozac, but I had a horrible reaction to it. Then my doctor suggested I go on Xanax for the panic attacks.

I prided myself on being a very strong-willed and strong-minded person, so having to take this medication made me feel like I was weak. However, I took it because I needed some sense of comfort that I had control over these attacks and I could make them stop.

In April 1995, we decided to return to Louisiana for the family reunion again. This time, my mother came with us. She was happy to meet the family, and they welcomed her with open arms. We went to New Orleans again, and this time we got to spend time with Aunt Carrie, my father's favorite aunt. She told us great stories about him when he was a child and growing up. She spoke so highly of him.

Then she handed down to me some of the gifts my father had given her. She wanted me to have them. Mom and I never told Aunt Carrie anything bad about my father. She was in her 80s, and at that point, there was no need to tarnish her fond memories of him with the horrific ones we had.

The family reunion turned out as great, as always. It was held during Easter. There was an Easter egg hunt and games for the children, a civil war reenactment on 'The Hill' again and lots of eating and sharing stories. My mother really enjoyed her trip there and liked everyone.

Mom and I also visited my father's grave together. We held hands tightly and stood there at the foot of his tombstone in silence.

I think we both realized it was time to let go. Let go of the pain, the anger, and the secrets. Life is short. And we were alive because of each other because we both suffered through physical and emotional pain to save the other. The love and bond that we have could never be broken. We were survivors, and there was nothing the two of us couldn't do or wouldn't do for the other.

As we stood there, staring at his tombstone, I felt my heart being put back together. There, mom and I shared a tissue to wipe our tears, and finally, we walked away. We let it all go so we could begin to heal.

Once we were back in Maryland and settled back into our routines, mom asked me to come over for dinner one evening. She wondered if Mike would watch the children so she and I could talk alone. It wasn't like mom to ask me not to bring the children. I felt worried. Was something wrong with her health?

I got to mom's house, and of course, as always, mom was cooking her delicious Korean dishes. She always made all kinds of food when the children and I came over. It was her way of spoiling us. The children were eating Korean food as soon as they were off the bottle, and they loved all the Korean dishes. The aroma from the foods filled the air in the house.

I lifted all the lids to see all she had made and couldn't wait to dig in. That evening, we enjoyed dinner and cleaned up afterward. Then we sat at the kitchen table, eating a fresh bowl of fruit for dessert when mom looked at me and said, *"I'll tell you what I know."*

"Know about what?" I asked, perplexed.

"Your adoption and about your family in Iran," she answered as she held back tears and choked on her words.

My eyes widened. I got up from my chair, knelt down, held her hand, and said, *"Are you sure? I know it makes you uncomfortable, although I don't know why. I would love to know, but not at the expense of making you sad or uncomfortable talking about it."*

"It is time you know the truth." She assured me.

That night my mother let go of all that was holding her back from sharing my origin with me. She sat in her favorite chair in the living room and started.

"You were born in Iran, and your biological family is Armenian. You are the youngest of five children. You have two sisters and two brothers. Your biological mother passed away after your birth, and your biological father

148

didn't want you. Therefore, your father, George, and I adopted you while we were stationed in Iran."

There it was. The truth. Finally, she told me. I sat solemn gazing at my mother, as it took my breath away. I felt relieved although my head was spinning. *"But mom,"* I said, *"How did you find out I was up for adoption? How did you know my family?"*

"George and I were stationed in Iran. We lived off of the Army base and had a nice house we had rented. I enjoyed being in Iran, liked the food, and loved the shopping. I even learned a little bit of the Persian language. Your father and I had been trying to conceive a child for a few years, and three times, I had a miscarriage. I was heartbroken and desperately wanted a child of my own. However, the doctors told me that I would never be able to bear my own child." She paused, pain evident in her eyes, and swiped a tear off her cheek.

"Then, while in Iran, I had a dream one night that I looked under my bed and saw a dragon. This dragon spoke to me, telling me that because I was a kind-hearted, generous, and loving woman fit to be a mother, I would be blessed with a child soon. In Korean folklore, it is believed that a dragon brings you good things. A few days later, towards the end of June, a Korean friend that I had met while we were stationed in Iran came to my home and showed me a military newspaper. My Korean friend had been wanting to adopt a child. She looked at the ad in the paper, and it said, **'infant girl for adoption to a Christian family available right away,'** *with an address listed. So, my friend asked me to go with her to look at this baby. I had an Iranian butler named Hassan. I asked him to drive us to the address listed in the ad. We gathered our purses, got in the car, and drove to the house. Once there, we knocked on the door, and a man opened it. He only spoke Armenian and Persian. My butler had to translate our communications. We could tell the family was very poor. The house had dirt floors, they had very few things, and the two children looked uncleaned. It was a young boy and his sister. They were sitting on a bed, holding the baby girl and trying to feed her with a bottle. We walked over and tried to speak to the children, but*

the language barrier prevented much communication. We asked my butler, Hassan, to translate for us." She paused, then looked at me with so much love and smiled a teary smile.

"You were so dirty and desperately needed a bath. They didn't have any clothes for you, so you were wearing a dress that belonged to your eleven-year-old sister. The dress was tied off at the bottom. The bottle of milk that the kids were feeding you was too big and dirty too. I asked the little boy and girl if you were their sister, and they said yes. Then I asked them what their names were. They said Vazgen and Emma. I asked them what their little baby sister's name was, and they told me it was Sonik. I asked your father if I could hold you. He allowed me. It felt so comfortable holding you and rocking you in my arms, and I felt immediate love flood through me. Then, I handed you to my friend so she could hold you as well, and I could have Hassan ask your father for some information as to why he was giving you up for adoption."

I sat even closer to mom, so immersed in the story she was telling me as she continued.

"He explained he has four other children. One son, nineteen, two daughters, one eighteen and the other eleven, and the youngest son, nine, and then you. But only the two youngest live with him. The older two are married and lived further away. He worked hard and made little money. His wife always took care of the children, but she died after you were born. He said he was upset because he had no wife, and the children had no mother now. He told me he couldn't take care of a baby and that you were no good for him. He explained that you would only remind him of the death of his wife that he believed you caused, and so he just didn't want you. I was practically speechless."

She cleared her throat, wiped tears from her face, and proceeded. I did the same.

"Then my friend handed you back to your brother and walked back towards the door. I stood there for several minutes, watching the little boy sit there,

rubbing your head and smiling at you. My friend kept motioning for me to come to the door so we could leave. I asked her when she was taking the baby, so we could let the father know. But she told me no way was she taking you. She told me you looked sickly, malnourished, probably had some kind of infection or disease from the filthy home, and most likely won't last a month before you would die. Hassan told your father we were leaving, and we headed out to the car. Hassan started up the engine. But before he could drive away, I got out of the car and asked Hassan to come with me to translate again. My friend asked me what I was doing, and I told her, **"If you are not taking that baby girl, then I will because you are probably right, she may die in a month or so if no one takes care of her."** I knocked on the door and told your father that I would take the baby and adopt her. I asked him what he wanted in return. He told me that they were Armenian. Whoever adopted the child must also be Christian. He did not want any Muslim with Islamic values to adopt the baby. He also wanted enough money to give his wife a beautiful and proper burial and some money to feed his children for a little while. I told Hassan to tell his father that I would come back the next day with some money. But your father told me to take you now and bring the money tomorrow. I walked over, picked you up, and held you in my arms again. I looked into your eyes, and then and there, I knew I couldn't leave without you. We were meant to be mother and daughter, and God had brought me there to you." Her voice was trembling and cracking as she continued to tell me the truth.

"I asked him, **'Don't you want to spend a little more time with your daughter?'** But he said no. He wanted nothing to do with you because he blamed you for his wife's death. So, with you in my arms, Hassan and I walked back to the car where my friend was still sitting. My friend kept telling me that it was a huge mistake, but I insisted it was not. I couldn't leave you there because I was already in love with you." Mom smiled at me.

"I dropped my friend off at her home and went to the store to buy some diapers, formula, and some clothes for you. Then I took you back to our home and bathed you. You had a horrible case of diaper rash. I couldn't believe how bad the rash was. I noticed a necklace around your neck when I

151

undressed you. It was of the Virgin Mary. Finally, after the bath, I put some clean clothes on you, fed you, and held you in my arms until you fell asleep."

"That day, your adoptive father came in just as you were waking up, crying. He asked me what that noise was, and I told him, ***'that is our daughter, Sonia.'*** *You can imagine the shock on his face when I said those words."* Mom laughed.

*"He was upset that I did that and frustrated because we only had about eight months left in Iran before we were going to be sent to the USA. He didn't want any complications, and adoption could cause legal issues. He asked me to return you, but of course, I refused and stayed by my decision. That's not going to happen. We argued, but finally, he agreed. He knew how happy you made me. I told him that your birth name is Sonik and that I would like to keep that name to honor your biological mother but just change the K at the end to an A. I told him that in Korea, the pronunciation of Sonia **is** SUN-YA, and it means angel. I told him that's exactly what you were, our Angel."* She paused, and I smiled, holding back loads of fresh tears.

"The next day, Hassan drove you and me back to your biological father's house, and I gave him the money, enough to give your biological mother a very nice burial, and for food for the children, and to put towards his home. I brought you back with me to show him how I had cleaned you up. I asked if he wanted to see you, and he refused. Then I asked about the necklace you had on. He said his wife put that on each child they had. ***'We are Christian, and it is the Virgin Mary. It was our tradition at birth to place the necklace on the baby. Sonik's mother placed one on Sonik too.'*** *As we were talking, your brother and sister begged to hold you and play with you. They were crying. I asked your father if he would be willing to let me adopt your brother and sister, too, because I would like to take them as well, but he refused.* ***'They are older and can work.'*** *He said."*

"He needed them, but you were useless to him. You were just in the way. You were a thorn in his side and bad luck, he said. I think he had to tell himself that so that he could convince himself not to hurt letting you go. I let your

brother and sister hold you. I asked why your older siblings didn't want to take you and care for you, but he said they didn't have money and were poor. He said he tried numerous times, leaving you at different orphanages, but his son, Vazgen, and daughter, Emma, would go to the orphanages and sit on the front doorsteps crying and begging for their sister. So, he would bring you back. He said it was best for you to leave the country and go far away, so it would not distract his children and family, and they could move on. When I was ready to leave, I carried you to the car. As I was putting you in, your brother and sister begged me to give you back and not take you. Hassan started the car, and I got in, but as we started to drive off, your nine-year-old brother Vazgen started chasing the car, crying as it drove off. It broke my heart." She choked, tears now flowing freely.

"Over the next five and a half months, your father and I took great care of you. You were thriving. The diaper rash went away, along with the heat rash. You even picked up a few pounds, got some immunization shots, and the doctors on base said you were healthy. We also got all the legal paperwork for the adoption and your visa completed because we were being stationed back in the United States in December."

"A few days before we were scheduled to leave Iran for the US, I went back to your residence. I wanted to show your father how much you had flourished in those couple of months and to give him a picture of you from your passport photos. When I got there, your father said very few words. I showed him how good you looked and let your siblings see you one last time. Your father did not hold you or even look at you. I handed him your photo, but he refused to take it. So, I left it on the table so he would never forget you, his daughter. I'm not sure why he wouldn't hold or look at you. I want to believe it was because it was breaking his heart to let you go. That was the last time he or your siblings saw you. As I headed back to the car with you and Hassan, your brother and sister were crying and screaming hysterically, trying to stop me. Your brother, Vazgen, chased the car again as far as he could until it was out of sight. And that was it. We never saw them again." She finished and closed her eyes.

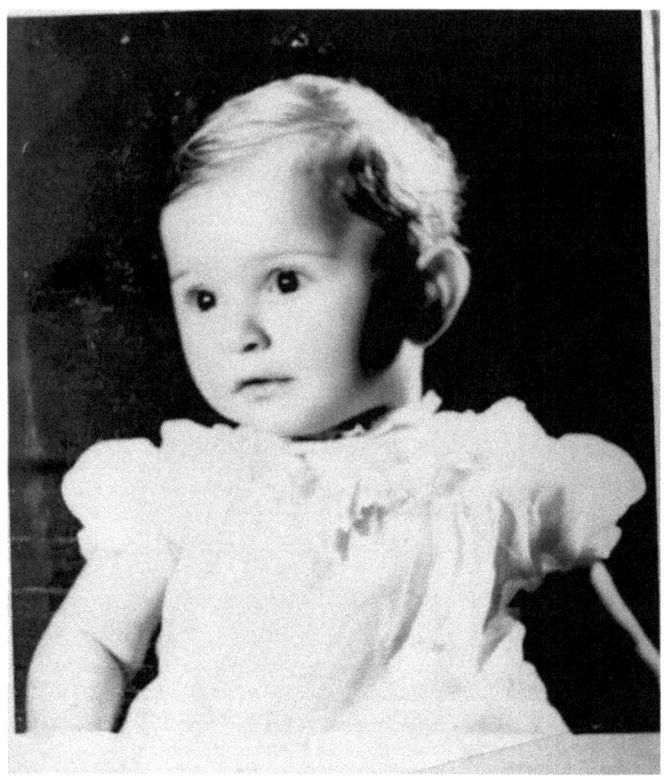

I let out a shaky breath. It was so much to take in. I sobbed. Now I understood why my mother did not want to share all this with me. She knew it would break my heart, too, so she never wanted me to know.

"You know, I was so shocked the first time you said out loud that you have a brother, and each time you asked me where is your brother and sister my heart skipped a beat. I didn't know how to answer you. Your constant insistence that you had a brother and sister, and could feel and see them, was unbelievable, yet amazing." Mom smiled at me.

"Some religious leaders didn't believe in the adoption of their own people and then leaving the country. Apparently, when doing the legal paperwork, word had gotten out about us taking a baby out of the country for adoption, and we received a few scary threats. Someone even threw a rock through our window. I had you sleep in the bed with me, just in case anyone tried to break into the house in the night and take you. Since we didn't live on

the Army base, we didn't have the added security of the Military Police. The Iranian conservative insurgents found out about the adoption and tried to harm your father and me on multiple occasions. They tried to stop us from leaving the country with you. Your father had to ask his Major for any kind of help from the Army to ensure the safety of getting you out of the country when his tour of duty ended in Iran. The army provided three vehicles and put you and me into one vehicle as we drove to the airport. George and I were scheduled to depart together. However, for safety reasons, they changed my flight, and you and I left the country two days before George. We all met up in Germany, and all of us flew to the United States as a family. They even tried to attack us at the airport, but we were able to get to the plane and board as quickly as possible without any harm." Mom let out a long breath.

After hearing the entire story, I was shaking and crying. I got up and hugged her. We both cried, like *ugly* cried. I was so happy to finally know the truth.

"Why didn't you tell me this years ago?" I asked.

"I never thought of you as an adopted child but rather my very own." She answered.

"Oh, my God, I am your child. I was meant to be your child. That was God's plan. He just brought us together in a different way." I cried.

Then she said, *"I was afraid if you knew everything, I'd lose you."*

"Are you kidding me? The love we have, the life we shared, and the sacrifices we made for each other, you could never lose me. You are my world, my heart, my soul, and my angel. You saved me in Iran and nurtured me to health. You gave me a wonderful life full of immeasurable love. You are the epitome of what a mother should be, mom. You are my role model and my hero. If I am one-tenth of the woman you are, then I am honored. You are stuck with me, momma! I am forever your daughter." I replied.

"All those years, I felt in my bones that I had a brother and sister. I could see their faces. I remembered them feeding me. To think I was less than six months old when my brother and sister held me, and yet, those memories and visions were etched in my mind tells you how powerful the human brain and memory are." I said, awed.

"What did you think each time I brought up my brother and sister?" I questioned her.

"To be honest, it gave me goosebumps. The first time you said it, I froze. It was so crazy to think that you knew you had a brother and sister. You were so young when you started saying it, and because of that, I couldn't explain it to you. I didn't know how to answer it, even when you got older and still questioned about your brother and sister. I wish I could help you find them, but I have no idea how to do that since, most likely, they are still in Iran." She said.

"Don't worry about it, mom. Right now, I need to absorb all of this, but in time, I will find them." I sighed.

"I know you will." Mom smiled.

After absorbing all this information, now, I was more determined than ever to find my biological family.

Chapter Eight

The Origin Search

Easter was behind us as we celebrated it at the family reunion in Louisiana, and now, we were celebrating Shelby's second birthday. I was still reeling from the fact of finally knowing the truth about my adoption. It wasn't that I was bitter about being adopted. No, not at all! It was just that I wanted to know more about myself. My adoptive parents rescued me from a third-world country, and my mother gave me a chance at life I would have never had if I hadn't been adopted.

Now, mom and I were more comfortable discussing the topic of my adoption. She even told me that this was why she was so worried about me each time I was pregnant. She told me since she never really knew why my biological mother died after my birth, she worried about me during childbirth.

It all made sense. Her panic in the hospital, arguing with Mike when I was in labor for so long and Brandon was in distress, and his lung collapsed. The joy, yet fear she had when I told her I was pregnant again with our second child. Anytime I'd ask her about our family medical history, she'd say to me just because she or other family members have a condition doesn't mean I will, too, so I shouldn't list anything on any medical forms and just leave it blank. Maybe there were signs through the years that I just couldn't or didn't want to see.

It took a couple of months to think about everything. Finally, I came to the conclusion that I don't have to be biologically Korean to say that's my heritage. I was raised with all the Korean customs and traditions.

I respected the culture, learned how to speak a good portion of the language, cooked the traditional foods, savored the foods, celebrated their traditional holidays, and defended the people of South Korea.

That's what defined my heritage, not my origin, so I could proudly say that my heritage is Korean.

Now, my mission was to find my biological family. I knew the last name was apparently Gharabi or Gharabian from what my mother told me, so that was a start.

I figured if I couldn't get ahold of my adoption papers because they were sealed in the divorce, shouldn't there be some record of how I entered this country through Immigration and Naturalization Services (INS)?

I had to become an American Citizen or Naturalized at some point, so there had to be a record of that somewhere. So, I took a chance and called the Immigration and Naturalization office and requested my entry documents along with my adoption papers. I wasn't sure if they would even allow me to have it. But to my surprise they told me it might take up to ten weeks to get it. Once they retrieved them, then I would have to pick them up in person at the INS office in Baltimore, MD.

I waited patiently. Then I received *the* call—the documents were available for pickup. Mike and I drove to downtown Baltimore which was about an hour and ten minutes from our house. I picked up the packet, and we dashed to the car, eager to open it up and see what was inside.

We settled in the car on that busy street in Baltimore and opened the large envelope. It was there that I read the names of my biological parents for the very first time and the name of each of my siblings from my Iranian birth certificate.

Apparently, in Iran, when my birth certificate was issued, it listed my birth name, my parents' names, and each sibling in order of birth, along with the city I was born in.

"My birth name is Sonik Gharabi." I smiled.

Then I read my biological parents and each of my siblings' names aloud multiple times. My mother's name was Benoosh, and my father's name was Kamal.

I noticed my birthdate was different on the Iranian birth certificate versus my American birth certificate. It must have been translated differently. I am not sure which was correct, but it was only a difference of three days. I had always gone by the date on the US birth certificate and decided to continue to do so. But I do think it is really cool and unique to have two birth dates.

I was on top of the moon and smiling from ear to ear. I had been looking for my origin for the past two and a half years. I had been weaving through government loopholes to get the answers I needed to find out about myself and my biological family. At that moment, I felt some sense of victory.

Mike said he was so proud of me, and that meant a lot to me. He was always so supportive of my search for answers and my journey. I was never a quitter. I learned to persevere at an early age. It didn't matter what obstacle was put in front of me. I would find a way around or through it.

I looked at Mike and said, *"My next step is to find my brother. Let's go. I've got work to do."*

"Let's celebrate with a dinner first." He answered. We smiled at each other and drove off.

The next day, I got right to work. Over the next several months, I called several Armenian churches in Washington, DC, to ask if they could help me locate my family in Iran. I couldn't really get an answer from anyone, and it seemed as though they just didn't understand what I needed. I called the Iranian Embassy to ask them for help, but the language barrier proved to be quite a significant problem.

I called the Swiss Embassy, and they said they could take a letter from me and submit it to the Swiss Embassy in Iran and hope that they would be able to give it to the Iranian government, but there was little hope that would work. I called the Iranian and Armenian newspapers and asked them if I could put an ad in it, stating that I was looking for my family in Iran with some information so people could contact me.

They agreed, and I did do that but got no responses. I tried one door after another, only for them all to close in my face. But no, I wasn't about to give up. So, I continued.

One night in November, as I lay in my bed sound asleep with my husband by my side, I was awakened by a sense of someone standing over me. I opened my eyes, and at the foot of my bed, I could see an outline of a man. I became petrified and tense. I blinked my eyes several times, hoping for it to be just another figment of my imagination. But the silhouette remained. I pulled the blanket up over my head, closed my eyes, and started praying. This was unusual. I dozed back off, and in the morning, I told Mike about it. He brushed it off as a bad dream. I thought, perhaps, he was right and let it go. I was still having those horrible panic attacks, and dealing with them was exhausting—perhaps, that figment was due to the exhaustion.

Mom and I were as close as ever, preparing for Thanksgiving, which is my favorite holiday of the year. For me, it was about time spent with family, good food, and giving thanks for the blessings we have in our lives. Even with all of my life's ups and downs, I have always been blessed and had reasons to be thankful.

A few nights after seeing that vague figure at the foot of my bed, it happened again. As I lay in bed asleep, I felt the same sense that I was being watched. I opened my eyes, and once again, I saw the image of a man. I closed my eyes, lay there stiff as a board, and just prayed that it wasn't something evil. I felt like I was losing my mind. But again, nothing happened. When I opened my eyes, the silhouette was gone.

I was able to fall back to sleep after my heart stopped racing from the fear. I told Mike about it again, as well as my mother. Mike still found it hard to believe that it wasn't a nightmare, and my mother told me to make sure I kept my faith in God. Christmas was around the corner, the children were so excited, and the tree was full of presents. On Christmas morning, Brandon and Shelby raced to see what Santa had brought them. Mom always spent the night on Christmas Eve so she could be there to see the look on their faces when they saw the presents.

After Christmas, we went to Pennsylvania to visit Mike's family to celebrate it with them too, and to be there for the New Year's Eve family party. Mike's cousin, Sharon, was married to a charming Iranian man named Farhad. Everyone loved him.

I told him about my story and how badly I wanted to locate my brother and family in Iran. I told him what my family's birth name was and the names of my parents and siblings. It felt rather exhilarating to be able to say I had siblings and to express their names out loud. I told him I wasn't a hundred percent sure if I was Iranian or Armenian. But he told me I had the typical look of an Armenian woman, not to mention the family name on my birth certificate was an Armenian name. He told me the story of my quest was terrific, from finding the truth out to gathering that much information all on my own.

Then he said to me that if there was anything, he could do, he would be happy to help. As the New Year's Eve party continued through the evening, he walked back over toward me.

"You know, I was just thinking, my sister's best friend is Armenian. I will talk to my sister and tell her a little about your story to see if, perhaps, there is anything her friend can do to help." He smiled at me.

We rang in the New Year 1996. The children were banging pots and pans outside, and the adults were toasting drinks and giving each other a New Year's kiss. As we stood outside watching the children parade around the yard, banging the pots and the adults lighting some sparklers, I gazed up at the sky, looking at the stars, and smiled. For now, my biological family might be worlds away somewhere, but soon, we will be together.

We enjoyed our visit with Mike's family for New Year's, and now we were back home. I was more determined than ever to keep going full force in search of my biological family.

I was still figuring out ways to find them. I hit several roadblocks. My frustration was building up, causing more frequent panic attacks and more visits to the ER and my family doctor.

My family doctor advised me that with the number of visits I was having between the ER and his office, it may come to a point where he may have to issue a referral for me to have a psychiatric evaluation and depending on the outcome, it may at some point affect my parental role.

He told me that I had crossed from a few routine visits to the ER to an obsessive-compulsive disorder. He told me he was concerned that my constant trips to the ER and his office, along with my *'hallucinations,'* as he called it, of a man standing at the foot of my bed during the night, that perhaps, there was an underlying issue that needed to be looked at now.

'Was he implying that I was becoming mentally unstable?' I asked myself.

I could see why he was concerned, but I was not crazy. Sometimes, I felt a little overwhelmed with the search, but I certainly wasn't crazy or losing my mind. So, I told myself I had to get it together. I couldn't allow myself to keep doing this. I needed to figure out how to make these panic attacks stop. I also had to be careful who I told about the figure of a man I often saw at night standing at the foot of my bed.

My doctor put me on Prozac, but within a few days, I had to get off of it. It was horrible and caused me to have real hallucinations and thoughts of wanting to kill people. I think not knowing what health issues ran in my biological family made me start to wonder if my family had a history of heart issues.

I could feel my heart palpitate so hard and fast, then slow way down. It sometimes felt like something in my heart would explode. I would get so scared that I would throw myself into another panic attack, and it became a vicious cycle. My panic attacks were paralyzing me with fear.

Finally, my family doctor suggested I go see a cardiologist just to ease my mind because I was constantly frustrated that no one was listening to me. I found myself yelling and complaining to the doctors and nurses at my primary care doctor's office and the ER that my heart was bad and I didn't want to die from a heart attack.

I took him up on the referral for a well-known cardiologist. He listened closely to my heart, performed an EKG, sent me home with a Holter monitor that I had to wear for forty-eight hours, and performed a sonogram of my heart.

The conclusion, I had a Mitral Valve Prolapse, and I was born with it. Apparently, you don't notice it so much until you hit your early to mid twenties.

I didn't have to go on any permanent medication but just had to take a pill before any major surgery or dental procedures. Finally, in February 1996, I turned twenty-nine.

My last year of being in my twenties. One day, I got a call from Farhad saying that he spoke with his sister and got the contact information of her Armenian friend, Anita. He said he explained my story to his sister, who then, in turn, told her friend, Anita, about it and asked her if she could offer any help to me.

He said, Anita told his sister she would do anything she could and to give Sonia her phone number so I could call her. I thanked him and his sister for giving me the information on Anita. I told him I would give her a call.

He wished me luck and hoped Anita, and I would make some progress.

I gave Anita a call and went over my whole story with her. She was amazed at how much information I was able to gather on my own about my adoption and the measures I had taken. Then, we discussed possible ways of searching for my family. We said we would brainstorm and put a few ideas together. We spoke again a few days later and discussed placing an ad directly in the Iranian and Armenian newspapers in Iran.

We had to think it through, though. Since the papers were controlled by the Iranian government, our use of words had to be careful. We tried to come up with a few more ideas and decided to touch base again in a week or so.

In the meantime, I was coping with my panic attacks and, then again, with the crazy vision and that sense of someone watching me as I slept during the night. It didn't happen every night. Just every now and then.

I just couldn't make sense of what it was. I was a firm believer in God and Jesus, my faith is strong and every room in our home had a cross above the doorway or on the wall, so I didn't think anything evil could get in.

Then, at the beginning of March, I got the next call from Anita. She told me that her father was going to Iran for four to five weeks on business. She said that he would be leaving at the beginning of April. He said he wouldn't mind passing out some kind of flyer regarding my search for my family while he was there on business. She thought it would be a fantastic idea, and since her husband worked in printing and graphics he could make the flyers for me.

So, we began putting together a flyer by figuring out what information we wanted to put on the flyer, and if we were going to put pictures on it, etc. We knew her father, Mr. Edgarian, would be staying at a hotel, so we knew we had to list him as the contact person and the hotel he would be staying at as the location of the contact.

We thought the front of the flyer should say *"In Search of Biological Family"* or *"Searching for my Brother."* Then we figured we should mention something about an American woman born to an Armenian family and given up for adoption in 1967. We didn't want to mention that my adoptive mother was Korean or about the necklace. We figured if we found my brother or sister, they would know that and mention it. We included on the flyer the city and village where I was born and that I had several siblings.

Anita's husband printed up many flyers, and Anita's father, Mr. Edgarian, packed them for his trip, ready to hand out to anyone who would take one. Before he left on his trip to Iran, I sent him a copy of my Iranian birth certificate, along with a copy of that passport photo that my mother said she had left on the table for my father.

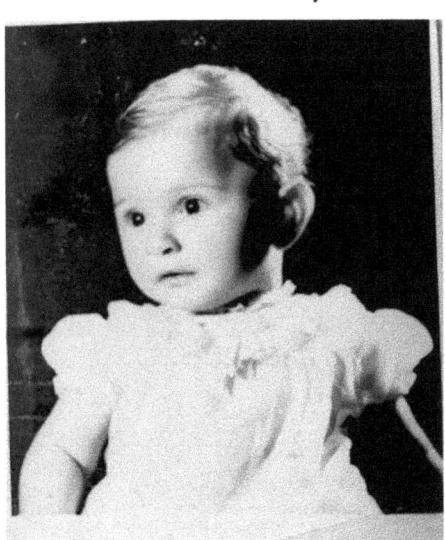

Mr. Edgarian didn't speak English, only Armenian and Farsi, so Anita always translated for us. I wanted Anita and her husband to know how much I appreciated all their efforts and that her father, who was willing to take the time during his trip to help me find my family, was so kind. We were basically strangers. None of us had ever met each other. Yet here they were, with their hearts and mind open, offering any help they could.

Whether he would find my family or not, I knew I would forever be thankful for their acts of kindness. I told mom about Anita and how she has been trying to help me. Then I told her that her father was going to Iran and was going to try to pass out flyers to see if he could find my brother. Mom said she didn't want me to get my hopes up only because she didn't want to see me heartbroken, but hoped that Anita's father could locate my brother. She said she would say some prayers for Anita's father, my brother, and me.

In April 1996, Mr. Edgarian went to Iran. We had Easter coming up and Shelby's birthday at the end of the month. My little girl was turning three. I was trying to control my panic attacks the best I could. I was still awakened sometimes during the night by the image of the man standing at the foot of my bed.

As time went on, each time I saw him, I started feeling a little calmer and not so frightened anymore. I felt convinced that this man was not there to hurt me. Otherwise, he would have done so by now. I decided the next time I saw him. I would try to figure out what and why he was coming at the foot of my side of the bed.

Then one night, I sensed he was there again. I took a deep breath, sat up in my bed and stared at him. Now, I could see an image of a man in some sort of suit. He was wearing a hat, and his head was slightly tilted to the side. It almost felt like we both acknowledge each other. It was odd because I didn't feel afraid, not even uneasy. For some reason, I kind of felt safe. By now, I knew it was best that I kept these visions at night to myself.

Brandon and Shelby enjoyed Easter and all the goodies in their Easter baskets. The Azaleas in the backyard had bloomed as they did every year around Easter, and they were such a beautiful array of pink, red, and white.

I felt somewhat relaxed during the month of April. I knew Mr. Edgarian was in Iran, and I just decided to take a breather from my constant ongoing search and truly enjoy myself with my family.

On the morning of April 29th, at 2:00 am, I was awakened by the phone ringing. I jumped up and answered it, fearing that perhaps, something had happened to my mother. I sat straight up in the bed, and with a crack in my voice, I said: *"Hello."*

On the other end of the phone was Anita. She apologized for calling me during the night and waking me up. I assured her it was okay.

Then she said, *"I just couldn't wait to call you. I had to tell you right away that my father has found your brother."* There was a pause as if she herself was trying to believe what she had just uttered, then she proceeded, *"I just got off the phone with my father, and he and your brother just finished talking. This is a miracle, Sonia."*

I started crying the moment she said her father had found my brother.

I kept saying, *"Oh, my God, Oh, my God. I can't believe it."*

Mike jumped up quickly, thinking something was wrong with my mother because I was crying and shaking. He kept trying to ask me what was wrong, but I was crying so hard, trying to get the words out of my mouth.

Anita told me she would call me back later so we could talk and I could go back to sleep, but could I really? There was no way I was going back to sleep. I was wide awake, adrenaline pumping through my veins, and excited beyond belief. I wanted all the details. I wanted to know how he found my brother. I walked down the hallway, eyes filled with tears, to check up on my babies and found them peacefully asleep, oblivious to the world. I kissed them on the forehead, pulled the blankets up over them, and gently tiptoed out of their room.

I couldn't fall back to sleep, and I didn't want to keep Mike up since I knew he had to get up at 3:30 am for work, so I decided to go downstairs and sit on the couch. A few minutes later, Mike came downstairs and sat next to me on the couch and held my hand.

I shared the blanket with him, and even though he didn't say anything, I knew he was there to support and comfort me while I cried tears of joy.

Later that afternoon, Anita called me back. But till then, I had quite a lot of time to dwell on the facts and figures. I started thinking, how do we know for sure this is my brother? What if it's someone pretending to be him? I told her what I was thinking, and she assured me that this was a hundred percent without a doubt, my brother.

She invited me, Mike, and our children to her home in Philadelphia that coming Saturday, May 4th, so we could actually meet for the first time. She, her husband, and her mother wanted to prepare a traditional Armenian meal for us and explain in detail how her father found my brother. I was very excited and eager to go and meet them.

She said, *"My father, your brother, and your brother's wife and his children will all be together at your brother's house, and they will be calling so you can talk to your brother for the very first time ever. When my father gets back from Iran, I want you to come back again for dinner on May 18th, so you can meet my father."*

I definitely wanted to meet him because I wanted to thank him personally. This was so overwhelming. I just couldn't believe this was happening. So much time was spent searching for answers, looking for him, and the years upon years of seeing his face in my mind and

168

memories to now being able to talk to him. It was almost unbelievable. It felt surreal.

I invited mom over for dinner that evening after she got off work. I wanted to tell her that I found my brother, and I wanted to let Mike and mom know that Anita invited us to her home this coming Saturday. Mom was pleased and excited to hear that I had found my brother. She hugged me and told me this was wonderful news. She told me that since I will be going twice in May and that on the first visit, I will be speaking with my brother, perhaps, it would be best if she stayed home and kept the children so Mike and I could go and meet Anita and talk with my brother without any interruptions from the children.

Then when I go back on the 18th, I could take the children. We agreed that it would probably be highly emotional and a lot of crying, and the children would most likely not understand why all the adults were crying.

On the morning of May 4th, 1996, Mike and I headed to Anita's house in Philadelphia, a three-and-a-half-hour drive from ours.

It was a bright and sunny day. During our drive to Anita's, I kept telling Mike how excited I was to meet her and talk with my brother. I was also very nervous. I didn't know what to say to my brother or what questions I should ask. I wasn't familiar with the Armenian culture, so I wasn't sure what kind of questions would be appropriate or considered rude or disrespectful.

I was a chatterbox full of nerves. I tried to stay calm during the ride, but it seemed like it took thirty hours. The anticipation was driving me crazy.

When we arrived at Anita's at 10:30 am, she, her husband, and her mother were also anxiously waiting for me. We all hugged each other. It was as though we had known each other for years. Her family's part in helping me locate my brother created an unspoken bond between us. It

169

was wonderful for all of us to put a face to the voice we had been talking to on the phone. She showed us around her home and smelling the Armenian foods that she and her mother were preparing for our lunch had my mouth watering and my tummy growling. I was so excited to try the food.

We knew the call from her father with my brother and his family would be coming at around twelve noon. It would be about 8:00 pm in Iran, as they are about eight hours ahead of us. Mr. Edgarian was invited to my brother's home for dinner and to be there on the phone with all of us for the call.

Anita and I met for the 1st time on May 4, 1996. This is the 1st time I spoke to my brother. Anita translated.

She wanted me to know everything before my brother called. Mike and I sat on the couch, and she and her husband sat on the armchairs. Then she started telling me.

She explained that her father had gone to a particular street corner for two hours or so a few evenings during his trip to pass out the flyers to people walking by, asking them to please take them and read them.

Then he would switch it up and go for an hour or so during lunchtime. Some people would take the flyer he handed them, and some didn't even bother. A few days went by, and he didn't receive any calls. So, he decided to go back and try it again.

He stood on the corner for a couple of hours. He passed out as many flyers as people would take. Some people seemed annoyed with him and would throw the flyer in the trash. Still, he got no call.

He headed back to his hotel to rest for the evening and get something to eat. As soon as he got to his hotel, he got a phone call. A man on the other end of the call told her father that he was a hundred percent sure that the woman in the flyer looking for her family was his sister.

He kept telling her father he was sure of it. Mr. Edgarian asked him for any information he could provide, any proof to back his statement up. He told Mr. Edgarian that if they could meet, then he could explain and show him.

So, they agreed to meet at 7 am in the morning in the hotel lobby.

There was a large area with comfortable couches where they could sit and talk with complimentary coffee and tea. She said when her father walked into the lobby. There sat an entire family.

A man, his wife, and his four children. This man shook her father's hand, introduced himself as Vazgen, introduced his family, and said that he had brought a box of pastries.

They all sat down, and her father asked the man what made him think the woman in the flyer could be his sister. He then began to tell her father his story.

The man said, as Anita narrated, '*Last night, a friend of mine came to my home. He described an older man standing on the corner, passing out some paper about a woman looking for her Armenian family. It gave me chills, so I asked my friend where that paper was. He wasn't sure if he had put it in his pocket or thrown it away. I made him go through all of his pockets and his jacket. He pulled out the crumbled paper, and when I read it, I knew this was my sister that I have been looking for, for so many years, and that is why I called you. When I was just nine years old, our mother gave birth to a baby girl, my sister. Then within a few weeks, our mother died. My baby sister was the youngest of five of us children. My oldest brother and sister didn't live at home. My oldest sister was married, and so was my brother. Our family didn't have much money, and my father had to work hard every day. He couldn't stay home with a baby when he had to work. He was angry and sad because our mom had died. He tried to put the baby in an orphanage a few times, but each time, my sister and I found out where the place was, and we would walk there to sit on the front steps and cry, begging for our sister. They made my father come pick her up and take her back home. We had just lost our mother and didn't want to lose our sister either. We thought we could take care of her for our father. Then one day, a woman came by and took her. We thought maybe she was a nurse and was going to make sure our sister was okay. She came back the next day, and our sister looked so pretty. But then, when she left, she took our sister with her again. Our father said he was giving our baby sister to another family. I remember crying and begging that woman not to take my baby sister.*

Our father looked at me and my sister Emma and said, 'she is gone.' My sister and I cried for months. We couldn't stop thinking about our sister. We lost our mother and our sister both. Then months later, that same lady came back with our sister in her arms. She had gotten bigger, was so cute, and wearing a white dress. We were so excited, thinking our sister was back. We had her back. We got to hold her and make her laugh. The man with her was telling my father that she was leaving Iran with our sister and that this would be the last time he would see his daughter. But my father didn't want to see her. He didn't hold her. He just turned away.'

Anita said her father was starting to choke up but asked, *"What else can you tell me? Can you describe the woman that took your sister?"*

At this point, there wasn't a dry eye in Anita's house.

Then the man said, 'Yes, I can describe the woman. She was Chinese, or maybe Japanese. I am for sure she was Asian. Also, the day the Asian lady left with our sister she handed our father a photo of my sister. He wouldn't take it. She placed it on the table in case he changed his mind. Then she left. We never saw our sister again. My father refused to take the picture, so I did. I vowed to him and myself that I would find my baby sister no matter how long it took or what I would have to do. We will be together again. And my search began from that moment. I have never stopped searching for her.'

Anita said his wife and children also chimed in, verifying his statements.

They said, *'He always talks about his sister. He contacted many Embassies in search of her. He didn't know where she had gone. But he kept trying, telling anyone who would listen. He prayed she would come back.'*

Then he told Mr. Edgarian if you still don't believe me, I will show you this. He opened up a large envelope, pulled out the same baby picture of the passport photo the Asian woman gave to our father, and left it on the table, the same one I had too. Mr. Edgarian also had that identical copy because I sent it to him.

In addition, he told Mr. Edgarian that our mother placed a Virgin Mary necklace around my sister's neck as she did with each of us when we were born.

'I don't know if she has it, though.' Vazgen said.

And finally, he pulled out his birth certificate, which listed his parents and each of his siblings.

Then he smiled and said, *'I know this is my sister, Sonik, who I have been searching for. I am her brother, Vazgen.'*

Mr. Edgarian began crying. He, too, pulled out the same picture of me in my passport photo that I gave him along with my Iranian birth certificate and placed it next to Vazgen's. Everything matched.

'You are her brother.' Mr. Edgarian verified.

Soon, there were no dry eyes. She said her father told her that Vazgen, his wife, and children, along with her father, Mr. Edgarian, were all in tears. Your brother Vazgen wants to speak with you. So, he decided to have a dinner party, invite his friends, and tell everyone the good news.

Vazgen wants my father to come for the dinner party as well to thank him because he said my sister and I wouldn't have found each other without him.

Vazgen scheduled it for Saturday evening. Anita cried as she completed the story, and I was crying too.

Even Mike had teared up. We are all amazed at how it all unfolded.

I looked at the clock. Mr. Edgarian was at Vazgen's house, and in a few minutes, I would be receiving a call from my brother. At 12:00 noon, the phone rang. Anita had two phone lines in her house.

She picked up one while I got the other. My heart was racing.

"Hello," She greeted, and her father, who was on the other end, said the same.

They exchanged a few sentences with each other in Armenian, and then she looked at me and said, *"Your brother is coming to the phone."* My eyes swelled with tears, my body got hot and I had a flood of emotions racing through my body.

I heard a man's voice come on the phone and was talking in Armenian and sounded so happy. Anita nodded her headed at me and mouthed that is your brother. That was the first time I ever heard my brother's voice since finding out I really did have a brother. I couldn't understand exactly what he said. I'm sure it was probably hello. I heard him call me Sonik several times.

His voice was cracking, and I could tell he was trying to hold back his tears. He was talking so fast.

I said, *"Hello,"* my voice trembling like a child's as tears ran down my face.

I told him I was so happy to have found him and that I had been searching for him. Anita was trying to keep up with the both of us, translating back and forth. But at that moment, it didn't matter if I understood one word he said or the other way around.

Just hearing each other's voices and the both of us crying together on the phone, thousands of miles and countries apart, was more than I could have imagined. It was a miracle in the making.

Vazgen handed the phone to his wife and children because each of them wanted to say hi to me as well.

I told Anita to tell him that I wanted to see him and that I would be making plans to come to Iran and visit. After spending about twenty minutes on the phone, it was time for us to say goodbye. But neither of us could say the word goodbye.

So instead, we said, *"Until we meet again."*

The call ended, but my tears didn't. I cried for about another fifteen minutes. My nose and eyes were so red, and my face was so puffy from crying. But for once, I was crying happy tears.

Now it was time for us to eat lunch. Anita and her mother set the table and placed all the traditional Armenian dishes they had prepared on the table.

The spices smelled so good, and the colorful veggies, the stew, the sauces, and the delightful Persian bread tantalized me.

We sat at the table, and as we all passed the dishes around, Anita explained what each was. Everything tasted wonderful.

After cleaning up from lunch, we all hung out in her living room, sharing stories about our lives. They wanted to know about my Korean mother.

I loved talking and actually bragging about what an amazing and wonderful mother she is and how she would do anything in the world for me.

How blessed I was to have a mother who loved me so incredibly much and that I was as much her heart and soul as she was mine.

Anita asked Mike and me to come back to her home on May 18th for lunch again. She said that her father would be back that week, and she would like for me to meet him.

She also said that my brother Vazgen would be calling that day to talk to me again.

I, too, wanted desperately to meet her father, and very excited to get the opportunity to talk to my brother again.

My brother couldn't call my house directly because I couldn't speak Armenian, and he didn't speak English, so for the time being, we had to schedule calls when I was with Anita or someone who could translate for us.

I wanted to thank Mr. Edgarian in person for helping me find my brother. The fact that he gave up his own time to help me was so generous and selfless of him. We planned to be back in two weeks. Mike and I gathered our things and thanked Anita and her family again for all their help, a delicious lunch, and for translating our conversation today, and finally headed back home.

"I am happy you got to talk with your brother today. I know how much this means to you and how hard you worked to find him." Mike smiled at me, and I smiled back.

"I have an idea." I grinned.

He looked at me, and the first thing he said was, *"Oh, boy."*

He knew when I *had an idea*, that meant I was making plans to do something.

"And what would that be?" He raised one eyebrow.

"I have to do a little research first. I will tell everyone in two weeks when we return to Anita's." I answered and gave him a wink. In return, he laughed.

I smiled and just stared at the sky through the window, finally feeling complete fulfillment.

Mr. Edgarian found my brother on April 29, 1996. Picture taken May 18, 1996. First time we met face to face.

CHAPTER NINE

THE SURPRISE OF A LIFETIME

I couldn't wait to tell mom all about being at Anita's and the excitement of talking to my brother.

"He doesn't speak English, but Anita translated for us," I said and then proceeded to narrate the entire experience.

She was so happy for me. We also told Mike's family about it, and I made sure to tell Farhad everything too. I wanted to thank him and his sister for getting me in touch with Anita. Everyone was so excited to hear about my journey to find my brother. Some friends and family members said that it gave them chills just listening to the story about me, knowing in my heart that I had a brother and sister and the struggles I went through to find them.

During the two weeks before we went back to Anita's, I made some phone calls, researched the surprise I was planning, and priced out a few things. I noticed that I didn't have as many panic attacks as I used to. Although I kept seeing the man at the foot of my bed, I felt a calmness in his aura this time. It almost felt like he was at peace somehow now.

I acknowledged he was there and then rolled over and fell back to sleep. By now, I knew whoever this person was, he wasn't there to harm me.

On May 18th, we headed back to Anita's, but this time, along with our children. Mom had some obligations with her church and couldn't make it. When we arrived and entered her home, there he stood, Mr. Edgarian. The wonderfully kind and selfless man who helped make my dream come true. We both locked eyes, hugged each other, with sniffles, trying to hold back our tears.

He didn't speak English, but that was okay. Anita, of course, translated for us. I got to listen to him tell me the story that Anita told me two weeks ago when we were here about the day, he discovered that we had found my brother. He then told me my brother had a nice home, four beautiful children, and a lovely wife—he was doing well. He told me that I had many family members in Iran that came to the dinner at my brother's house, and they all wanted to meet me someday.

We presented Anita and her father with gifts of appreciation. Then we hung out in the living room, chatting like we had been friends for years. Her mother was making food for a small gathering at Anita's later that afternoon.

She had invited a few of her other Armenian friends as they wanted to meet me since they knew about my journey through Anita. The phone rang, and like a child, I jumped up and asked, *"Is it my brother?"*

She nodded her head and put it on speakerphone. I could hear lots of people in the background. Through her translation, I got to learn that my brother was having a large family party. That I had so many family members, and everyone wanted to say hello to me. I could hear everyone in the background yelling their hello to me.

My brother asked me about my mother—if she was alive and how she was doing. He told me he wanted to thank her for taking such good care of me and giving me a good life. I started crying. I told him I would tell her. I asked about his children and their names, what kind of work he did for a living, and how my other siblings were doing.

He also told Anita that my sister Emma and Seda were there beside him and wanted to say hello too. It was surreal to think that just a month ago, I knew I had siblings but was not sure I'd ever find them, and now I was talking to them on the phone. What a whirlwind it was. I then asked Anita to do me a favor.

To ask my brother to have everyone quiet down so she could tell him what I wanted to say. After two weeks of keeping it a secret—I couldn't wait to get it out. Everyone on the other end of the phone got quiet, and then Anita translated to my family what I was saying.

I said to my family, *"Since finding my brother just twenty days ago and talking to him two weeks ago, I made a few calls to see about learning Farsi so I could communicate a little better. I am sorry that I want to try to learn Farsi instead of Armenian, but it was a little easier to learn in such a short amount of time. I called a few government agencies to ask about a US Citizen traveling to Iran and what the US guidelines, recommendations, or restrictions are. I also did some research on getting a Visa to travel to Iran. I priced out plane tickets and asked my mother if she would take care of our children for two weeks if I could go to Iran. She said yes. So, I want to let you know, my brother and sisters, that you will get to see your baby sister again in just four months. I am coming to Iran to see you all."*

And there it was. The reaction I was anticipating. I could hear screams of joy and crying, hands clapping, and my brother yelling *'thank you, thank you'* multiple times. I told them that I would give Anita all the details and she could communicate them with him.

His daughter, Elvin, spoke a little English as they learned it in school as a second language. My brother gave me his phone number, and I told him I would call my niece, Elvin, to keep her updated with flight information, departure, arrival, etc.

We talked for a few more minutes and finally ended our call on an excited note.

Mike looked at me and said, *"So, we are going to Iran?"*

I felt horrible that I didn't tell him until now, but I wanted to research everything first. I told him he didn't have to go. I didn't expect him to. Mom was going to watch the children, and it was probably best if he stayed here in case anything happened to me. Who was to say that something wouldn't happen—I could be detained and held in Iran without the possibility of leaving. I didn't want to put him in that position or leave our children without any parents.

"I am not going to let you go alone. I have been by your side, supporting you since you discovered your adoption and through this journey. I am not about to leave your side and let you go alone now. Nothing is going to happen other than you getting to meet your biological family, and we will be fine." He assured me.

I smiled at him, knowing how lucky I was to have him. Then he said, *"Alright then, I guess we are heading to Iran."*

The rest of the evening went great. We met Anita's friends, talked about everything, enjoyed delicious Armenian food, took some pictures, and then called it a night.

Over the course of the next four months, I took Farsi-speaking classes every Saturday in Arlington, VA. Mike and I got our Visas on our American passports, booked our airline tickets, and I shopped for the appropriate clothing to enter Iran. I needed a hijab to cover my hair and a long coat. We shopped for gifts to hand out to my family, assigned the Power of Attorney to my mother while we were out of the country, and then started packing.

My mother sewed pockets inside of my underwear so I could fold up photocopies of our passports and hide them in there. It sounds crazy, but we had watched the movie *"Not without my daughter,"* and other shows and documentaries and wanted to be prepared in case our passports were confiscated.

We figured if we had to make a run for it to the Swiss Embassy, we would at least have a photocopy to show that we were American Citizens.

The night before we left for Iran, the image of the man appeared again. I woke up, and there he stood at the foot of my bed. For some reason, now I could see him much more clearly than I had the other times. He wasn't tall and wore a brimmed hat and a suit jacket. His hand hovered over my foot as though he was reaching out to touch me. His head was slightly tilted, and as I continued to stare, he grinned and nodded his head up and down. This time, for some reason, he looked so calm and at ease. I kept staring at him until he faded out and was gone.

On the morning of September 22nd, 1996, we dropped the children off at my mother's. Brandon was five years old, and Shelby was three. They were excited to be at grandma's house as always and to get to stay there for two weeks. They had no concept of time, but two weeks without our children seemed like a lifetime for us. The thought did cross my mind what if I never saw my children or my mother again? Was it really worth it to go and leave my children behind? Was I making a mistake? I trembled and cried as I hugged my mother and my children.

My mother whispered to me as she hugged me, *"God is with you, you will be safe, and your children will be fine. You need to do this for yourself. We all will be waiting for you when you get back. Always remember, I love you."* Then she kissed me. We kissed Brandon and Shelby and hugged them so tightly. I kept repeating *"I Love You"* to them as my tears streamed down my face. Finally, we said our goodbyes and drove off as mom and the children waved at us from the doorstep.

We flew out of Dulles International Airport in Virginia on Lufthansa Airlines. During our flight, I was filled with excitement, knowing I was finally going to see my brother and sisters. We had a layover in Frankfort, Germany, for about nine hours.

During that time, I paced the floors of that airport so many times and walked through every gift shop in that airport. So many thoughts ran

183

through my mind. Then I became filled with anxiety, panic, and fear. I thought about getting on the next plane back to the states. But I had come too far to turn back. Finally, we heard the boarding call for our next flight, which was also Lufthansa, headed directly to Iran. This was about a five-hour flight which for me meant five more hours of thoughts running through my head.

As the plane started to descend, the stewardesses instructed all women to completely cover their hair with their hijab and to make sure all sleeves were pulled down to cover their wrists and that no skin was exposed. I felt my breathing getting erratic. I was panting and felt hot and flushed. I kept thinking to myself, *'this is really happening.'*

The plane landed at 12:50 am, Iran's time, and everyone gathered their carry-on items and exited the plane. I kept sitting in my seat, frozen with fear. I couldn't move.

I did as instructed by the stewardess and put my hijab on, and covered my skin, but for some reason, my legs wouldn't move out of the seat. I was paralyzed with fear. Mike assured me it would be okay and to get moving.

The stewardess came back to my seat to see if everything was okay and if I needed assistance. I took a few deep breaths, got up from the seat, and walked towards the exit. Once again, I froze. I wanted to go back to my seat. The airline crew was commanding that I needed to depart the plane. So, I closed my eyes, slowly took a deep breath in, exhaled then I stepped out of the plane and placed my foot on the ground.

I was now officially in the land of the country I was born in, IRAN. I finally returned twenty-nine years later. Now we had to walk to the terminal inside the airport.

Customs checked us in and looked over our American passports, our luggage and our carry-on bags. They asked why we were in Iran and what purpose did we have.

I told them it was to visit family. Then the customs agent stamped our passports and welcomed us to Iran.

We had to go to baggage claim to pick up our luggage and now had to walk down the hall to the set of doors that opened to the waiting area for incoming passengers. I knew my brother would be on the other side of those doors. This was the moment we had both waited for, for so many years. It was finally happening.

We pushed open the doors, and there stood a crowd of people. None of whom I recognized. Everyone was holding bouquets of flowers and screaming out, 'Sonik, Sonik!'

There were balloons and cameras flashing. People were racing towards me. The man standing in the front held his arms wide open and smiled so big and started shedding tears. I saw the resemblance in his face, felt the connection and I knew he was my brother. I ran to him, and we hugged each other and couldn't let go. He kept talking, but I couldn't understand him. I told him I was so happy to finally see him. That I never forgot him. I stood in that airport, crying like a baby.

His wife, Roza, hugged me so tightly and said something in Armenian. Everyone took turns coming up to me, hugging me, and touching my face or my hands.

My brother brought a friend with him named Vaughn, who spoke English. He came up to me, introduced himself, and said he would be with us to translate everything. His daughter, Elvin, who was my niece, could also help with a good amount of translation. Everyone gave me so much love that I couldn't even distinguish between family members, friends of the family or strangers in the crowd.

People were coming up to me, asking to take a picture with me, and some people had video cameras recording everything and asking questions. With all the commotion we were making, the airport security told us to move along. We walked outside of the airport like a mob. My brother walked Mike and me to his car. We put our luggage in, and he motioned for us to get in. Everyone else got in cars as well, and it was like a procession, one car after another pulling out of the garage and onto the highway, each one following us to Vazgen's house. Mike and I sat in the car's back seat and looked out the window. We couldn't see much as it was about 1:30 am in the morning.

When we arrived at my brother's house, the lights were on, music was playing, and the place was full of people, mostly immediate family members.

We walked in and witnessed a party that was planned for me. There were balloons, banners, flowers, and tables filled with so much food.

As I walked in and made my way through all the people, my sister Emma walked up to me, I remember you I thought holding me as a baby, she hugged me so tightly. I closed my eyes as we hugged each other and I could vividly see her and Vazgen holding me when I was a baby. The interpreter translated everything she said.

She had tears running down her face and expressed she missed me and didn't want to let me go when I was a baby. She walked me over to my oldest sister, Seda, who was sitting on the couch. She has two children.

Seda suffered from health issues and was basically confined to a wheelchair. She was petite and frail. Her husband, Nashan, and son, Varoojan, had to carry her from room to room. She has a beautiful daughter, Alina who doted on her mother.

My sister, Seda, and her husband, Nashan, held my hand and kept apologizing to me. The interpreter, Vaughn, told me she and my brother-in-law were so sad that they couldn't take me when I was a baby. They said they wanted to, but for specific reasons, they just couldn't.

I learned that my brother had four children. His oldest son was Edris, his daughter Elvin, and his two younger sons were Arbi and Argin. They all hovered around me, calling me *aunty*.

I was told that my oldest brother, Vahik, was killed in a car accident in Armenia. He was married and had three children too. They told me that his wife and I could pass for twins. She and the children live in Armenia. Everyone said I was so beautiful, and I appreciated it, but I certainly did not feel beautiful. I was so ashamed of myself for being overweight.

I found myself turning to food all the time because of stress or anxiety and truly wished I could have lost weight before I came to Iran.

It was early in the morning when the party wrapped up. I think everyone was exhausted. My brother showed us the room we were to be staying in, and it wasn't long before we were fast asleep.

When we got up later, I was told there was a big party planned for me that evening. I couldn't believe it. Another party? I felt so honored. This one was to be filled with immediate and distant family along with their friends, co-workers, and neighbors.

That afternoon, my sister Emma and her two daughters, Marietta and Meganoosh, came over. She has a son as well; however, he was serving in the military. We sat around the living room, chatting as my niece, Elvin, translated. My brother, nieces, and nephews brought out several photo albums for me to look through family photos.

I flipped through each page, smiling as I looked at pictures of how cute my nieces and nephews were. There were lots of pictures of Vazgen and his wife too.

Then I flipped the page, and it was as if I saw a ghost. My eyes grew big, and a cold chill ran down my back. *"The man in this picture, who is this?"* I paused.

"Oh, my God! That's him!" I exclaimed in disbelief.

The man in the picture had on a brimmed hat and a suit jacket. The way he stood and the frame of his body was that of the image of the man that I kept seeing at the foot of my bed. My niece, Elvin, came over next to me and looked at the picture, and chuckled.

She said, *"That is your father."* Then she asked me, *"What is wrong?"*

I took a deep breath and then exhaled. I explained how I saw him several times in the middle of the night at the foot of my bed.

Her only response was, *"What? Really?"*

I wasn't sure if she understood what I was saying with the language barrier or not. I didn't want them to think I was crazy, especially since we had just met less than twenty-four hours ago.

So, I didn't say anything more about it. However, it did rattle me. I thought about the last time I saw him, and I remembered he smiled and seemed at peace as it appeared that he was trying to touch my foot or leg. I couldn't explain it, but that image was him.

I asked when did he die, and they told me about eleven months ago from a heart attack, and he was seventy-two years old. That was just about the time I started seeing the image.

My biological father, Kamal

That night, there were even more people and more food. Music was playing, and everyone was trying to teach Mike and me how to do the Armenian dances. We danced and laughed and had a great time. Then my brother stood up and asked Mike and me to stand up. Vaughn stood next to us and translated.

My brother proceeded to tell everyone the story about how he lost his sister twenty-nine years ago. He talked about the struggles he dealt with in life. That was because our family was so poor that he learned to be street-smart.

He went into business with our brother-in-law Nashan that manufactured plastic for plates, cups, etc., and exported them to other surrounding countries. The business did well and he was able to own several homes and had a good life with his wife and children. He said the one thing he was missing was his baby sister and that he never gave up hope in finding her.

Then it was my turn. I also talked about my story, about how I so often had a flashback of a memory where my brother and sister were holding me in their arms. I explained that I felt it in my bones that I had a brother and sister and often asked my mother about them. I talk about my childhood, my teenage years, my wonderful mother, whom I love so much, and our incredibly close bond, and how I found out on my own about my adoption. What I did not mention was the molestation I suffered or the abuse my mother and I suffered from my adoptive father.

I talked about my husband, who always stood by my side through the search and my two beautiful children. I told them about all the people I reached out to for help, the countless hours I spent digging and searching for information, and the determination to never give up.

Everyone raised their glasses in a toast to our reunion, and then my brother, sisters, and I exchanged gifts.

Over the course of the two weeks that Mike and I were in Iran, we visited my mother's graveside, toured my brother's company, went to some parks and bazaars, ancient ruins, beautiful architectural Armenian Catholic churches, ate food from street vendors, and did all sorts of shopping. My brother took us on a five-hour drive to the North side of Iran to visit his friend's house by the Caspian Sea.

We had a cookout at his friend's and spent the day on the beach, walking along the shoreline. I picked shells and rocks as souvenirs from the Caspian Sea.

Almost every night, a different family member hosted dinner at their place. My brother took me to apply for my Iranian Birth Certificate. We drove by the military compound, which was very secure and off-limits, and there, I saw a large mural of the Ayatollah Khomeini.

My sister-in-law's father passed away, so we attended his funeral, went to a wedding, drove to the King's Palace, and visited some museums.

Outside the Museum of animals & wildlife, this is a view of the city.

One of the highlights was that I got to go back to the home I was born in, the place where those memories of my brother and sister holding me and the home my mother first laid eyes on me and adopted me.

This is the house where I was Born.

Every day was filled with all sorts of things I got to experience. My family wanted to ensure I got to experience as much as possible, and I did. Everywhere we went, the people of Iran were very nice and kind. Many of them gave us free food and desserts when we ate at their restaurants or stopped by to get some pastries. Some shop owners gave us some free trinkets too.

Everyone came over to me and talked about how good the USA was. Many said they had previously traveled to the US and liked it.

Life was different in Iran from what it is here in the US. Their customs and traditions are different as well. We learned to adapt and embrace all the differences between the two cultures.

I learned that it wasn't the people of Iran that we were led to believe by media and news in America as bad, evil, or terroristic people. Every stranger we met treated Mike and me very friendly. They didn't look at us any differently because we were American. But rather, it seemed more so that our governments didn't get along.

During my time in Iran, I tried to gather as much information about my family's medical history as possible. I learned that my mother died almost three months after giving birth to me. She had diabetes and very high blood pressure. Apparently, her cause of death was due to high blood pressure that went out of control after giving birth to me.

They said our family was poor, and they couldn't afford proper medical care for her, and childbirth was extremely hard on her. So, having no medical attention, she passed away.

I saw that my brother also had a prescription for Xanax, and I told him I did too. I asked why he took it, and he said because he suffered from panic attacks. I raised my eyebrow and wondered if it was hereditary. In some sort of way, it felt comforting knowing that my brother and I shared the same panic attack diagnosis.

We called the children and my mother several times during our two-week stay.

Each time we called, my brother wanted to talk to my mother and the kids. He thanked her for everything she did to take such good care of me.

He cried and told her he would kiss her feet because she was an angel. He told her if Sonik couldn't have our own mother, then he was glad I had her for a mother.

My brother and sisters bought so many gifts for me, the children and my mother. Between all the gifts that my family gave us and all the things that Mike and I had bought, we had to buy a few extra suitcases.

I purchased an authentic handmade Persian carpet and quite a few pieces of jewelry.

Finally, our last day approached. It was October 6. Our flight was to leave very late that night, at 11:00 pm. My brother, my sisters, and I enjoyed the evening together and took lots of pictures of the four of us. I couldn't get over what a large family I came from.

So many cousins, nieces, nephews, aunts, and uncles I had.

I had a wonderful time, and everyone made Mike and me feel so welcome. The whole experience of finding out I was adopted, to the miracle of locating my biological family and then traveling to Iran to meet them and getting to enjoy my time with my family and being in Iran is something I couldn't have imagined in my wildest dreams. The day I walked off the plane in Iran, I had no idea how happy, and how loved I would feel.

I cried uncontrollably when it was time to say goodbye at the airport. I was leaving my biological family and the land where I was born, where it all began. I think I was so overwhelmed with emotions.

We could never go back and recapture the years we lost, but we could now look forward to sharing the memories and time together in the coming years. In our short time together, we had gotten attached to each other. There was so much love, laughter, and joy that saying goodbye seemed almost impossible.

My brother hugged me and said, *"Goodbyes are forever, so we will say see you later because we will see each other again."*

Meeting my biological brother and sisters was such an incredible and emotional experience. It was so surreal.

We all compared our looks, even the fact that my brother and I both have a cleft chin, our health history, our lives, our likes and dislikes, our hobbies, and our childhood—we talked about my adoptive mother.

They all said she was a wonderful woman for taking me and raising me so well. We also talked about politics and governments, sports, food, and literally everything.

We talked about everything we could think of, and my stay now felt so short to me. It truly felt like God, and our biological mother felt the time was right for us to now reconnect. It was a feeling that no amount of money or object could ever come close to.

A strong bond that spanned over twenty-nine years, thousands of miles and countries apart, and yet by the grace of God and the people in our lives, we were able to come back to each other.

We boarded the plane and headed back home to the United States. Mike and I were so excited to see our babies. I missed them and my mother so much. I was excited to give them the gifts we got and the ones my family sent with us and to tell mom and everyone about our trip.

A few days after we arrived back home, I was still engrossed in the excitement and jubilation. Now, as I stared into the mirror, thinking about how often people questioned if I really was half Korean and how I could have a Korean heritage, I got my answer.

I held up a picture of my biological mother that my brother gave to me. I held it next to my face, and I could clearly see that I resembled her. It made sense now why some people questioned my features.

My entire journey from discovering my adoption by mistake to my search efforts, the resistance of people or places who shut the door in my face, the sense that I felt my entire life that somehow, somewhere, I had a brother and sister, the determination and dedication to never give up is probably one of the most incredible and unexplainable things anyone could think of. But it happened, and I'm blessed it happened to me.

Actually, going to Iran, the country from which I was adopted, and visiting my biological family was one of the best experiences of my life. It was like that journey of finding me had come full circle. I proved to myself that I could do anything I set my mind to. I now believed in my own inner strength to never give up—I accomplished my goals. Through all the heartbreak and challenging times, I am so thankful I had my husband and my mother by my side and that God brought people into my life for specific reasons, such as Anita and her father.

As suddenly and unexpectedly as the onset of my panic attacks had started at the discovery of my adoption and all of the unknowns about who I was and where I came from, they subsided once I left Iran after meeting my family.

I was at peace and no longer stressed over my adoption.

Today, who I saw staring back was a woman who was raised to believe she could do anything she set her mind to. She is an intelligent woman who is strong-willed, determined, persistent, relentless, and a protector of those she loves and who has a compassionate and loving heart.

All of these traits I have, I didn't get because I resemble my biological mother. I got them because of my adoptive mother. Everything I had become, I had because of her. She raised me, she loved and nurtured me, and she taught me. Now, I understood why it was hard for her to say that I was adopted.

Perhaps, she thought that meant I wasn't truly her child. But I was. I was forever going to be her daughter, and she was forever going to be my mother. The adjective adopted was a word that was irrelevant to us. I now had peace of mind and a massive sense of accomplishment, knowing that I had found my family.

I was a woman who was blessed to be biologically Armenian with an American/Korean heritage. I was very proud of that and planned to carry that with honor and pride.

Chapter Ten

A Bittersweet Reunion

S ince the time Shelby was eighteen months old, I wanted another child. I discussed it with Mike, and he was good with it. But when I told my mother that we were trying for baby number three, she had reservations. She was worried and afraid for me to go through childbirth again.

By now, I completely understood the odd fear and panic I saw in her eyes when I was in labor with Brandon a few years ago. It all made sense because now I knew her secret. I was a little nervous too, but my faith and desire for more children wouldn't let me give up on my dream of having more children. She knew I wouldn't give up, so she did what she always did; prayed to God to take care of me.

We had been trying for a little over a year and a half before I got pregnant with our third child. I was feeling nauseous in the mornings again and decided to take an at-home pregnancy test.

I was so excited when the result came out positive. I couldn't wait to tell Mike.

I wanted to tell him as soon as he came home from work, but I waited until we put the kids down for bed. Then we sat in the sunroom, and I told him. It seemed like it had taken forever, but finally, I was pregnant. He was pleased about it. We told Brandon and Shelby the next day that they were going to have a brother or sister. They both were excited too.

My pregnancy with Noah was probably the easiest. This time I learned my lesson about gaining weight. I only gained 32 lbs. My mother had recently retired from State Farm Insurance after serving twenty-three years with them. She was so excited to be able to enjoy being with her grandchildren all day. My brother and I remained in constant contact since I left Iran in October of 1996.

In August of 1997, he told me that he and his wife were granted a visa to come to the US to visit me. I was surprised and thrilled. He said they wanted to come to see how my life here was and to also see parts of America. He provided me with their flight information and the date of their arrival.

My brother, Vazgen, and his wife, Roza, arrived on October 28th, 1997, as I was very pregnant and just a few days away from my due date with our third child. They had plans to stay in the US for six weeks.

My brother picked up a little bit of English from his daughter. His wife, my sister-in-law, actually was able to speak broken English.

She spent a reasonable amount of time learning from her daughter, so we were able to communicate without a translator now. Mom kept the children at her house so we could pick them up from the airport. This time, the tables were turned. Just a year ago, I stepped off a plane onto a foreign land to see my brother, how he lived, and what the country Iran was like. And now, a year later, my brother was doing the same to see me, his sister, how I lived, and what the United States was like.

I waited for him as he came through the baggage claim. We hugged for what seemed like five minutes.

We both had tears in our eyes and almost simultaneously said, *"See? No goodbyes, as we are meeting again now."*

It was evening when we left the airport and headed back to our home. It had already gotten dark, so they really couldn't see much on our drive back home. Once we arrived back at the house, we showed them around the house and made them comfortable. Then we sat a bit and chatted. For a brief moment, my mind wandered.

All I could think was just a few years ago, the thought of my brother and I sitting together on my couch talking to each other was inconceivable, yet here we are.

I knew they were tired. It was a long flight, and the time difference worsened the jet lag. I told them to go ahead and get some rest and a good night's sleep and that we would start our day in the morning. Since the children stayed at mom's house last night, she said she would take Brandon and Shelby to school so I could spend the day with my brother. I had planned on picking up the children from school at the end of the day and asked mom to come by for dinner so she could meet my brother and his wife.

I spent the day driving my brother and sister-in-law around our town and Frederick so they could see where I grew up. I drove them by the apartment mom and I used to live in and my schools. We stopped for lunch and did a little shopping so they could buy some things for their children. Then we headed back home so I could pick up Brandon and Shelby from school and start cooking dinner. This was the first time they met my children.

It was so incredible to say to my children, *"This is your uncle, Vazgen."*

Being raised as an only child, I never expected to tell my children that they had an uncle, my brother. The children were a little shy, and of course, they didn't fully understand what was going on. In the evening, Mike came home from work, and we finished preparing dinner. Mom just pulled up in her car, and my heart was racing for Vazgen and her. I knew at this moment this would be the first time in thirty years that the two of them would see each other since that day when he chased her car, begging her not to take me.

I watched mom walk up to the house and come in through the door in the sunroom, where we always entered the home. Vagzen and Roza stood in the dining room, waiting for mom to join us as she took off her shoes and jacket. I walked in with mom, and immediately, I could see and feel the years of wonderment and gratitude my brother had for my mother.

I could clearly see how elated my mother was to see him. They hugged each other as though they had known each other for all of those thirty years. Vazgen kept thanking my mother over and over for taking such good care of me and raising me so beautifully.

My mother held his hand and apologized for the pain and anguish it caused him when she had to take me.

She said she wished so badly she could have taken him and my sister Emma too. She told him she thought about them and that, in the back of her mind, she was always worried about whether or not they were okay.

Then she told him his face still looked like that little boy he once was. She said she could undoubtedly recognize him and that he grew up to be a handsome man. She said to him that it was truly a blessing that we were reunited after thirty years. Vagzen kissed my mother's hands, and they hugged again. I stood there, taking it all in as we all had tears in our eyes.

My brother said to my mother, *"You are a wonderful mother to Sonik, and for that, my family is forever grateful to you."*

"You don't have to thank me, son. Your mother, God, and I ensured Sonik would be cared for and loved so much." My mother answered.

There wasn't a dry eye in the house. I told everyone to sit and eat. Dinner was good, and afterward, my brother and his wife brought down gifts from the bedroom that they brought for my mother, the children, Mike, and me.

This was such a bittersweet moment. The amazing woman that I was blessed to call my mother had let her guard down about this secret she had kept for so long and was now opening up and talking to my brother and me about the adoption.

Still being cautiously private, she didn't divulge our personal information, such as the abuse my adoptive father inflicted on us, but I could see some sense of comfort and relief in her heart that this was now out in the open. As the evening progressed, I put the children down to bed so they could be rested for school. Mom said she was heading home. She invited my brother and his wife to her home for dinner any night before leaving and heading back to Iran.

As she was putting on her coat, Vazgen said to her, *"Thank you again for saving my sister."*

My mother smiled at him, winked at me, and said to Vazgen, *"No, we saved each other."*

Holding back tears was absolutely impossible for me because I knew that God had picked the perfect mother in the world for me. After all, he knew I'd needed, an angel and a hero.

Our third child, Noah, was born in November, during my brother's visit, although not on the same day as his grandmother, as she had hoped. My brother and his wife were waiting at the house when we brought Noah home from the hospital. This time, I decided that I would wait until my water broke and I was in labor. I didn't want a C-section this time. I would endure the labor pains and wanted to give birth naturally. I went full term, and on the morning that I went into labor, we called my mom, and she came over to watch the kids.

We called my doctor, and he said we needed to come to his office so he could examine me.

We did just that. Upon examining me, he told Mike and me to go straight to the hospital. He asked if I had anything to eat or drink yet, and I said no.

"Good. Don't stop anywhere to grab anything to eat." The doctor advised.

"I am a little worried. Do you know why the doctor said that?" I looked at Mike.

He just shook his head. Neither of us knew. When we arrived at the hospital, they quickly checked me in and got me into the room.

Then the nurses came in.

"We need to get you prepped for a C-section." They informed me.

I spoke up, *"I am not having a C-section. I was planning on doing a natural birth."*

The nurse turned to me and said, *"That is not an option. By doctor's orders, you are scheduled for an immediate C-section."*

"Why? What's going on?" Mike and I questioned, troubled now.

"The doctor would be in to explain soon." The nurse answered.

When the doctor arrived, he explained to us everything he could.

"There is meconium in your amniotic fluid, and it can be deadly if the baby swallows it. So, we need to get the baby out quickly." The doctor explained.

Mike called my mom to let her know. He probably shouldn't have called her as I just knew she would worry herself to death.

"I will bring Brandon and Shelby to see the baby after the C-section is done." She said.

Then, I was taken to the operating room, and the C-section was performed with great success.

Finally, our third and last baby, Noah, was born in November 1997. He weighed 8 lbs, 7 oz. I loved the name Noah. It has this special place in my heart as it belongs to the kind-hearted and obedient servant of God. I knew my mother loved the Biblical name as well.

My brother and his wife got to experience Thanksgiving dinner for the first time. My brother wasn't too fond of the turkey and all the side dishes. He said he preferred a burger and fries. We all laughed. While he was visiting the US, we took him to Washington, DC, toured some museums, Baltimore and the inner harbor, the beach, and a few other places. Then they flew out to Las Vegas and then California to visit some friends and distant relatives.

He did come back for his final week at our place so we could spend more time together, do a bit more sightseeing and shopping, and have dinner at my mother's house before it was time for them to head back. It was wonderful having him visit me. I was happy that he got the chance to visit and see how I lived and where I grew up. Time flew by so quickly and it was time for them to head back to Iran.

Both of our kids were in school now. Brandon was six years old and in first grade, and Shelby was four years old and in Pre-K when our third child Noah was an infant. I made it a point to be very active with the school and the PTO, volunteering my time. I was the PTO Fundraising Chairman and then became the PTO Vice President and President over time. I wanted my children to know that their mother was supportive of their schooling and anything that they did. I was also their homeroom mom and chaperoned their field trips.

Everyone from the teachers, staff, children of the school, and their parents knew me because I was so actively involved in the school.

Mike was always a hard worker and very good at his job. He worked for Defense Mapping in Washington DC, so often, he had to work overtime, including on the weekends too.

When different military oppositions happened, he was required to work seven days a week, long hours each day. But he never minded. He was always a go-getter at work, and the extra pay was helpful.

He later transferred to another Federal Government Agency in DC.

Brandon and Shelby were the doting older siblings. Watching them with their baby brother gave me immense joy. My heart is filled with love and happiness. Even though Brandon and Noah were six years apart in age, Brandon was very gentle with Noah, and Shelby was very nurturing with him.

I loved having the children with me. It wasn't hard having three children at all. I did everything with them. With my mom retired now, the children wanted to be at grandma's house all the time. It was the same house that mom bought for us when I was fourteen years old. The neighborhood was full of children, and all the kids enjoyed riding bikes in the cul-de-sac, running back and forth to each other's houses, and just playing. All the neighbors were very close to each other as we all felt more like close friends than neighbors, and they looked out for each other and the children.

With my mom being retired, it gave her ample time to help me with the children. My mother did play a big role in helping me with the children. Mom and I took the children everywhere we went.

Yard sales, the mall, grocery shopping, no matter where or what, the children came with us. One of the fondest memories I have with my mom is when the children and I, along with her, went strawberry picking. Mom loved it. She would pick a berry and eat a berry. She and the children would make a game out of picking more strawberries than me, and each time it never failed, that mom would inevitably sit on some strawberries in the patch and have them smashed all over her bottom.

The kids would be covered in red as well, from their mouths to their toes. I swear mom was a pro at picking strawberries. She could have three buckets filled in the time it took me to get one filled. We would freeze a lot of the strawberries and enjoy them all through the winter.

Mom spoiled her grandchildren so much with a kiddie pool, all kinds of outside toys, a trampoline, games, and toys for in the house, new clothes, jackets, and shoes, and each time the ice cream truck came through the neighborhood, she would hand them money and take them out to the truck so they could pick out their own ice cream. She would chase them around the yard and play all sorts of games with them.

She let them do things that I wasn't allowed as a child, like letting them eat in the bedroom and on the floor while watching TV. She even let them jump on the beds and much more. She said that's what grandmas are for.

It was so fulfilling to witness the amount of love my mother had for her grandchildren—my children. Heck, my kids enjoyed being at their grandma's house so much they would call her anytime I yelled at them or put them in time out for her to come to pick them up. They even told me they wanted to move in with grandma because they loved being with her all the time. I knew my children loved me more than anything, so I found it endearing that my children so deeply loved their grandmother, the perfect mother I was so blessed by God to have.

Mike and I also did so much with the children. We took them camping, to amusement parks, to the beach in Ocean City, MD for vacation, cruises, as well as various other places for vacation. All three of our children were in various sports, which kept us all busy. We always went to each of their games and practices.

Of course, my mother came to all of their games too.

Any chance we got, Mike, the children, and I would go back to Pennsylvania to visit with his family. I always felt close to his family, and I enjoyed going on our visits.

The children enjoyed visiting and especially during the big Mummers Day Parade, the town carnival, going back during Christmas break and being there for the New Year's Eve celebration, and of course, the family reunion picnics each summer. Usually, each summer, I would take the children by myself to Pennsylvania for a week so they could spend time with their father's side of the family.

I so desperately wanted to have more children, but we stopped at our third baby. I always talked about wanting six children. We halted because I was very busy finding my biological family and visiting them. I was thirty when Noah was born. I was afraid that by the time I had a fourth child, I would be thirty-three or thirty-four, and I worried about having children being older since my biological mother died after giving birth to me.

Also, a few years after Noah was born, Mike and I started to have some marital problems, so having another child probably wouldn't have been the best thing to do.

My years of being married to Mike had their ups and downs too, like most marriages. Turned out that being married wasn't always a walk in the park. The expectations I had from Mike and the expectations he had from me increased tenfold when we tied the knot.

In the initial phase, life was wonderful. I did work sometimes, but mostly, I was a stay-at-home mom. Mike never said I had to work as he made good money, and we could afford for me to stay at home with the kids.

But personally, I wanted to work because I wanted to feel some independence and to have some time in the workforce chatting with co-workers and feeling like I was contributing somewhat financially to the family income. I started working full-time when Noah was two and a half years old. I went back to work at River & Trail Outfitters as the office manager. A company that I had worked at as a raft guide and shop girl when I was in high school and college. Since my mom was retired, it made it easier for me to go to work because she took care of my children when I worked. When they had school, she would pick them up after school, and sometimes, she took them to school too. But usually, I dropped them off, and she picked them up. It was while working at River & Trail that I met my dear friend Amanda Mendez, my co-worker

Over the course of our marriage, Mike did develop a little bit of a pot belly. However, I never lost the attraction to him. He was a jokester at times, but he was always a hard worker and could fix anything in the house, including gutting out plaster walls and replacing them with new studs, insulation, and drywall. He could fix almost any issue or repair on our cars, and he was wonderful at taking on as much overtime as he could so he could save money for our retirement. He was a great provider for his family.

He would do anything to help his friends. And he was very helpful to my mother doing anything she needed. He wasn't the greatest father. He would lose his temper with the kids and often said things that were out of line to embarrass them, but his heart was in the right place at times. He watched them during practice and games for the sports they were enrolled in. He was active in helping them with their Boy Scout activities. He wasn't good at communicating his feelings nor was he a good disciplinarian to the children. The kids never took him seriously when he tried to discipline them. I think it was the way he spoke to them, how he said it, the way he said it, his facial expressions and that he never followed through with the discipline. But he was my husband, the father of our children and good or bad, I loved him.

CHAPTER ELEVEN

THE SECOND VISIT

In the summer of 2000, Mike and I decided to visit my brother and family in Iran again—this time, with our three children. This time, I went as an Iranian Citizen since I was given my birth certificate when I was there four years ago. So now, I was able to obtain my Iranian passport.

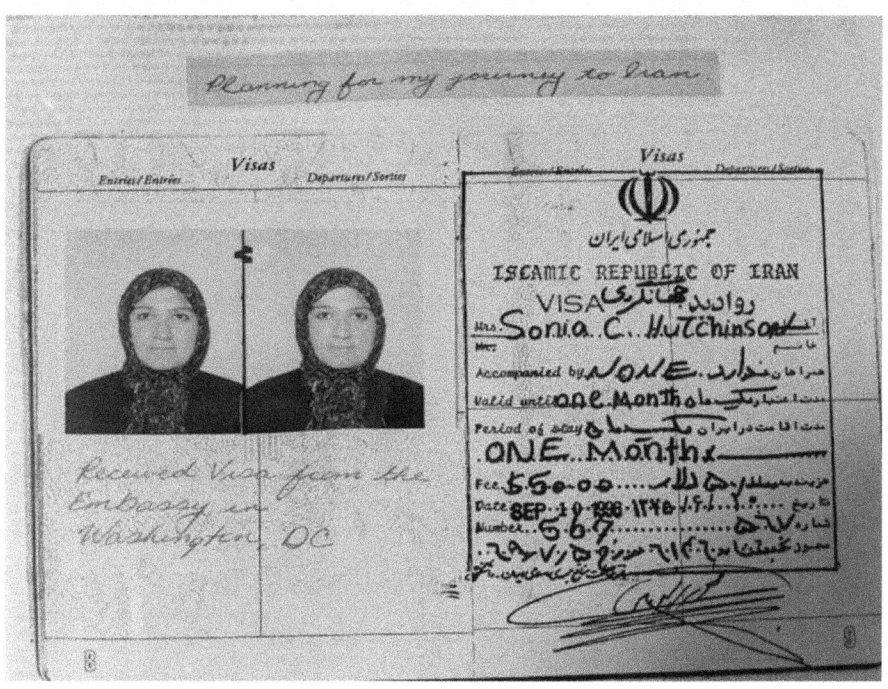

Also, the Iranian government told me that the next time I returned, I must do so with my Iranian passport because they considered only you their citizen first and foremost if you are born in Iran.

Mike and the children went with their American passports, obviously. I still planned on taking my American passport as well and hiding it. I also planned on making copies of all of our passports, just as I did before, and hiding the copies inside a secret pocket in my underwear and socks.

We asked my mother if she would like to go, but she declined. She had recently been to Korea to visit her family and wasn't up for another overseas trip so soon.

So, at the end of October of 2000, me, Mike, and our three children flew to Iran and stayed at my brother's house. Everyone was so excited to see us again and meet our children. They absolutely adored them. When my family saw me this time, I had lost a significant amount of weight and was much smaller than I was on my previous visit four years ago.

Every family member's home we visited spoiled our children. It was a great learning experience for the children to be able to go to Iran. I did take Brandon and Shelby out of school for three weeks. However, I got it approved through their schools, and their homework assignments were to write about their trip. They had to write something every day detailing what they did, where they went, what they saw, how they felt, and what they liked and disliked. The journal they had to keep of their trip covered their history and grammar.

They also had a math book in which they had to complete a certain number of pages or sections each week. These things had to be turned in to school upon their return for grading. Brandon and Shelby were diligent and wrote in their journals every day.

Life in Iran was different for them. They quickly realized the difference in the dress codes, the music, the foods and customs, and even the toilets. While on our trip, the children also got to visit an elementary school to see how schools were in Iran and the structure of their classroom studies compared to ours in the US. They were allowed to visit the classrooms and meet some of the teachers and students. They also visited a fire department and got to sit in the fire trucks. We visited my brother's business and watched how plastic is recycled and made into plates, cups, and other items.

We visited parks, museums, candy shops, bakeries, toy stores, arcade centers, and malls. The children experienced eating from street vendors and buying freshly made Lavash (Bread) each morning from the men on the streets baking them in the hot urns.

They witnessed people smoking Hookahs in both indoor and outdoor restaurants. They quickly realized that there were no fast food restaurants like McDonalds', Burger King, or even Pizza Hut. They did have pizza restaurants, but even the pizza wasn't quite the same as we had in the US. They didn't have any fried chicken restaurants like KFC that we were used to, but Brandon and Shelby adapted very well to the Armenian foods and, of course, enjoyed the pastries and candy without hesitation.

Noah, on the other hand, was a bit more difficult when it came to eating. He was a picky eater. All he wanted was pizza and chocolate pudding. But for a child who was just about to turn three years old, what more could be expected?

It seemed as though every day, we were invited to a different family member's home for dinner or lunch. Everyone was so hospitable. Everyone really went above and beyond to make us feel welcome and a part of the family.

I remember, one day, my sister Emma invited us to her home for dinner. It was her husband and children, along with my brother, his family, Mike and I, and our children. I will never forget while at dinner, Brandon asked to go to the bathroom, so I walked him down the hallway to the bathroom. Their bathrooms are typically the same as ours, with one exception. They have squat toilets and spray hoses to clean after the deed instead of toilet paper.

None of us really cared for that style of toilet, but we knew that while traveling, we had to acclimate ourselves.

With Brandon being nine years old, I shut the door and told him to join us back at the dinner table after he finished.

About fifteen minutes later, I heard Brandon yelling, *"Mom!"* Multiple times.

I ran down to the bathroom and stood outside the door, and asked, *"What's wrong?"*

"I'm stuck!" He replied.

"What do you mean you are stuck?" I asked, confused.

Then he said in a broken voice, clearly in pain, *"I've squatted so long that my legs are stuck, and I can't stand up."*

I opened the door, ran behind him, put my arms under his armpits, and lifted him up. However, his legs still stayed in the same squat position and wouldn't straighten out. He tried to straighten his legs as I held him up and was finally able to do so just slightly. I had him pull his pants up and then sat him on the floor while I rubbed his legs.

He told me that he squatted so long that his legs went numb, and fell asleep. Once he got the feeling back in his legs, he was able to come back to the dinner table, embarrassed, and to state how much he disliked those toilets. I know, at the time, it was embarrassing for him. However, we all were able to laugh about it later on.

217

Noah, on the other hand, loved the squat toilets. He thought it was funny to be able to squat over the toilet and actually see his excrement go down into the toilet.

He would laugh and say, *"Poopy go down the hole!"* Sometimes it's the little things in life that make you laugh.

Noah turned three during our visit. My brother and his family threw a special Armenian birthday party for Noah and invited lots of family members. It was a wonderful birthday party with lots of families, food, cake, and, of course, gifts for Noah. One of his favorite gifts he got was from his Uncle Vazgen, which was a tricycle. He rode that tricycle every day in the house and on the street where my brother's house was.

I think one of the most traumatizing things for the children during the visit was witnessing the slaughter of sheep outside of my brother's home by the neighbors. Mike and I were unaware of what was going on, and the children were playing on the balcony of my brother's house and looking down at the street below. We were in the kitchen grazing on snacks and chatting when I heard Shelby yell for me and cry.

We ran to the balcony to see what was going on, and there, in the street, we saw a group of men with a knife with the beheaded sheep, and blood was pouring out of its body. I grabbed the children and made them go inside. I, myself, was taken aback by it as well, although I did understand that all countries and customs are different.

But I wanted to know why they did that in the middle of the street with other adults and children around. My brother explained that it was an important day for Muslims, called Eid-ul-Adha, which is known as the *Feast of the Sacrifice.*

This told me nothing, as I was still confused. So, he continued to say that it marks the end of the Islamic Pilgrimage and that Muslims worldwide celebrate this day in remembrance of Prophet Ibrahim, who was willing to sacrifice his own son until Allah ordered him to kill a sheep instead.

"So, this is a religious sacrifice and event?" I asked.

He replied, *"Yes. It is something that the Muslim people celebrate. We are Armenian, so we do not celebrate this day or event with them."*

I tried to explain it to the children in the simplest terms possible so they could understand and not be frightened.

Our family trip to Iran was a great success. I was able to learn more about my family and my medical history on this trip. I learned that my biological father basically sold my sister Emma to her husband when she was just thirteen or fourteen years old. He was a much older man, but my father wanted the money. She told me she had never loved him but was forced into a marriage with him. It broke my heart to know that my sister had always been in an arranged, loveless marriage for the sake of our father making money.

They told me that, more than likely, our father would have sold me as well by the time I would have turned twelve. I found out that my brother Vazgen became very street-smart at an early age to hustle money. Our father also basically sold Vazgen at an early age possibly around 12 years old as a laborer to his son-in-law Nashan (our sister Seda's husband) to work in his plastic company he owned. And rather than pay Vazgen the money for working our father demanded that the paycheck be given to him. I guess that's how Vazgen learned the business well enough to become a partner and buy in on it. I assumed it worked out well for him because, financially, he was doing very well.

Luckily, my oldest sister, Seda, did marry the man she was in love with, her husband, Nashan. Maybe she was able to do that because our mother was alive and wouldn't have allowed our father to do anything otherwise.

Unfortunately, my sister Seda's health declined from the time I first visited her four years ago. We had a late-night departure.

She became so tiny and frail. She was on a kidney transplant list and was still waiting. It was such an eye-opener to learn as much as I did. I greatly appreciated everything they shared with me.

On our last day, again, we did not say goodbyes but instead said, "*See you later*," to each other, and then my brother drove us to the airport. We had a late-night departure.

family members came to wish us well on our trip back home to America.

During our first trip to Iran, when it was only Mike and me, I made a few mistakes that were purely unintentional that frightened me. Such as, when my brother and I went to the government office to obtain my birth certificate, I smiled at a high-end government official while I was seated and waiting for my brother in the hallway, and he was in an office getting the paperwork completed for me.

When I smiled at the government official, he walked towards me with his cavalry of bodyguards, started yelling at me, and his men drew their weapons and pointed them at me. I was so startled and terrified, not knowing what I had done and why they wanted to shoot me.

My brother ran out of the office and into the hallway where I was sitting and asked them what was going on.

They told him that, I smiled at them. Apparently, the man I smiled at was one of the members of the Guardian Council. My brother explained it was a mistake and that I was from America, and that I didn't know I could not smile at a government official.

After a few minutes of getting him to calm down, my brother grabbed my arm and walked me into the office and out the door after we got my birth certificate. Once we were in his car, I asked him what that was all about, and he explained that in Iran if you smile at a government official, you are implying you are a prostitute and can be stoned for that.

My immediate thought was, *'Oh, my god! I could have been killed for a smile!'*

I also learned at that time that a thumbs up meant a bad word, apparently the F word, whereas, in America, it means, *'Good to go, okay, or all is good.'*

Also, on my last visit in 1996, while my niece Elvin and I were shopping at the mall, a security officer followed me for several minutes and nodded at me several times. I had no idea what that meant, so I just kept walking and looking around.

Finally, after he nodded about four or five times, he walked up to me and pointed his rifle in my face, and shouted.

I had no idea what I had done wrong. I wasn't shoplifting if that's what he thought. He continued to yell at me, and I shook my head no because I thought he was accusing me of stealing.

But my niece had to come over, and she immediately started shoving my hair on my forehead into my hijab. Apparently, my hair was sticking out and not fully covered, so it was a religious violation. Me shaking my head no he thought was me saying I was refusing to cover my hair. Yikes! I couldn't believe the simple things I took for granted at home in the US could cause such pandemonium here. But I know we must respect other cultures and their country's rules.

This time, I made sure I didn't make any mistakes and even asked my family what were the proper protocols before I left their houses.

However, this was something new. This was clearly an oversight on my part. As we arrived at the airport to depart, my brother walked us in and helped with our luggage. We hugged and waved at Vazgen as we headed to the check-in counter. Vazgen said he would wait at the airport until we boarded the plane, and he knew everything was good.

They checked in Mike and the children with no problem, along with their carry-on baggage. However, when it came to me, there arose a huge problem.

My airline departure ticket said, *"Sonia Domarasky,"* however, my passport said, *"Sonik Gharibi."*

The people at the check-in counter said I could not leave with that airline ticket because it was not in my name. I tried to explain that it was me, but they said the departure ticket must match the passport. I couldn't believe I could make that mistake.

I knew going over my airline ticket from the US to Germany was for *Sonia Domarasky*, and then my airline ticket from Germany to Iran was for *Sonik Gharibi*. So, coming back, I should have done the same. I should have had my departure ticket as *Sonik Gharibi* when leaving for Germany from Iran, then switched back to my American passport and used my American name for my ticket from Germany to the US.

They pulled me aside and said I could not leave. My children and husband were upset and stressed. I was a nervous wreck on the inside, but I couldn't let my children see how scared I was. I needed them to stay calm.

I told them to go ahead and fly back without me and that I would fly out when all this got sorted out.

Mike and the kids refused to leave without me and waited with me. I called my brother as he was still waiting at the airport and asked him for help.

He came in, and they explained what was going on. He immediately jumped in and had them make some calls. He showed them my two passports and explained the mix-up. After forty-five minutes of him talking to them and some government officials, they escorted us into another room, where they allowed me to talk to the staff at Lufthansa and have them reissue me a new departure ticket.

We had to wait another thirty minutes for them to reissue a new ticket for me, but finally, we got it, and the Iranian government said I was cleared to depart on the flight.

We just barely made it to our flight on time, as boarding was about to begin in five minutes. We still had to run to the departure gate. I hugged my brother, thanked him, and told him that I loved him and that I'll see him soon. And then, the kids, Mike, and I ran to the gate.

One last time, I turned around again and looked at my brother's smiling face, yet sad eyes.

Feeling a heavy stone in my heart, I smiled back a teary smile and finally dashed to catch my plane.

Chapter Twelve

The Greatest Tragedies of All

A s I said before, the trip was fantastic. We arrived home safely— it felt wonderful to see my mother again. The kids couldn't wait to tell their grandmother all about their trip, and, of course, Noah wanted to show grandma his new way of using the toilet by squatting over it. He continued doing that for a month or so and then finally stopped.

During the course of 2001, I reflected back on the things I had accomplished, my life in general, and the many challenges. I realized what a strong woman I had become. I was a wonderful daughter, an exceptional mother, a great wife, a fantastic friend, and a community volunteer.

Now, I felt ready to take on a different type of challenge. I knew with the amount of determination, persistence, and will that I beheld, I could do anything I set my mind to. So, I decided I would run in the Walt Disney World™ Marathon in January 2002 for the Leukemia and Lymphoma Society and raise money for a little boy named Mikey.

I certainly was not a runner and never had been, so this was completely new to me. I started by running a quarter mile and walking a quarter mile. Then, I gradually increased each week. I trained with some other runners who were also planning on taking part in the marathon.

In January 2002, I flew to Orlando, Florida, with Mike, the children, and my mother by my side as my cheerleaders. I ran in the marathon and completed my first-ever marathon. My feet were sore, and my body ached, but seeing my family there cheering me on, was priceless. I wasn't worried about where I was placed. I just wanted to get across the finish line to say I accomplished what I had set out to do and to raise the money for Mikey, the Leukemia patient.

We spent the rest of our week at Walt Disney World™, Animal Kingdom™, Hollywood Studios™, and the Epcot Center™. We all loved it so much, and it was truly a magical time.

Over the course of the next two years, life became busy. Mike and I were both working while the kids were active in sports and busy with school. Brandon played baseball for several years, and my mom was always at his games, cheering him on with us.

Mom watched the children every day after school as she picked them up. They always stayed with her on the weekends because they enjoyed being at grandma's house. They could ride their bikes in her cul-de-sac and the neighborhood was filled with so many children. They played outside in the neighborhood every night on the weekend until the street lights came on. I was usually at mom's house on the weekend, as well during the day when I could, unless Mike and I had errands to run or unless we all went on a day trip or outing together with mom and the children.

During summer vacation, I dropped the kids off at mom's house every morning on my way to work. They were just as attached to their grandmother as I was. Brandon was often bullied in middle and high school, particularly because he was a little overweight. He confided in his grandmother how he felt and how much it hurt him, and throughout all of that, she was his confidant, his listener, his cheerleader, and his constant supporter. She gave him the strength to face each day as she lifted him up. He confided more in his grandmother about the bullying than he did in me, I think.

Perhaps, it was not to worry me, or that he knew the protector I was and that I would confront the issue head-on at the school with the instigators, or maybe, he was worried about being embarrassed with me going in to correct the issue.

In 2004, mom decided to go to Australia to visit her sister and her niece and nephew. They lived in Australia and had their own business there. She decided to go for her 70th birthday and planned on staying for a whole month. Mom got her tickets, and as usual, she provided me with all the information on the date and times of the departure and return. I asked her for the address of her sister's home and her sister's phone number so the children and I could call her on the day of her birthday to sing to her over the phone.

She did provide me with all the information. However, what she didn't know was that I was planning to fly to Australia with the children and surprise her for her 70th birthday there.

We took mom to the airport, wished her well, and she flew to Australia. We called her two or three times to see how she was doing. Then, I booked a flight for us to go there during the last two weeks of her visit to Australia. Brandon decided he didn't want to go as he really wasn't much on traveling. So, I bought the tickets for myself, Shelby who was now 11, and Noah who was now 7. We flew to Australia, and we landed there on the day of my mother's 70th birthday.

I had to figure out how to get to my aunt's house, which I had never been to. I had already booked a hotel room for us in advance since I didn't know if my aunt had enough room for the kids and me.

We got a shuttle from the airport to the hotel to check in. Once we were settled in, I called my mom from my cell phone to tell her that the kids and I wanted to sing Happy Birthday to her and see if she was at her sister's home and if they had plans on going anywhere. She asked where Brandon was, and I told her he was at a friend's house and that we would call back again as soon as he got home. I had to make up some kind of story so she wouldn't suspect anything.

We left the hotel and took the subway to my aunt's town. When we got off the subway, I asked a few people how to get to the street we were looking for. We walked several blocks, but I couldn't find where my aunt lived. I stopped at an auto repair shop and asked the manager for help. He offered to drive my children and me to the exact location. So, we hopped in his car, and he dropped us off in front of her home. I know it was crazy to get in a car of a stranger with my children in a foreign country, but I felt safe, and my gut told me it was okay.

I knocked on the door of my aunt's house with Shelby and Noah both standing beside me. My aunt opened the door, and her jaw dropped. She looked at the children and me as I said I was there to surprise my mother for her birthday. She didn't speak English but she knew who we were and that it was a surprise. Still in shock, she gently closed the door and called for my mother to come to the door as it was for her.

When my mother opened the door and saw me, Shelby, and Noah—we yelled out together, *"Surprise! Happy Birthday!"*

She was so shocked, and tears started running down her face. *"Oh my god, how did you get here? When did you get here? Why didn't you tell me?"*

She shot one question after another at me.

Then she said, *"Come in, Come in."*

We were just as excited to see and surprise her as she was to see us. I told her there was no way I was going to let her celebrate her 70th birthday without me. I had it planned as soon as she said she was going to Australia. We called Mike and Brandon to let them know we got there safely and were with Mom.

Brandon and Mike wished her *a happy birthday* as well. She thanked Mike for allowing me and the kids to come to Australia to surprise her.

Mom came to the hotel and stayed with us for the remainder of the time. We did so much while in Australia. We went to the Sydney Opera House, toured around Sydney, spent two days at Bondi Beach, went to the zoo, hand fed the kangaroos, took pictures with the Koala and peacocks, went shopping at the malls, took a double-decker tour bus through Sydney, and ate at some great restaurants.

We also tried Vegemite with our breakfast toast and realized we didn't like it.

Noah got to play the Didgeridoo with the Aborigines and got his very own Didgeridoo. We spent time with my aunt and her adult children. Mom bought all three of the grandchildren gifts from Australia. She bought Noah a Spiderman blanket that he absolutely cherished.

In Australia, we had the most wonderful time, and the memories we took from this trip were priceless. But like all good things come to an end, this trip also finally concluded. We all flew back home the first week of December on the same airline and same flight, just as I had planned.

Now we had just two weeks before Christmas to finish up any shopping we needed to get done. As usual, Christmas was wonderful. It didn't matter how old the children were. Mom was always there on Christmas eve to spend the night and to see the twinkle in their eyes, dance with them to the singing Santa that sat on top of the TV, watch them set out cookies and milk for Santa, sprinkle oats for the reindeer and wait with them until Santa arrived who was always played by our next-door neighbor, Mr. Bob Ward.

He dressed up every year as Santa, unbeknownst to our children, and came to the house to talk with each of them to let them know how good they had been and that they needed to continue to be good.

He told them he had lots of presents for them, and they needed to go to bed now so he could finish delivering all the presents to the children in town. Even though Brandon and Shelby were old enough to know that Santa wasn't real, they never wanted to spoil it for Noah since he was only seven years old.

Mr. Ward was also the Santa for the town of Brunswick and had been for many years, and his wife, Shirley, was Mrs. Claus. As our neighbors, the Wards and their family was a big part of our lives as the children were growing up.

But little did we know, this was our last Christmas with mom. The New Year came in peacefully. We had returned from visiting Mike's family, and we were back to our normal daily lives.

Winter break was done, the children were back in school, and Mike and I were back at work. Spring came, and then summer. The children enjoyed spending their summer months with their grandmother. Brandon was now about to enter the 9th grade and had signed up for football at the high school. He spent the month of August walking up to the high school for football training. He loved the sport and was eager to play football. He shared this love with his grandmom as she loved football too. Her favorite team was the Washington Redskins, and Brandon's favorite team was the Pittsburgh Steelers. His coach had him mainly on the defensive line and occasionally on the offensive line.

School started, and every Friday night, no matter how cold it was or if it rained, mom was right there beside me, Mike, Shelby, and Noah cheering Brandon on at his football games. We were so proud of him.

We celebrated Brandon's 14th birthday in September and mom's 71st birthday in November.

Mom was always an early bird and had already started her Christmas shopping. She pretty much finished the rest of her shopping when we all went out on our annual Black Friday excursion. We would gather up the children and leave by three in the morning so we could stand in line to get the newest games or dolls that the children wanted for Christmas. They loved it when we did this on Black Friday. By ten in the morning, we were usually done and headed for breakfast somewhere.

November 30th, 2005, my company sent me on a business trip to Reno, Nevada, for a conference. The conference was for three days—November 30th - December 2nd. Then on December 3rd, I flew to Los Angeles to visit my niece, Alina, the daughter of my oldest sister, Seda.

She had recently moved to the US. I stayed in Los Angeles for a few days with her and flew back home on December 7th.

I spoke to my mother almost every day, and she mentioned that she wasn't feeling well, so she didn't go to the school show that Brandon was in. It concerned me because it was odd and so unlike my mother to ever miss anything her grandchildren were involved in.

I asked her multiple times if she was okay and if I should come home, but she insisted that she was absolutely okay.

My flight back from Los Angeles was on December 7th, and I arrived back at Dulles Airport very late in the evening. Our next-door neighbor watched the children while Mike picked me up at the airport.

The next morning, December 8th, mom came to pick up the children to take them to school. Where work was concerned, I was off for the rest of the week. That day, Noah stayed home with me because he said he wasn't feeling well, but I think it was because he missed me.

That day, I noticed mom's face was very swollen, and she seemed a little off. I asked her if everything was okay, and she replied with a quick yes.

I was so tired and jet-lagged, and the three-hour time difference threw my body off as well, so when she said she was good, I didn't push the issue. But I really wish I would have. She asked me to come over for lunch with Noah because she missed me and wanted to make lunch for me so we could catch up. I told her that sounded great and that I was planning on taking a nap in the morning to catch up on some sleep and not to bother me but that I would be there for lunch.

I tried to nap a bit while Noah was still asleep, but then I got a call from work asking me to come in because an employee needed a check. I called mom to let her know I couldn't make it for lunch and to move it to dinner if possible. I asked her if she could pick up Brandon and Shelby from school.

"Of course!" She said.

"I may stop by the grocery store and pick up a few things before I come over. Do you need anything?" I asked.

She gave me a short list with only three to four items. She told me I could drop Noah off at her house while I went to work, and she would watch him.

"I can tell you are not feeling well, mom. I'll take him with me so you can rest during the day. We'll be there for dinner if you're up to it. Then we can catch up, and I can tell you about my trip. I love you." I answered.

'Okay, I love you too." She replied.

Then, I called Brandon and Shelby's schools to let the front office know to tell them that their grandmother would be picking them up after school today since I had to go to work.

Around 3:30 pm, I got a call on my cell phone while at work from Brandon and Shelby that they just walked home and asking me where grandma was because she never showed up to pick either of them up after school. My heart sank immediately. There was no way my mother would forget to pick up her grandchildren. Even my children knew that.

I hung up and immediately called mom's house phone three or four times. Then, I tried her cellphone a few times, all the while gathering

Noah's coat, his coloring book, and my purse and jacket. I loaded Noah into the minivan and drove as fast as I could to mom's house. I only worked about six miles from her home.

From the moment I pulled into her cul-de-sac, I could see her car backed into the driveway with the passenger door opened. As I pulled up in front of her house, I saw my mother slumped over into the passenger seat with her bucket of water and hose out. I immediately ran to her, but she was somewhat stiff and cold.

It was then that I let out a blood-curdling scream.

"Oh, God! No! No, no, no! Mom!" I screamed.

"Help! Someone! Help!" I kept screaming. I was in a state of panic.

Then, coming to my senses, I raced into the house and called 911 on mom's portable phone. I told the dispatcher I needed help for my mom.

"Something has happened, and I don't think she is breathing." I ranted.

Noah opened the door of the minivan, came over, and stood by me as I was crying and begging my mother to wake up.

"Please get up, please, mom. Don't do this! I need you, mom! Wake up!" I cried uncontrollably.

Just then, a car came racing into the cul-de-sac. A man jumped out, pulled my mother out of the car, laid her on the ground, and began doing CPR. I scooped Noah up and put him into the van, and told him to stay there. I didn't want him to see what was going on with his grandmother. He had just turned eight; I was worried he wouldn't understand.

Finally, the advanced life support personnel showed up along with the ambulance company and the state police.

Some of the neighbors came outside, and all I could do was beg the ambulance crew to please tell me that my mother was going to be okay.

"Please, don't let her die!" I cried.

I could hear Noah beating on the side window of the mini van crying and begging to come out. He was yelling for his grandma. When he saw the ambulance, advanced life support, police and neighbors gathering he knew something was horribly wrong. I opened the door and took him out and had him stand next to me shielding his face but he continued to yell for his grandma.

Then, still crying, I called Brandon and Shelby to let them know that I was at grandma's house and that something has happened, and that they would be taking her to the hospital.

One of my neighbors said they would go pick them up so I would have all my children with me.

But Brandon and Shelby both ran out of the house and started running to grandma's house, crying the whole way. The neighbor found my children running on the sidewalk on their way to their grandmother's house.

The medical personnel worked diligently on mom and even injected an epi-pen into her heart. They loaded her into the ambulance and drove her to the Frederick Memorial Hospital.

I called Mike to tell him to come to my mother's house so we could go to the hospital, and he said he was just a few minutes away. Just as the children and Mike arrived in front of the house, the ambulance pulled off.

I locked mom's house, gathered my things from the minivan, loaded the children in Mike's car, and we drove to the hospital as fast as we could.

When we arrived, I told the front desk that my mother had been brought to the hospital and I needed to see her. They asked me to have a seat and said that someone would be with me very soon. I called her preacher at her church and one of her closest friends to come to the hospital so we could pray for her wellbeing. They said they would be there shortly.

Then, a doctor came out and asked me if I was a family member of Soon Nam Lee.

"Yes, that's my mother! How is she doing, and when can I see her?" I asked.

But I didn't get an answer but rather a request that I move into a family room. Me, Mike, and the children all went to the family room and waited. Another doctor came in and asked me if I was her daughter, and I said yes and then repeated my questions.

"How is she doing? When can I see her?"

The doctor looked at me and said, *"I am so sorry to inform you that your mother has passed away. She suffered a massive heart attack and was pronounced deceased before she arrived at the hospital. Her estimated time of death was approximately 1:30 pm."*

I looked at him as though he was crazy. Clearly, he was mistaken. He couldn't be talking about my mother. No. My mother couldn't have passed away. He must be talking to the wrong person. It must be someone else's mother, not mine. God wouldn't do that to me. He wouldn't take my world away from me.

"No, you are wrong!" I said. *"I want to see my mother now!"*

He said, *"I will walk you down to the room. Just follow me."*

I walked behind him, thinking what a horrible thing this was to say to someone when it was not true. We arrived at the room, I walked in, and there was my mother lying on the bed, covered with a sheet up to her neck.

I walked up to her, leaned over her, hugged her, and said, *"I am here, mom."*

She was so cold and stiff. I grabbed every blanket I could find and covered her.

I yelled out, *"My mother doesn't like being cold! She needs more blankets! Where are more blankets?"*

The children were all crying, and Mike was trying to calm me down through his own tears. I knew at that moment that she was gone, but I couldn't accept it. She was supposed to live until she was a hundred. I still needed my mother so badly. How was I supposed to live without her? She was my rock, my hero, my heart, my soul, and my world.

Her grandchildren need her. How dare God take her away from us. I got no warning, and I didn't even get to say goodbye. What kind of God does that?

Mom's preacher, his wife, and her close friend were escorted into the room. They hugged the children and me and then stood over mom with tears and said a prayer in Korean.

I sat by the bed and just cried. I stroked her hair and tenderly rubbed her cheek. Then, I held her hand and then placed her hand by my cheek.

I sat beside her, rocking myself with her hand in mine and against my cheek, constantly repeating, *"I can't do this without you, mom. I need you, I need my mom"*

I saw my three children crying, and I tried to console them. They knew and understood that grandma had died and we couldn't have her in our lives anymore.

I wanted to comfort them, but I was so paralyzed with grief myself that I couldn't. I was still processing this nightmare. Mike tried to comfort us all, but it was a difficult feat.

The doctor came into the room and said they would be taking my mother down to the morgue. I told them absolutely not. My mother didn't like the cold, and I wanted her to stay right here in this room with me so I could keep warm blankets on her and sit beside her all night.

Even though my mother had just passed, I was still her protector, and I wanted to protect her from being cold. Mom's preacher, his wife, and her friend gathered their things and left, but I refused.

The doctor pulled Mike to the side, talked with him briefly then left.

Mike came over to me and said, *"They cannot keep your mother in this room. They need the room for other patients. We have to go and let them take her. Besides, you need to go home and be with the children."*

I reluctantly agreed while crying uncontrollably. My children had never seen their mother this emotional and so distraught. I had always been so strong and in control, and now I felt utterly helpless, like someone gutted me and ripped my heart out.

Before we left the hospital, I hugged my mother again tightly, kissed her cheek and her hand, and repeated over and over, *"I Love you."*

It was always the last thing we said to each other, and this time was no different.

CHAPTER THIRTEEN

AUTOPILOT

Mike drove the children and me home. We left my minivan parked at mom's house. On the drive home, there were no sounds in the car other than crying and sniffles. It was around 8:45 pm when we got home.

I walked the children up to their bedrooms and got them ready for bed. The children were so upset and crying for their grandmother. They kept saying they wanted grandma. I hugged each of them and explained that it was grandma's time and that she had to go.

God must have needed her. It didn't matter what I said or how I worded it. The simple fact was that we needed her more. How could God take her now? She was only seventy-one and in good health. She exercised every day, ate healthily, took good care of herself, and was a devoted servant to God, bringing people to church and spreading the gospel. She was a Deacon.

She had so many friends, and most importantly, she had a family that desperately needed her. Why did God do this? My head hurt, my throat hurt, my eyes hurt from crying so much but most of all my heart was broken just unimaginably broken in pieces. I don't even know how I am going to process this and hold it together. I have to plan a funeral and it was only seventeen days until Christmas; how could we even consider having Christmas without her.

We always kept a nightlight on in each room for the children. Brandon and Noah shared a bedroom, and Shelby had her own. I tucked them into bed and told them that I was there for them and I was going to be in my bedroom if they needed me. Then, I turned on their nightlights and walked out, closing the door behind me.

Later that night, I crawled into our bed, and Mike tried to talk to me, but I couldn't think or comprehend anything. This whole day had been a nightmare, and I just wanted to wake up from it. I lay in bed staring at the ceiling with tears rolling down my cheeks. Nothing made sense. She had been to the doctors just two weeks ago, and they never said anything about a bad heart or heart problems. I knew mom had high blood pressure and Crohn's Disease, but that was it. And she managed those with medication.

"How could she have a heart attack?" I wondered. *"This is my fault. I killed her. I knew her face was swollen in the morning and I didn't force her to go to the doctors, I didn't take her. Then I should have been there for lunch and I cancelled to go to work and chose to come for dinner instead. If I would have been there, I could have saved her. It's my fault she died. Oh God! I screamed and cried in fetal position. It's my fault!!!!"*

That night, I didn't sleep at all, and I knew the children didn't either. So, the next day I allowed the children to stay home from school, and even Mike took the day off.

I had so many calls to make. I had to call all of her friends and her family in Korea and Australia. I needed her friend to tell our family in Korea and Australia that she had passed away. My Korean wasn't fluent, so there was no way I could relay the message properly. The hospital called me and said I needed to arrange funeral services and asked who would be picking up her body. I just couldn't understand how anyone expects you to make calls and plan funeral services when you are grieving so badly. But it was my duty and obligation to make sure my mother was given a wonderful service so that everyone who loved and adored her could pay their final respects.

Mom always said when it was her time to go, she wanted to go peacefully in her sleep without any pain and suffering. She died while washing her car, something she enjoyed doing as she loved her car. So, she was outside in her sweat suit with her pink rubber gloves, hose, and bucket, washing her car before she was to pick up the children at 2:45 pm from school. The doctor said the massive heart attack took her quickly, and she did not suffer much. Knowing that brought me a little comfort.

But then the guilt I had was so powerful. I blamed myself for her death. Noah and I were supposed to have been there for lunch. I called mom to tell her I had to go to work and couldn't make it until dinner. So, the overwhelming guilt I had made me sick. If I had been there, perhaps, I could have gotten her to the doctor that morning, or I could have called 911 before the heart attack began. It was definitely my fault. What kind of daughter lets her mother die? I just wanted to die too!

How could I spend my entire life protecting her and, in the end, let her die from my negligence? I felt like a horrible daughter. I felt worthless. I was angry at myself and furious at God and the world. Why does God always inflict so much pain in my life? I questioned my faith.

I had to go to the hospital and pick up the clothes that mom had on when the ambulance brought her in. They also needed me to sign some documents. I had the children with me in the car as we circled the hospital parking lot many times in search of a parking spot. Finally, I resorted to waiting for a person to back out of a parking spot so I could pull in.

I sat there for about three to four minutes with my turn signal on, notifying other drivers that I was waiting for that spot. When the driver backed out of the spot, another car came from the other direction and whipped right into the spot I had been waiting for. I was so angry. I put my window down and told the man that I had been waiting for that

241

spot and had my turn signal on. He was an older man and said he didn't care and that his wife was in the hospital and he needed to go.

I was already angry, an emotional wreck, sleep deprived, heartbroken, and distraught, and now this man just did that to me. I watched as he walked towards the front door of the hospital and revved up my car, and pushed the gas pedal so hard as I had planned on running him over. But something made me stop within inches of running him down. My children were in the back seat, terrified. What was I doing? Not only did I feel like a horrible daughter, but I also felt like a horrible mother. I felt so bad for my children. My mother wouldn't want me to act like this. I was so focused on how I felt I forgot about how sad and heartbroken my children were. I apologized to them and drove around until I found another place to park. But secretly I was hoping he would fall down a flight of stairs and crack his head.

The funeral was as good as could be expected. It was beautiful and respectfully done. There was a large turnout of her friends, church congregation and coworkers. The flower arrangements that her church and friends sent were beautiful. I made two large billboards of pictures with mom throughout the years, reflecting on her life with her family, friends, vacations, and hobbies so everyone could see what a happy life she had. And mom looked at peace in the casket.

It was held at her Korean Baptist Church. Her pastor performed the services in Korean, and my pastor spoke in English for it. There was no gravesite, as mom always said she wanted to be cremated.

My goal was to someday go back to Korea and spread her ashes over Haeundae Beach in Pusan, where she often reflected back on her wonderful teenage memories. After the church funeral services, I invited all guests to a restaurant for a memorial supper.

Everyone told stories of what a wonderful woman my mother was. I listened with pride in my heart, but only I knew how truly wonderful she was. She was a true angel and my hero. She was and always will be *MY MOTHER*.

From the time the children were infants, every night when I put them to bed, I would say to them, *"Night night, sleep tight, don't let the bed bug bite. I love you."*

Then I would turn their night lights on and leave with the door closed. Their night lights were touchable lamps, which brightened up with every touch. Touching it the third time made the light come on to the full wattage.

A few nights after mom's funeral, I was still heavily grieving and couldn't sleep. I walked down the hallway to the bathroom and noticed a bright light coming from under the door in Noah and Brandon's bedroom. I opened the door, and the lightbulb in the lamp was on the highest setting. So, I tapped it twice. Once to turn it off and then once again for the lowest nightlight setting. I figured Noah got up and turned the light up on high.

The next night, I noticed it again. And, of course, I put the setting back down. The third night when I tucked Noah into bed, I told him not to change the light setting on the lamp.

He replied, *"It's not me, mommy. It's grandma. She was here beside me, talking to me. She told me she was here with us and always will be and to tell you not to worry. We would all be okay. She said she loves us. Then she touched the lamp and turned it up to the brightest setting."*

I cried. I was absolutely stunned. I didn't know what to say. I undoubtedly believed him. Noah couldn't make that up. I was so happy mom was visiting Noah and hoped she would visit the rest of us too.

Christmas came, and it was the worst Christmas our family had ever had. It wasn't the same. I didn't get to make our traditional Korean Eggrolls at Christmas with mom like we did every single year. Grandma wasn't there on Christmas Eve with the kids, and there just wasn't any joy or excitement.

We drove over to mom's house on Christmas day, and I let the children open up all the presents she had gotten during black Friday and before she passed. But all we could do was cry as they opened each present because she wasn't there to watch us all open them.

For the next six months, I was on autopilot. I functioned daily but as a zombie. I took my children to school, tried to help them with homework, went to work, and cooked meals for the family. I would get in the car and drive to work or the store but couldn't remember the road or highway that I had just driven on. I just knew I got in the car, and then I arrived at my destination. I would often drive to her house and open her closet to smell her clothes. I would take out an outfit and sit on her bed, hold it close to my heart, and talk to mom. It was comforting and calming because they smelled like my mother. I just wanted to hold onto her and talk to her.

So many times, out of habit, I called her number because I saw something I wanted to tell her about or ask what she was doing or see if she wanted to come over or go to the store with me. But the phone would just ring.

Everything was a blur. Half the time, I didn't eat. I merely existed. Other than that, I honestly have no recollection of anything that I did, places I went, or people that I saw during those six months. I was lost.

Mike couldn't handle my grief. He didn't know how to console me. I begged him for his support. According to him, I should have gotten over it.

I merely existed in body, but my mind and heart, and soul were not present. I felt completely incapacitated.

At that time, I needed my husband the most, but his only comment to me was, "It's sad that your mother passed, we all miss her, but you live, and then you die. That's life. You have to get over it and move on."

I couldn't believe the man that I married, had three children with, loved so much, and needed now more than anything could say that to me. I needed his support not a lecture.

Perhaps, he needed more than what I could give him at the time. I was suffering through the loss of my mother, and so I guess that was his excuse to be distant from me, whereas, in reality, he was preoccupied with something or someone else.

My grief and his attitude couldn't allow me to perform as a wife. I struggled to cope with my mother's death. I tried, but perhaps, it would have helped if I had I some emotional support from him. I knew it was bothering Mike. But I was hurt by his lack of support.

On top of grieving, I started thinking back to all the years of our marriage and how he never was the family protector. It was always me who protected the family. He never once stood up for our children when they were bullied or even for me when comments were made about my weight or my mother. He just chuckled. It was me who had to confront the bullies. How he was never the disciplinarian, that was all me too. How often he would make sarcastic comments about the children or me and how he made lustful comments about other women in front of our children and me. Thinking back on all of that and dealing with my grief, I became more distant.

All I wanted was the man I thought I married, who would risk his life for me and go to a foreign country just to be by my side. Or perhaps, he did that only because the excitement interested him.

I was so unhappy with my life and the current state of my marriage. I just couldn't figure out how to live my life without my mother. I found myself rocking myself to sleep again, just like I did in my childhood until I got married. It was the only comfort from my fears and anxiety I could find. And, yet, I felt so overwhelmed and so alone.

But now, that man that I so loved wasn't making me feel I was loved. Perhaps, he was grieving too, but maybe, he had some sense of relief, knowing that now without my mother around, our marriage was truly just him and I and not my mother. I can't say for sure because he wasn't one to always open up.

But what I did know was that I had been having some suspicions about infidelity going on. It was hard enough trying to deal with and accept my mother's passing, but now to think my husband was cheating on me was completely breaking me down and destroying me.

The children and I talked a lot about grandma. Brandon said how much he missed her and how much she meant to him.

How much he loved and adored her, and how she made him feel better anytime he confided in her about being bullied.

He said he loved looking up in the stands at the football games and seeing grandma sitting next to me, watching him play.

Shelby also adored her grandma. She was grandma's precious little girl. Mom would buy her cute clothes and dress her up. Shelby loved going through her grandma's jewelry and trying it all on. And she loved trying on grandma's dress shoes and walking through the house. Mom loved turning on the music and dancing with Shelby. One of mom's favorite things was when Shelby would hop and scoot on her butt from room to room.

Mom would call her *hop hop* and laugh. Mom really got a kick out of Shelby doing that. And we always got a kick out of how she pronounced Shelby as Sha-bee with her Korean accent. She would call her a little princess and always told me Shelby was the perfect little girl.

I would joke with mom and say, *"But what about me; I thought I was the perfect little girl."*

And she would say, *"Okay, I have two perfect girls."*

Noah was the baby, and of course, he was extremely spoiled by both mom and me.

He knew grandma let him do anything, from jumping on the couch, or the beds, eating what he wanted, buying him toys each time they went to the store, building forts with blankets, pillows, and the kitchen chairs so he could climb under them. Noah was her sidekick. She was retired by the time Noah was born, so she was basically with him every day, all day, just as she wanted. Once, he was there when grandma had taken a little fall, and he was able to help her.

Then he stated that he was there to protect her. It warmed my heart to hear him say that. He knew he was her sidekick and her little man.

My children were still grieving, just not as much now as several months have passed. We always talked about grandma and all the funny things she did or said. The children and I all needed to grieve together and hold onto the memories of my mother; we often cried together. There were times when Shelby or Noah would wipe the tears from my face. I saw how much it pained my children to see me cry all the time.

It was summer 2006 now, which brought along happy, sunny days. I knew my children deserved to be happy, and my crying all the time in front of them wasn't good.

So, I decided to grieve and cry on my own time and in private and to love, nurture, support, and raise my children just as my mother did with me. I wanted to continue to teach them Korean customs, cook Korean foods with them, and let them experience all the wonderful things that I did with my mother.

Therefore, the memory of their grandmother would live on forever. We also found that doing these things helped us cope with mom's death a little.

On the other hand, tension was mounting in my marriage. By this point, Mike's infidelity was very evident. We tried to make the marriage work. We bought a new big, beautiful house in Charles Town, WV, in November of 2006, and still, the children and I weren't happy. They weren't happy because it moved them out of their school district. So, I used my mother's address since I kept her home in Brunswick and didn't want to sell it. That was an issue in our marriage as well. Mike had hoped I would sell it and contribute the funds towards our marital home.

We tried to muddle through Christmas of 2006. It had only been a year since my mother had passed, and again, Christmas just wasn't the same.

The new year of 2007 started. The winter was gloomy and cold and seemed to drag on. I think we all were looking forward to the summer and brighter days.

Summer of 2007 came and went quickly, and now school started back up. Brandon was in the 11th grade.

I was always so close to my children. So, I could immediately tell something was off with Brandon. I wasn't quite sure what, perhaps, it was being a teenager, but I noticed some changes in him.

He seemed reserved, quiet, and dark. He seemed a bit distant from the family. I thought it was a phase that teenagers went through, so I let it be, but I was worried. I tried to talk to him, but he assured me everything was fine.

Shelby was in 9th, and Noah was in the 5th grade. Brandon was back to playing football now for his junior year. He also started wrestling when football season was done. He requested and got the number 71 put on his football jersey for the start of his sophomore year of football.

He wanted that number because that was the age of his grandmother when she passed away. Each time we went to his game, I always left an open space next to me, so he knew when he looked up in the stands that grandma was sitting next to me watching him play. He was able to keep number 71 on his jersey until he graduated.

I didn't want the school to know that we were living in Charles Town because then they would force the children to change schools. So, a few nights a week, the children and I would stay at my mom's house. Typically, it was on Friday nights after the football game and one night during the week. I could tell at times; Mike was growing more distant from me.

Mike's idea of fun was always hanging out at the Moose Lodge. He took us there all the time so he could drink and play the tip jars and gamble. He was big on playing the tip jars, signing the book there, and buying lottery tickets. When Noah and his father would go out, Mike's idea of a father-son day out was to take Noah to the Moose Lodge with him. He did the same with Brandon.

While he flirted and gambled, he gave money to Noah to play the arcade games. When I would come home from work, Noah would tell me that daddy was talking to women at the Moose Lodge. Shelby told me on several occasions that she saw long blond hairs in daddy's car.

I was receiving phone calls at the house in the mornings while I was getting ready for work and getting the children ready for school from women at the Moose. They would tell me they were sleeping with my husband and would describe the inside of my home, my furniture, and what color sheets were on my bed and what bedspreads were on the kid's beds.

Once, when the children and I came home with a new puppy, we walked into the living room with a random woman sitting on the couch with Mike. I knew he was cheating, and the children did too. But each time, I would forgive him. There were nights that I cooked dinner for our family, and he would show up two hours late from work. I wasn't stupid. I knew what he was doing.

My daughter walked into our master bathroom and saw me curled up in the fetal position on the cold ceramic tile floor, crying because my heart was broken. She wiped the tears from my face and rub my head.

She even said to me, *"Mommy, I don't know why you stay with daddy when he hurts you so much."*

Children are wiser than we think they are. How ironic, there she was, my daughter, protecting her mother—me.

I wanted so desperately for my marriage to work. I loved my husband so much that I kept forgiving his infidelities. Maybe I felt he was all I had left other than my children. Maybe I was afraid to live without him. But each time I found him cheating with another woman it broke me down even more. He was ripping my heart out and the pain I endured was horrible. When was enough going to be enough? Why did I allow myself to hurt like this?

February of 2008, I told Mike that we couldn't keep going like this. I was depressed, eating my emotions, and gaining so much weight. Also, it wasn't healthy for the children to see me crying all the time. I told him that the children and I would go live at my mother's house temporarily so I could gather my thoughts. But I think, in his mind, that was his free pass to chase more women.

So, I filed for separation. But within a month, I canceled the separation and tried to work things out with him. I was still so in love with him. I couldn't let go without one more fight to make our marriage work. He told me he loved me and promised he would stop cheating.

I suggested we go for a marital counseling weekend retreat. He agreed, so we went at the end of March, and my friend watched the children. I thought the weekend retreat went well, and we agreed to both make changes, and I told him that the children and I would come back home at the end of that week. Little did I know he had been seeing a married bartender from the Moose, and the same day we got back from the marital counseling retreat, he met up with her.

The children and I were back at the house with Mike at the end of the week. There were times I think we all felt like we were walking on eggshells.

We agreed to continue to work on our marriage. It was the end of April, and I wanted to celebrate Shelby's 15th birthday with a party and have her friends come for a sleepover. We were living in our new home in Charles Town, WV, and my daughter had several girlfriends over for a sleepover birthday party. She was so excited, and the girls were having a blast. The party was a success, and Shelby was very happy.

But that night, I could tell something was bothering Mike. as the girls slept in the theatre room of our home, watching movies all night, he lay on our couch in the living room, quietly sobbing. I could see him from the walkway of the upper level.

In the morning, I asked him if everything was okay. I had plans to take my two sons out that morning to get them a toy and lunch since they were so good for their sister's party.

Once the last parent picked up their child, I begged him to tell me what was wrong. There was nothing we could not work out. Mike asked me to sit down next to him, and as he cried, he told me that he had been cheating on me again. And that when we came back from the marriage counseling weekend retreat, he met up with his mistress, the bartender, within the hour that we got back in town.

Then he proceeded to tell me that the bartender he was having an affair with was married, had two children of her own, and that she just told him that she was pregnant by him and that the sonogram showed twins. She said she knew she was pregnant by Mike because her husband had a vasectomy a few years before. She wanted him to pay her cash, thousands of dollars to have an abortion, so her husband or I wouldn't know. I couldn't believe it. Why? How could he do that? He kept asking for my forgiveness over and over and again and again, but I felt too stunned to speak.

But the next thing he said, I felt the walls close in on me. He continued to cry and said he had one more thing to tell me and that it was even worse. But I couldn't imagine anything worse than what I had just heard.

He then proceeded to tell me that, unfortunately, he was on an antibiotic for a curable STD that he contracted from unprotected sex with some other woman or maybe it was from the woman that was pregnant. Who knows, my mind was spinning and I felt like I was sucker punched. All I could think was 'What the Fuck!!"

Now, I was shaking, terrified of what else he may have had, but worse, what he may have given me. What if he gave me AIDS. How will I raise my children? How could he do that to me? How could he put my life at risk? Who the Hell is he to play Russian Roulette with my life? At that moment, I went into total shock. I was back in the shoes of the child I once was, standing in that long dirty, dingy bathroom of my father's apartment, crying as he abused me.

I felt sick, nauseous, tormented, and frightened. My heart was racing. After a long time, I felt that same feeling, that I had to protect myself and my mother, only now, it was my children that I had to protect. I started having a panic attack.

My children were there and saw what was happening. They saw me race out of the house, and I told them to just stay there until I came back. I had to run. I needed help.

I drove to the hospital, my heart about to explode. I begged the ER for help, screaming and crying that I needed an HIV test and STD testing. They told me they couldn't do it because insurance doesn't cover that being done in an ER if you walk in and that I should go to my OBGYN in the morning.

But I couldn't breathe. I felt like I was dying, and I just couldn't stop shaking. I drove back to the house, took all three of my children, and we left and went to my mother's house, yet again. Then, I called work and told them I couldn't come in to work the next day. I went to my OBGYN that next morning and told my doctor everything. He was the one that delivered all three of my children.

He did all the different tests. For some, he could give immediate results, and for others, he said it would take about a week. So far, the immediate tests came back negative. I just had to wait and pray that the rest would come back negative as well, especially the HIV.

And thankfully, they all did. I did go every three months for the following year to be tested for HIV because I was absolutely terrified that it would be positive. However, I believe God, my mother, and my biological mother were watching over me to protect me because every test came back negative for the entire year.

After a few days of staying at my mother's home with my children, I had time to think things through, and I spoke with my husband and said things just didn't add up about this woman's pregnancy. She had told Mike that her husband had a vasectomy, and she couldn't tell him she was pregnant and she needed to abort this pregnancy but needed money to do it. She was emailing Mike from her work email to his work email.

I asked him to forward me all those emails, and I asked him for the proof she gave him that she was having twins and who her OBGYN was. He gave me a copy of the ultrasound that she provided him. I did some research and discovered that it came from the internet and it was fake.

So, I told him not to send her any money. Then, I went to her workplace. When I walked in, she had a look of fear on her face. I confronted her about it, and threw a pregnancy test kit at her and told her to walk to the bathroom with me to take the test or I'd drag her by her hair into the bathroom myself. Her supervisor walked over to see what was going on. She asked me not to say anything to them. I thought to myself, who the hell is she to ask anything of me? She was the homewrecking bitch. I spoke with her supervisor and the owner of the company. I told them that she has been sending my husband extortion letters via email from their company email on their company time.

In the end, she apologized for trying to scam us. I told her to stay away from my husband and my family, or I would seek legal action against her. And thankfully, that was the end of that affair.

Again, I protected my family and my marriage. I was so angry at her when I should have been angry and pissed off at my husband instead. All I wanted was for someone to protect me. As crazy as it was, I found myself still wanting to make my marriage work. Perhaps it was seeking a genuine love that I desperately wanted from a man, whether it was from a father or husband.

Maybe I had it once at the beginning of our marriage from Mike. Maybe I just needed to be loved by someone since I no longer had my mother's love for me. Regardless, I found myself reluctantly forgiving him and trying again.

I tried for several more months to make our marriage work because I wanted it to work. I loved this man, and yet, all he could do anymore was constantly hurt me. I was the doting wife.

I always kept an immaculate home, took great care of the children, was very active in their school and sports, volunteered when I could, worked full time, cooked homemade meals, and continued to teach my children the Korean customs and traditions along with teaching them how to make the Korean eggrolls that my mother and I did as a tradition.

I thought I had to work harder and try harder to be a better wife, blaming myself for his infidelities. But Mike was distant. He still came home late sometimes or ran to the Moose Lodge in the evenings for a beer or two leaving the children and me at home, and there were days when I called his work to ask him something just to be told by his coworker that he had taken the day off. I became an emotional mess.

I ate my emotions and picked up more weight and had gotten up to 303 lbs. My health was in danger. I still got several phone calls from other women who said they were having an affair with my husband. My children knew exactly what was going on. They heard the phone calls, and Mike and I arguing. Eventually, it became unhealthy for myself and my children to see him carry himself in such a selfish manner and treat me, the mother of his children, with such emotional disrespect by being unfaithful time after time.

I observed my children, studied their demeanor, asked questions, and at night, I opened their bedroom doors and just stood in the doorway, looking at how precious they were.

They were my legacy, my blood, my life, my heart, and my soul. They were so innocent, and yet, they are also victims paying the price, living in a home where they saw their own mother being mentally and emotionally abused. I knew what it was like when I watched my own mother be mentally, emotionally and physically abused and how traumatizing it was for me. I know the pain I carry from that. I couldn't allow him to do this to me or our children anymore.

I thought in the beginning, I was doing what was best for my children by keeping the family together.

I wanted so badly to have one man, once in my lifetime, to not hurt me or discard me like a piece of trash, and I really thought Mike Domarasky was the one, and for a while he was.

I was tired of feeling like that frightened little girl who wouldn't speak up and just allowed a man to hurt her over and over again and keep it hidden, of constantly reliving the emotional pain and hiding the scars.

I missed the man I fell in love with. He just wasn't there anymore. I wanted to be happy, but I felt broken and exhausted again. I had to find my strength, my courage to come to terms with where our lives were headed and I needed to protect my children.

Everyone has a breaking point, and mine came one evening at the end of August 2008 at the dinner table when the children and I sat there eating the dinner that I had prepared as I looked at Mike's empty chair. He was late again.

I held back my tears because I didn't want the children to see their mother cry again. It was so hard to swallow the food when choking back tears. I couldn't understand why I continued to allow myself to be treated this way. Why did I constantly feel that I needed love, affection, and respect from Mike or any man?

After dinner, I sat on the couch while the children were finishing up their homework in their rooms. I reflected back on my childhood. I thought about the many times I was abused by my father and other men and never spoke up about it.

The fact that I couldn't in order to protect my mother, although I never regret staying silent to protect her. I thought about the multiple times I had been beaten up and bullied at school myself.

I thought about the mental anguish I had suffered all these years because of all of it. The horrible flashbacks and how certain smells would trigger memories.

How it sickened me all these years when I looked at something so benign as a Hershey® Bar that brought joy or happiness to most children and adults, but for me, it was a reminder of a sick man as a thank you for what I had to endure in order to protect my mother and me. But now it was time that I needed to protect myself. I sat there until Mike walked in through the door.

"Where do you see yourself in five years?" I asked him.

I prayed in my heart that he would say with my lovely wife and children, living a renewed life with them, with forgiveness of the sins I did to this family, with no cheating ever again, and that we would all be a happy, healthy family.

But his response was, *"I don't know."* I closed my eyes for a few seconds and thought, *"Is that his answer? I don't know"* I was already broken but those three words, *"I don't know,"* destroyed me.

And that was the last straw. My heart sank as I realized that this was it. Finally, I realized that I need to love myself enough to say no more, I have had enough.

Then I told him, *"I can't and won't do this anymore. I have forgiven you time and time again for cheating on me. Even when you cheated on me with my friends and neighbors and when you brought home an STD and thought you got another woman pregnant. I stood by you. But no more! I'm done. My weight has gone up, and the doctors have told me that I have high blood pressure now. I hate the crude comments you make at the children and me. I am sad all the time, and with you, I fear for my life because of your affairs. I don't know what woman will show up at our doorstep and try to kill me or what disease you may bring home. It is like playing Russian Roulette with my life, and you have made me look like a fool. But most importantly, because of our children. I never want our daughter Shelby to think that it's acceptable for a woman to allow a husband to treat her this way, and I definitely didn't want my sons, Brandon and Noah, to think this is how they should treat a woman. I need to protect our children. I needed to show them my strength and the immeasurable amount of love I have for them and myself."* I finished, and he remained quiet.

I had never lived on my own. I lived with my mother until I moved in with Mike. Now I had to learn to do it alone with taking care of our three children because I wanted a divorce. I really didn't know what to expect or what the future would hold, but what I did know was that I had finally reached a point in my life where I was tired of feeling like a victim.

I was ready to become a survivor—*the survivor!*

I found the inner strength that my mother had always instilled in me, loaded the last item in my car, along with my children, and walked out, not even glancing back once. I walked away from my marriage with my children.

The day we married, I felt happy. I felt content. But most of all, I felt safe. Safe to love and *safe to have my happily ever after*. But now that was gone—lost. I didn't feel safe, and I was not happy. How was I going to survive this betrayal?

I had to make a move with the children as smoothly and quickly back to mom's house as it was the start of the 2008 school year.

My mother's house was a two-bedroom rancher with a finished basement. I gave Shelby my mother's bedroom and Noah my old bedroom I had as a child. Then I gave Brandon the bedroom downstairs in the basement. I wanted them all to have their own bedroom so that when they had their friends come over, they would feel comfortable telling their friends to hang out at our house.

I chose not to take a bedroom, so I slept on a twin mattress on the floor in the basement in the family room.

During the day, if they had friends over, I would put the mattress in the closet to hide it and get it off the floor so they could enjoy the family room.

I wanted to make sure my children were happy and healthy, and I wanted them to know I was too. I even started exercising and had the children join in with healthier eating habits.

Brandon was now in the 12th grade, and this was his fourth year of football and his second year of wrestling. He loved playing sports. I didn't want our family issues to affect his performance in playing his favorite high school sports.

I was the proud doting mother and the football team mom, preparing food and feeding the whole team and coaches every Friday before the game. Everyone in each of the schools, from the teachers, students, and parents, seemed to know that I was Shelby, Brandon, and Noah's mom. I prided myself on always being involved with my children and their schools and education.

Shelby was in the 10th grade and her second year of cheerleading at the high school. Noah was now in 6th grade and at the middle school and exploring different sports opportunities. I had bought Brandon a used car back in September of 2007 for his 16th birthday, and so for Shelby's 16th birthday, I purchased a used car for her too. I had to sell my vehicle and my wedding ring and financed a portion of their vehicles.

But thankfully, I had my mother's car that I could use to take the children to school and go to work, and with both Shelby and Brandon having a car, they helped me with taking Noah to and from school, picking up groceries, and other things. I borrowed money and purchased things on credit to make ends meet, but I kept it hidden from my children.

The separation was hard on the children as well. They already knew about the issues and infidelity in the marriage. They didn't need to know any other struggles I was going through. They knew how angry I was with their father. I tried not to vent our marital issues to the children because they really didn't need to know as children.

However, I did make the mistake of telling them things at times about it, and they did overhear my conversations with my attorney and with my friend, Amanda.

Amanda, as mentioned above, was a co-worker of mine. We worked together at my current job. I was the office manager, and she was the payroll manager. I met Amanda when I started working at my current job as the office manager in 2000.

We talked to each other every day. We would spend time at each other's homes, and we would often go out for dinner after work with a few other female co-worker friends.

We were very close friends and could talk about anything. We shared our secrets and supported each other as best friends do. Also, we both were going through a divorce at the same time, which made us able to understand each other as no one could.

Amanda's father is famous, *Antonio Tony Mendez*, author of *Argo* and former CIA agent for the USA. He was the one who went into Iran in 1980 and rescued six American Diplomats that were held hostage.

I was thankful I had a few very close friends to confide in, like Amanda, and my dear childhood friend, Stacey Hahn.

But even though I had my friends, I felt so alone at times. I lost my mother, and now I was losing my marriage. We were losing our marital home as well to foreclosure because of some of Mike's indiscretions.

There was animosity for both Mike and me as we both blamed each other for just about everything.

Between their grandmother's passing and the constant moving I did, from our marital home, to my mother's home, along with knowing each of my three children were bullied at different points throughout their school years, had, in some ways, been affecting their emotional well-being. However now being settled in my mother's house and with our normal routines, I felt like the children, and I were slowly picking up the pieces of our lives, and perhaps, we were gaining a small sense of normalcy.

I could still see the pain in each of my children's eyes, from the heartache of their grandmother's death and the pending divorce, even though they tried to hide it from me as much as I tried to hide my own pain from them the best I could.

Brandon has just graduated high school. I was so proud of him. He had looked around at some colleges and had a couple of offers from colleges for partial scholarships.

Although I begged him not to, he reluctantly turned them down. He said he didn't want to put a financial burden on me since I still had to pay a portion of the tuition.

So, he decided to do one year at our local community college and then maybe transfer to a four-year college. And, of course, I was thrilled to have him home with me for another year before heading off to a four-year college.

All of the teachers at the elementary, middle, and high schools always complimented me on how well-behaved, respectful, kind, and smart my children were.

I had always been so proud of each of them. And I knew that the traits and mannerisms they had were a result of the love and nurturing that my mother and I bestowed on them.

261

During the summer of 2009, I worked long hours every day so that I could make as much money as possible. When I wasn't working, I would take the children out for the day so we could do something fun and spend quality family time together.

I continued to work full-time; however, I didn't make the income that Mike did, so it left me strapped to pay the bills at times. Credit cards were my best friends and I always managed somehow to pull through. Mike wasn't willing to pay child support or help financially with the children until the courts forced him to.

I think it was because Mike was angry with me for wanting a divorce. He begged me not to go through with it. In his mind, he didn't want to give me any child support because he thought it was money in my pocket to start a new life.

Money that I was going to spend on myself and not the children. I just couldn't figure out why he would think that.

Perhaps, his own guilt with infidelity made him have stupid thoughts.

Chapter Fourteen

The Separation

We both hired attorneys. We had to go to mediations and as each month passed, we were both racking up attorney fees. He lived in our marital home as it was in foreclosure status and continued to bring random women into our home.

He also threatened me a few times that he was going to fight to get full custody of the children, but it was evident to me that none of the children wanted to be with him as they showed no interest when he attempted to stop by sometimes to see them. He must have been out of his mind if he thought I wasn't going to fight tooth and nail for full custody of our children.

Throughout the divorce process, we both were bitter with each other. We couldn't even agree on things when we sat down with the mediator. The whole process was difficult and exhausting for both of us.

I do believe he loved me in his own way. And I think he just couldn't believe he was losing his wife and children. He hated losing his family, no matter how dysfunctional he made it with his infidelity and emotional abuse toward the children and me.

Also, I feel like his behavior was the way it was because of certain people he was around and the women he was screwing around with. I think they made him feel like he was a great guy and that I was the worst spouse.

Mike spent his time as a single man while I picked up the pieces of my broken heart and had to play the role of both parents for my children. I had no interest in dating, as my only focus was the love, safety, and security of my children. Along with healing myself, I needed to work on myself. My failing marriage, emotions, my anger, my need to be in complete control of everything, my insistence on perfection with everything I did or touched, my constant sadness from not having my mother by my side, my scars from the molestation, and my fears and my weight gain.

I needed to learn to forgive myself and those who hurt me and to be the best version of myself, so I could be the best mother, hero, and role model for my own children. I just needed to figure out where to start.

I tried to make everything as smooth as I could for my children. I tried everything in my power to show them how much I love them and to provide them with stability.

Still, I felt like I wasn't doing enough for my children. I could clearly see that each of my children were still struggling with pain. More so, I could see it in Brandon. I was becoming more stressed and somewhat fearful of how he was acting. He just wasn't himself. I just couldn't figure out what was going on with him. What was I missing?

His appearance changed, and he became more distant. He wasn't happy. He talked about things that I found disturbing about religion. It was as though there was someone else in my son's body. I tried harder to smother him with more love and affection. I started watching him more closely. I would search his room, looking for anything to explain why his personality was changing, but I couldn't really find anything. Maybe, I had overlooked something.

As teenagers, I know kids can become distant from their parents and, sometimes, a bit rebellious. My children and I were always close, but something seemed off with Brandon.

He became increasingly distant and dark as each week passed. He just wanted to be left alone, didn't want to communicate with us, and didn't want to be around us. I could tell he was very depressed, and no matter how much I tried to encourage him to talk to me, he wouldn't. It broke my heart.

I was trying to cope with my separation and pending divorce, with being a single parent and the fear of not being the best at everything I had going on in my life at that moment, and it made me resentful and angry. The anger I had been holding inside for so many years was now working its way outward.

It was time for me to say goodbye to the days of stepping back and being afraid to speak up or fight for what was right. I needed to change.

I have always celebrated special days with each of my three children since they were little. Where I did a mother-son day out with Brandon, a day with Noah, and of course, I did a mother-daughter day out with Shelby. It was my way of letting each of them know I wanted to give them my undivided attention and do something fun exclusively with each of them alone.

But during that summer, nothing I said or suggested for Brandon and me to do for our mother-son day out interested him. He wanted to be alone, and I could tell he was in a dark place. I asked his friends if they had any information to offer so I could help my son, but they had nothing. I tried to give him some space, but I was at a loss for what to do. I snooped around in his room, looking for answers. I checked the computer again and tried to keep tabs on where he went or who he talked to.

I told him I didn't want him listening to certain kinds of music because I felt it was making him more depressed. I literally tried to smother him with so much love, affection, and attention. But nothing seemed to make a difference.

Then, in the middle of a hot August night, I was awakened by a phone call from the Frederick Memorial Hospital. Waking up from a deep sleep and groggy, I answered the phone. A woman on the other end asked for Sonia Domarasky.

I replied, *"This is she."*

Then the woman stated that my son was in the hospital, and I needed to come right away.

I immediately became alert and said, *"There must be some mistake. My children are all home and in bed. Is it my husband, Mike Domarasky, that is in the hospital?"*

The woman on the other end replied, *"No, mam. We have your son, Brandon Domarasky, here in the hospital. And you need to come as soon as possible."*

I darted from the family room of the basement, where I slept on the mattress, and ran to Brandon's bedroom next to the family room; he was not there.

Then I ran outside, and his car was gone, and that's when my heart sank.

I screamed on the phone, *Oh, my God! Oh, my God! Is he okay? Was it a car accident??*

The woman on the other end paused as if contemplating something, then said, *"He is alive. The doctor will explain when you arrive."*

Shelby and Noah were upstairs in their bedroom, asleep. I threw the phone down and ran upstairs to wake Shelby up. I told her I had to go to the hospital for Brandon and for her and Noah to not worry and go back to sleep.

I called my friend Amanda and asked her to come to the house to watch my children as I went to the hospital for Brandon. I left the door unlocked for her and drove to the hospital, speeding excessively. When I arrived, they told me that my son didn't want to see me. I felt extremely confused.

But at least I knew he was alive, and that's all that mattered. It was already hard to decipher what was actually going on. What had happened? Because he was still seventeen and wouldn't be eighteen until September, they had to allow me to go into his room.

But just as I walked in, my heart was crushed, shattered into a million pieces. I saw my son lying on the hospital bed in a gown; he looked broken. He didn't look like my strong, fun-loving, handsome, and athletic son.

I sat next to him, reached for his hand, and asked him what had happened. But he didn't want to talk about it. Then the doctor came in and wanted to check on him, and Brandon asked that I leave the room. I didn't want to leave, but I didn't want to upset him either, so I stepped outside the room, and when the doctor finished, I asked what had happened. That's when he told me that my son had been cutting himself and self-mutilating for months, probably close to two years.

He explained that this time, Brandon had cut himself too deep and was bleeding out. He said that he was apparently driving himself to the hospital when he became weak and pulled over on the side of the road because he couldn't drive any further. Thankfully, his friends from high school drove by, saw him, picked him up, put him in their car, and brought him to the hospital.

I was in a state of shock. I couldn't understand why. My mind was racing with various thoughts.

Why would he hurt himself? Why didn't I see it? What did I do or didn't do? Why didn't he come to me and talk to me?

I couldn't help but blame myself. But for right now, I just needed to be by his side and let him know that I loved him and that I was there for him and always would be.

267

The doctor told me they needed to keep him in the hospital for twenty-four hours under observation, and then they could release him. I walked back into the room with tears running down my face. I couldn't help it, but I flooded him with questions. I wanted to help him, but he didn't want to talk about it.

I begged him to show me what he had done, and reluctantly, with anger, he moved the gown from his legs, and there it was so many stitches and scars and blood. His leg looked mutilated.

This was my baby, my firstborn! I so badly wanted to take the hurt away from him and inflict it on myself. He was my precious child. My gift from God. I thought I was protecting him, but I had failed. All I could think was, I failed my mother and now my son? I tried so hard not to cry. I wanted to be strong for him. But there is no way to stop the tears when you see your child hurting and in pain.

I stayed in the room with him as he drifted in and out of sleep, rubbing his arm and holding his hand. I tried to think of everything I did so wrong that would make him want to cut himself so badly. There was no way I could sleep, and I didn't. I just held his hand and prayed to God to heal my son.

In the morning, I told him I had to go home to check on Shelby and Noah and that I would be right back. I hugged and kissed him, but he seemed to have no emotions. Not only did I want to check on the children and let them know how Brandon was doing, but I also needed to talk to Mike.

I thought, perhaps, as parents, he and I could come together to do whatever it took to help our son. This was devastating and frightening because we could have lost our son.

I drove back to my mother's and called Mike at work but was told he had taken the day off. So, I called our home phone in Charles Town but got no answer. Then I called his cell phone, and finally, he answered.

I told him we had a huge family issue and that one of our children had an urgent medical issue that needed our immediate attention and help. I didn't want to get into the details over the phone, but I told him it was extremely serious.

Then I offered to meet up in the next thirty minutes so we could talk and figure out the next steps to help and protect our child. I wanted to tell him everything in person and thought we could go to the hospital together for our son. He seemed annoyed with me and his response was that he was busy and that we could chat about it later. He said he would meet me at my mother's house in about three to four hours.

Frustrated with his response, I hung up the phone. Then, I changed my clothes, grabbed some clean clothes for Brandon, made sure Shelby and Noah were okay and fed, and then I drove to our home in Charles Town, WV, so I could talk with Mike in person, and we could go together to the hospital and be there for Brandon.

When I pulled into our driveway, I noticed an unfamiliar red truck in the driveway. I walked into our home and directly upstairs. But when I opened our bedroom door, there, in front of me, was my husband having sexual relations in our marital bed with another woman.

They both looked at me and snickered. My head was spinning, my heart sunk, it absolutely took my breath away. My home, my bed (the one my mother bought for us), my husband. It was the worst type of gut punch you could imagine. The vision of seeing your husband engaged in sex with another woman in your own bed. Every day, I was dealing with more pain mentally and emotionally. I was so enraged that for a split moment, I really thought I could kill them both. He was disgusting and she was a piece of trash. I just didn't know how much more I could take. I had such rage come over me.

Partially because of what I saw but mainly because of his lack of concern for our child and his life. I wanted help from him to help our child and he couldn't and wouldn't make time for it. They both absolutely sickened me.

But Mike wasn't my concern. My first priority was my son. As I stood in the doorway of my bedroom, paralyzed with fear for my son's life and so angry towards my husband, I felt some kind of divine intervention as though someone lifted me from under my armpits and escorted me down the stairs and into my car. I believe it was my mother. For several years, my mother had always said she couldn't understand where my anger was rooted from. Even as I walked down the stairs and left the house, he never attempted to stop me and ask what child has the medical emergency or what he could do to help.

My anger frightened my mother because she thought that one day, my anger would get the better of me, and I would do something horrible that I would regret later. Even in death, I believe she was still protecting the children and me.

I left the house and drove back to the hospital for Brandon. They released him later that day, and I was so happy to bring him home.

Around 7:00 pm that evening, Mike finally called me to see what was so important that I had to come to our house to talk to him. He didn't even ask me which child had the medical issue. I told him not to worry about it. That I was going to take care of everything.

Then he proceeded to accuse me of coming to our marital home because I wanted to see him have sex with another woman. All I could think was *"This man is demented and sick."* Words could not even describe the anger I felt toward him.

I told him he was a worthless father and a piece of shit and hung up the phone on him. At that point, he didn't deserve to know what was going on with any of our children. How could a father not immediately put his child's health and well-being ahead of himself or his own sexual desires?

From that point on, I realized that I was the only responsible parent our children needed.

The family bond that my children and I have is unmeasurable. Shelby and Noah were so heartbroken that their big brother was cutting himself. They both wanted to do everything they could to help him. I am sure, in their minds, they were just as confused and frightened as I was. They both looked up to their big brother.

A few days after Brandon was home, he ripped out his stitches. I couldn't understand why. I cried and begged him to let me help. I begged him to let me know what I could do to help. I was willing to do anything.

I was so terrified that I was going to lose my oldest son. How did our lives twist like this? I prayed every day, asking God for help. I called out of work and stayed home because I was afraid to leave Brandon alone. I basically wanted to be attached to him like glue. I thought then he would know how much I needed and loved him. But I don't think it mattered.

We would have the stitches put back in, and he would rip them out again. I was so terrified that he was going to kill himself intentionally or unintentionally. I had already lost my mother. There was no way I was going to lose my son too. If he died, it would absolutely kill me. Our family just couldn't bear any more pain.

Shelby and Noah were teenagers and should have been enjoying their summer, but instead, they wanted to protect their brother. The time I took off from work to monitor Brandon's every move made it seem as though we both were prisoners in the home that was built on love and great memories of my mother and me.

I couldn't sleep or eat because I was so worried. Shelby and Noah felt the same. We all lived in a constant state of fear and worry, not wanting to leave Brandon alone in the house. The three of us took turns every night staying up and keeping an eye on Brandon. Each night we would take two-to-three-hour shifts, sitting near his bedroom door and monitoring each time he went into the bathroom since that's where he had been cutting himself. Shelby decided to give up her spot as the cheerleading captain so she could be at home more to help me with watching and trying to protect her brother.

Noah also gave up his sports and time with friends to help. I was so proud of my children, the strong bond we had, and how much we cared and loved each other to be there and protect each other no matter what it took.

A few weeks later, in September 2009, the judge granted our divorce. He actually granted it a few weeks early upon my request, and he granted me full and sole custody of our children.

When my lawyer explained to the judge the circumstances of my request, with how Mike handled our son's medical issue, he was appalled at Mike's actions and lack of parenting.

In less than four years, I suffered the loss of my mother, the loss of my marriage, the loss of my marital home, and now, almost the loss of my son. I felt completely alone and lost. I had no one to lean on. I cried so much that not crying almost seemed abnormal.

I cried in my car, in the shower, at night in bed, and sometimes, I would just sit on the toilet and cry.

But I didn't want the children to see me cry. I didn't want them to worry and question why I was crying. I didn't want them to think I was weak and couldn't handle things. I knew I wasn't weak. I just had so much stress and burdens to carry.

I constantly prayed and asked God to help me. I asked mom to help and watch over us too. I had to keep telling myself that God only burdens you with how much he knows you can handle. So, I figured if God knew we could handle this, then we most certainly could and that better days would come ahead.

The children were relieved that the divorce was final and, of course, that I had full custody of them. They were angry at how their father treated me. Shelby wanted absolutely nothing to do with her father.

When he did stop by on occasion, she was very short and sarcastic with him. Mike tried to help Noah with homework after school sometimes, but each time, he yelled at Noah, calling him stupid for not figuring out a math equation, and then he would pound his fist on the table to the point where Noah had tears in his eyes and would start crying.

He was only twelve years old. It got so bad for Noah that he stopped coming home after school, went to his friend's house, and walked home later when he knew it was time for me to come home from work and his father had left.

Of course, I was unaware of it all until I called the house one day after school, and Brandon and Shelby told me Noah wasn't coming straight home from school. I called the school and everywhere looking for him.

I called all his friend's houses until I found him. That's when he finally told me why he was afraid to come home after school. Now, I was even madder at Mike. All he managed to do was push the children even further away from him. Brandon tried to stay somewhat neutral as I think he really just wanted, and hoped, to have a good father-and-son relationship.

Mike never knew how to carry a meaningful or good conversation with his children. He always managed to say things that upset the children because he had a sick sense of humor.

But his humor always embarrassed the children. Even their friends were put off by Mike's sense of humor.

Sometimes, I think it was not so much his sense of humor as it was his not caring about what we felt when he said stupid or hurtful things directed at us.

Over the course of the next year, I flooded Brandon with more and more attention and love. And finally, we started seeing a little bit of progress in him. Sometimes, I could see tiny sparks of happiness starting to shine through.

But Brandon still wasn't ready to tell me why he was cutting himself, and as much as I wanted to know and sometimes begged him to tell me, he assured me that in time, when he was ready, he would. Years later, he did open up to me about it.

The children never made an effort to reach out to their father, and it didn't take long for Mike to almost completely stop reaching out to them as well. He made it a point to not pay child support for Brandon since he was within months of turning eighteen when we separated.

He also stopped Shelby's child support early and made sure he ended Noah's on the exact day of his 18th birthday.

I asked him to help the children with college tuition and expenses for books, gas, or utilities while they were in college, but he made it very clear when he stated, *"They are not my problem."*

I tried to wrap my head around what kind of parent says their children are a problem or doesn't want to continue to help them in college or no matter what the situation is? It's no wonder why the children lost respect for their father. It was up to me to be their only parent who would do anything and everything for their well-being, happiness, and success as long as I was living and breathing.

The following year, in 2010, Shelby graduated from high school. In August, she enrolled for a year at the local community college and eventually transferred to a college on the eastern shore of Maryland.

I moved Brandon to Pittsburgh in an apartment so he could attend college there. I was proud of the progress he had made so far, yet still nervous having him so far away from me. I wasn't a hundred percent sure that he stopped cutting himself.

Till this point, he still hadn't opened up to me about why he started doing it, but I had to trust him and give him some space. I visited him every other weekend and did his laundry and grocery shopping and cleaned his apartment as any other mother would in my place.

I just couldn't cut the umbilical cord. Plus, for me, it was my way of seeing him, hugging my son, and feeling some sense of security that he was okay.

Noah was becoming a young man and was in the 8th grade. He was always so sweet and kind. I was thrilled to spend so much time with him, and he was my sidekick. I was so happy to have Shelby still at home during her first year at the community college.

I think we all were starting to heal. Every day, life became a little easier and happier for each of us.

Over the course of the next few years, lots of changes occurred. I focused on my mental and physical health, my own personal strength, my finances, my future, and the love, happiness, and prosperity of my children and our family. I realized what an incredibly strong woman I had become and that I could move any mountain when I put my mind to it.

I didn't need to remarry and was content with being a single woman. I was blessed and had such gratification with all the wonderful gifts God had given me. I didn't always see it, but he never left my side. He allowed me the time to learn to love myself and to stand up for myself. All three of my children were maturing into their own person and becoming wonderful adults.

Over time, Brandon fully recovered from his dark days of cutting himself. Each of my three children taught me things throughout the years. It's amazing what you learn from your children.

I always assumed I was the one teaching them. They brought me so much joy and happiness, and without a doubt, they were, are, and will always be my whole world.

I found out that my brother, Vazgen, his wife, and all of his children were moving here to the US and would be living in California.

I also found out that many other family members, such as cousins, aunts and uncles, and nieces and nephews, were also moving to California or had moved there recently. It was a great relief to know that I could see them more often.

In February 2011, I developed pre-cancerous cells and had to have a partial hysterectomy.

In September, I tore my ACL and meniscus and had to have knee surgery.

Then, on December 24th, I moved all three of my children to Georgia for a change of scenery and what I thought would be a fresh new start for our family, only to find out a few months later that the children and I missed our hometown, Brunswick, and moved back. I think, mentally, none of us were quite ready for the move.

Within a few months of our move back from Georgia, I purchased a brand-new home in Brunswick in July 2012. Life was flourishing for all of us.

In November, I started working out with a fantastic personal trainer named Chip, "The Animal," Gerber, and over the course of the next four years, I lost 150 lbs. He taught me so much about health and nutrition and was a mentor to me.

Shelby graduated college in 2014, and Noah graduated from high school in 2015.

In 2016 Brandon, Noah, and I participated in our first Tough Mudder™ in Pittsburgh, PA.

In 2017, Shelby got married, and I was honored to walk my daughter down the aisle. That same year, I participated in a half marathon. I felt like a new woman, being able to do the things that I couldn't do when I was so overweight for so many years of my marriage.

I found participating in these events was very therapeutic for me as it was a sense of releasing my anger and exchanging self-doubt for self-accomplishments. I loved the new, healthy, and happy me.

In 2018, Shelby and her husband gave me my first grandchild, a precious grandson, Callen. Later that summer, Shelby and I completed a Muddy Princess run as mother and daughter.

Then, in September, I went to California to visit my brother, sister-in-law, nieces, nephew, and many other family members. It was like a dream come true.

I wouldn't have to go back to Iran now, and it was just a plane ride to California to be with my brother. God really is great!

In 2019, I sold my home in Brunswick and moved to Sevierville, TN. I had always loved that area when we vacationed there when the children were younger, and it was a dream to live there.

I decided to move to Tennessee because it was time for me to do something in my life that was truly for me. I wanted to take time away to reflect on my life and how I could tell my story.

I wanted to take the time to write about my experiences and provide a written book as my legacy to my children so they could truly understand the trials and triumphs that their mothers had gone through.

To apologize to them and hope they understand that I tried to be the best mother who raised and protected them the best she could with her entire being.

When I came to Tennessee, I bought an authentic cabin and transformed it into a beautiful overnight rental cabin. I succeeded well at it and became a five-star host.

In August 2020, I studied to become a realtor and became licensed in the state of Tennessee in November.

In October 2020, I traveled back to California to visit my brother and family.

Brandon's career in mortgage financing was going well.

Noah became a first responder as a paid firefighter/EMT.

In 2021, Shelby and her husband gave me a second grandchild. My beautiful granddaughter, Sophie.

Shelby kept up with our mother-daughter tradition, with our first names starting with *S. Soon, Sonia, Shelby, and Sophie.*

About me, I spent my free time traveling back and forth from Tennessee, Maryland, Virginia, and Pennsylvania to visit all three of my children.

281

In March of 2022, I spent a week with my son Brandon at the home he and his girlfriend shared. I absolutely had the most wonderful time bonding and spending great quality time with my son. We even sat up until one in the morning on the couch talking. It was twofold because finally, after all these years, my son was ready and willing to open up to me about his dark and depressed days and to cut himself.

He proceeded to tell me his story. He explained that he was depressed from his grandmother's death, the constant bullying he was subjected to in school, having a girl that he liked, who started talking to some other guy, not feeling like he was good enough, the stress of the divorce, the constant fighting between Mike and I, the arguments that he and his sister would get into, the disagreements between him and I, the constant moving and then feeling like he had to step up and be the man of the house and protect me, Shelby and Noah.

For him, he felt emotionally overloaded and lost. It was too much for a sixteen-year-old boy to have to take on and endure. I think I knew he was dealing with the stress of the divorce, the arguing between his father and me, the financial issues, and that his grandmother's death still affected him, but I honestly had no idea my son felt like he had to be the man of the house, or for that matter, that he was being bullied in any way because he was so good at football and wrestling, his school work, and his teachers and coaches loved him. He explained that he held it all in, and eventually, it became too much to handle.

At the time, there was a huge surge in 'Emo and Goth' popularity, where kids were dressed in black, dying their hair black, using black makeup, and cutting themselves to release emotional stress. It was almost like it was the in-thing to do or be.

He said he didn't consider himself emo or goth, but after hearing so much talk about cutting one's self and how it could help relieve the emotional pains, he wanted to try it for himself because nothing else seemed to help.

He narrated that the first time he cut himself, he felt a sense of opening up and relieving the pain he had been enduring. Soon, it became an addiction for him, and he found reasons to cut. Each time he was at a boiling point, he would cut himself to relieve the pressure. He admitted that he never intended to kill himself, but if it did happen, then he was in a place in his mind where it was okay. He said he knows now how wrong it was and realizes now how it would have killed me too.

I choked up as I absorbed every word he said. In ways, it was like a dagger through my heart. But I truly understood every word he said about an emotional overload and wanting some relief.

I asked him if there were signs or something that I missed that he was cutting himself, so I could have gotten him help.

He then continued. "You didn't miss anything mom, I just hid it well."

All in all, that night was an extraordinary night. After years of waiting and I finally came to know the truth. I could tell Brandon was ready to talk about it, and I think it was a way for him to let go of the past as well. Perhaps, to forgive himself and me.

What I do know is that night brought us even closer as mother and son. *I felt so proud of him for opening up and honored that he shared everything with me.*

CHAPTER FIFTEEN

I AM A PROUD SURVIVOR

L ife has a strange way of teaching you things. I'd say what life taught me is how to be a survivor—a warrior! There are plenty of dark days in our lives. I don't think any of us are excluded from having them. But as each new day dawns, it's another day and another chance to learn, work and grow from those darkest days. It's never going to be easy to overcome trauma or tragedy, but little steps, little changes, little progresses will help and you will discover that you can prevail.

Now that I look back at life, I feel the most blessed to have a mother like my adoptive mother. Whatever I am today, and whatever I am to be, I believe it is because of her. I will always be proud to have a Korean heritage. And very proud to be an Armenian woman

Would I still be here if she hadn't saved me all those years ago? Would I still have achieved all the milestones that I have? Both my biological and my adopted mother are Angels in my life. If it wasn't for my biological mother, I wouldn't have come into this world.

And if it wasn't for my adopted mother, I would not be alive today. I feel like they are still watching over me.

The bond I had with my adoptive mother is absolutely incredible. I adamantly believe that she saved my life by choosing to adopt me from Iran, and I, without a doubt, know that I saved her life as well by succumbing to my adoptive father's mentally ill desires. I know I could keep my mother alive as long as I did what he wanted. There is nothing in this world I wouldn't have done for my mother.

She was my protector, my cheerleader, my supporter, my role model and so much more. She gave me unconditional love and taught me to be the best version of myself. She always looked at me as though I was the perfect child. No matter how hard her life was, she never considered placing me in foster care or an orphanage so she could escape and return to her family in Korea.

And the fact that she never wanted me to know that I was adopted just tells me that she never considered me adopted but rather as her own biological child. Mom and I, there was nothing that we didn't do together or talk about. We were literally joined at the hip.

Even though now she has passed away, there is not a day that goes by that I don't think of her, kiss her Urn or talk to her. I miss her more than words can ever describe—more than is probably considered ordinary.

Sometimes, I am just so amazed that she never considered just giving me away to foster care or an orphanage and returning to Korea. I told her to do that many times when I felt like life was difficult for her here in this country or to pack us both and move to Korea. But she wouldn't do it. She said she wanted the best life for me, and she felt the best life for me was here in the USA.

She represented so many things to me. She was a mother, father, brother, sister, aunt, uncle, grandparent, and best friend, all rolled into that tiny petite Korean stature. She was and is my everything.

God brought us together because he knew how much we needed each other.

My mother was a very strong-willed woman. She was, without a doubt, my hero. There was nothing that she could not overcome. This was a woman who lost her father at the age of nine, had to help raise her siblings, overcome an abusive marriage, fight doctors not to amputate her leg after a tragic car accident, learn to walk again, learn multiple foreign languages and overcome racism in the early '70s and through the '80s, all while raising a daughter as a single parent and building a new home for us. That's why she's my hero, my role model, and my inspiration for why I can do anything I set my mind to, simply because my mother taught me so.

She had the biggest heart anyone could have. She was my God-given protector, my angel, and *my mother*.

She raised me with the traditional Korean customs and was very stern. She taught me that I could break down any obstacle in life, knock down any brick wall, or move Mount Everest to achieve whatever goal my heart was set on. Afterall, I watched her do it so I knew I could too.

287

She raised me to be strong, tough, smart, and never procrastinate. That education was extremely important, to be passionate about my dreams and follow through, to be respectful to my mother and my elders, and to help others if I could. My mother loved to help people, and she loved cooking and sharing the foods she cooked with the neighbors and her friends.

Everyone knew of my mother's *'almost famous'* Korean eggrolls. It was our mother/daughter tradition to make those eggrolls several times a year, especially on Christmas. She would pass them out to the neighbors throughout the year and as Christmas gifts. She also gave eggrolls to her co-workers and my children's teachers. Soon everyone started requesting that she take orders and charge by the dozen for her delicious eggrolls. So, that's why we even started taking orders that required us to make anywhere from a thousand to two thousand eggrolls.

Every person who ever had the chance to taste them begged her for more. They wanted the recipe, and they wanted to order dozens of eggrolls from my mother. She never gave the recipe out, but she made more, and people paid her for our delicious Korean eggrolls.

But yes, my mother did hand me down her secret recipe for those eggrolls. And what an honor that was.

We turned that mother & daughter tradition into a three-generation tradition as my children (her grandchildren) also joined in making the eggrolls from a very young age. Although sometimes, my children would eat them faster than we could make them just as they came out of the deep fryer.

Until my mother died, we made those eggrolls several times a year. And, of course, my children were right there with their mother and grandmother, making them and distributing them to the neighbors, their teachers, and their friends.

Even though my mom passed away, my children and I still carry on my mother's legacy of making those special Korean eggrolls. We gather several times a year and make about five hundred each time. And yes, we pass them out to the neighbors, friends, and teachers. And to honor my mother, we still say they are Ms. Lee's eggrolls because, after all, they are her recipe and made with love from her daughter and grandchildren.

She always ate very healthily. She was never really into junk food or soda. She exercised every day by walking and doing yoga-style stretches. She was a hard worker and dedicated to her job. She worked for over twenty-three years at State Farm Insurance Company where she retired from.

She was one of the Deacons of the Korean Baptist Church and was also in the choir. Being in the choir and bringing people closer to Jesus was something that brought her happiness. She was tiny but mighty. She always said her daughter—me—and her three grandchildren were her life. There was nothing she would not do for us. And she did spoil us. She was not only my hero but my world, my heart, and my soul. I certainly would not be the woman I am today without the undying love, support, and guidance she gave to the children and me.

My mother was such a huge help with helping to raise my children. We were always together and always doing everything together. My mother's life was dedicated to God, me, my husband, and our children—her grandchildren.

I have always loved being a mother. It was and is one of the best things I have ever accomplished in my life. My children are my pride. They bring me so much joy and love. They have taught me so much. I want to give them the world. I want to shield them and protect them. They will tell you that I was extremely overly protective of them growing up. They will tell you that I was very involved in all their school activities and sports.

I can move mountains for my children. I may have been hard on them at times, but I always did everything for them to help them flourish, grow and become strong and independent. I am still very close with my children. Nothing can ever keep us apart.

My oldest son, Brandon, is very strong-minded. He is so handsome. He is 5'11, has dark brownish-black hair and brown eyes, and usually always has a beard and mustache. He has a beautiful smile with beautiful teeth and a sleeve of tattoos on both arms.

He has the looks of a middle eastern man from Armenia. He definitely looks like a mix of his father and me both.

He has such determination and accomplishes anything he sets his mind to. He is so much like me. He is brilliant. He is all about doing research and fact-finding. He will debate anyone all day about something he is passionate about, and of course, with his fact-finding and research in tow.

He has a heart of gold and will do anything to help someone. He is a family-oriented guy. He treats me like a queen. He is a calm person; it takes a lot to make him angry, but if he reaches that point, he is a force to be reckoned with. He loves his sports. He played football all through high school and did wrestling in his junior and senior years. He has always diligently worked out in the gym and stays fit.

My daughter, Shelby, is beautiful. She has the looks of a model. She is 5'5 and has naturally dark brown hair and brown eyes. She also looks like a mix of her father and I both, and carries the features of a beautiful woman from the middle east with her beautiful smile and her pretty eyes.

She is so strong-minded and such a go-getter. She is just like me in so many ways. She will be the first to speak her mind and speak up if she disagrees or is passionate about something.

At times, she can be confrontational when it involves the safety or well-being of her family. Pretty sure she gets that from me as well. She is a wonderful mother to my two beautiful grandchildren.

She also doesn't let anything stand in her way. No matter what life throws at her, she is a fighter, and she conquers it all. She takes great care of her body and exercises every single day.

My youngest son—my baby—Noah, has the kindest heart and soul. He is so handsome, standing at 6'0, and has brown hair and brown eyes. He looks so much more like me with very few features of his father.

He has a gorgeous smile and the kindest eyes. He is so sweet, loves to make you laugh, is a jokester, has a very calming and peaceful tone to his voice, and would do anything for his family. He is very much a family-oriented man. He is like a mediator; he always wants to help resolve any issues.

He is the first to be there any time his family needs him. There is nothing he wouldn't do in a heartbeat for us all. He, too, treats me like a queen, like his older brother.

If I even mention I need help with anything technical, he is on it right away. If he even detects the slightest change in the tone of my voice, he becomes worried, questioning if I am okay and what's going on because he wants to fix it.

His heart of gold makes him an incredibly sweet, caring, and sincere man. He is a calm person, and he often wears his heart on his sleeve.

He has taken the sibling abuse from his brother and sister as the baby of the family, like most kids that are the youngest in the family, and yet, he has grown into a man that can dish it back with a smile.

He loves his sports as well. He loves football and has a passion for ice hockey. He did some sports in high school, but his favorite has always been being on the ice hockey team. Even now, as an adult, he still manages to make time to play in the adult ice hockey league.

I am a proud mother because of the man he is and because my son puts his life on the line every day as a Paid Firefighter and EMT.

Sometimes, he underestimates himself, but he always pulls through with flying colors because he has more strength than he even realizes.

It takes a lot to make him angry, but when he reaches that point, he, too, is a force to be reckoned with.

My relationship with all my children is wonderful. We are all very close, and I love and respect the adult version of what they have become, and I couldn't be any prouder of each of them. They are my pride and joy, my life, my soul, and my legacy. *What a great gift God has given me!*

Although I have traveled most paths life has to offer, I still cannot forget about my childhood trauma. Sure, it's a distant memory now, a memory that sometimes creeps in, but that's when I see the warrior and survivor in me.

All of these so-called issues are not flaws, they are my badges each and every one of them because I earned them through the many challenges and traumas that made me a survivor.

Sometimes now I am asked, why I never told my mother about what my dad did when I became an adult. I look at it this way, if you are given the opportunity to save someone's life, and you save it, you don't tell them what you had to endure to save them and assume the role that you are the victim. You do it because you love that person or because it's the type of person you are to want to help or save someone.

I never wanted my mother to feel I had to sacrifice anything for her. I wanted her to know I would do anything for her because I love her. The various traumatic experiences and finding out about my adoption, have moulded me into a persistent, determined, strong-minded, competitive, and overprotective woman.

Instead of thinking of myself as cursed or a victim, now I choose to believe I am blessed. Instead of allowing this to take the joy out of my life, I choose to live my life to the fullest. If I didn't stop letting myself be the victim and dwell on it, then I am still allowing those men to hurt and control me. I have too much love to give and a long life to live to allow that anymore.

But as I have gotten older, I have forgiven my adoptive father for what he did, but I won't forget. As crazy as that sounds, I have learned to find some positives in the situation.

I have learned to thank my adoptive father for allowing my mother to persuade him to adopt me from Iran. Without his agreement, I would have been left in Iran, a third-world country, and possibly may not have lived too long in the condition I was in when my adoptive mother found me. I wouldn't have had the awesome mother that I had, and I wouldn't have had the amazing bond my mother and I created. I wouldn't have a Korean Culture upbringing that I absolutely adore. I wouldn't have become a US Citizen. I wouldn't have had a good education or the opportunity to marry who I wanted. I wouldn't have the freedoms in Iran that I have in the US. I wouldn't have had all the great experiences that I did with my mother's friends, or the schools, or boyfriends and girlfriends that I have had the pleasure of having in my life. And most importantly, I wouldn't have the children I have today.

So, I thank him for saying yes. I don't hate him; I hate his illness. I have learned to accept what he did. I understand that he did really love me as his daughter and that it was truly his mental illness that caused him to do what he did.

Although God took my biological mother early, he gave me the very best adoptive mother in the world. And although both of my mothers have now passed away, I know they are both together, watching over me and protecting me. By the grace of God, my entire life and all the events have been a blessing. I am a survivor of child molestation—the key word being a *survivor.*

Over time, I have overcome so many obstacles and traumas in my life. All of them have made me the person I am. Smart, strong, independent, confident, determined, loyal, compassionate, and faithful.

During those years after my divorce, when I truly had no one else to lean on, I realized life is what you make of it. You can allow yourself to be a victim, or find within yourself the strength to try each day to find one small positive thing about the situation and one thing you can do to overcome it and in time you will become a survivor if not, you will become a prisoner within yourself. It's easy to allow yourself to go into a deep dark place. I learned that, too, from my son Brandon. Try to find some positives out of it. Whatever your traumas are, just know that you are alive because you are strong and you are a survivor and in time you will be okay.

Telling myself that I was a victim took away my freedom to speak up for myself. It took away my confidence and my will, and it almost destroyed me. We always have a choice. We can choose to be destroyed, bitter or angry from events in our lives that have traumatized us, or we can even be a puppet to fears and anxiety, but if we can find within ourselves the inner strength to face our traumas head-on, little by little, day by day we can start to release it.

Me? I chose to be in control and fought to let it all go. It wasn't easy and it took time. Years as a matter of fact. Somedays are great, other days not so much. But I did it on my terms and my way. I am not perfect, none of us are. I will always have those scars, it's part of who I am. I am a survivor of my traumas and I am okay. I found ways to occupy my mind and those horrid thoughts and flashbacks that would so often push their way through. I chose to focus on my weight loss, lifting weights and pushing my body through challenges such as the marathon, half marathon, Tough Mudder™, and so on. Because for me, it was only two things. My body and my mind that I could control.

Moving forward, I wanted to have complete control of both because, then, I had nothing to hold me back from being the best version of myself. Life's experiences moulded me, but it is up to me to decide what shape I allow it to leave me in. That's when I knew I could accomplish anything.

I forgave my biological father for discarding me like I was nothing and chose to look at the positive that he gave me a better life, I forgave my adoptive father for what he did to my mother and me. Forgiving him has helped me cope with and deal with a lot of issues that I have had. I also forgave Mr. Lee for what he did. I forgive myself for being too afraid to speak up and tell my mother, teachers, or police officers what I was forced to do.

I forgive myself for not being with my mother on the day she died.

I forgave Mike for the way he treated me at times. I forgave myself for the things I allowed my children to know about my divorce from their father.

Now, by letting everything go with forgiveness, I can stop looking at the scars so negatively but rather as a medal for the triumph of my strength and courage.

I will never forget them of course, because each experience made me realize the strength I have within to conquer those traumatic events, but now if by me telling my story and sharing my experience can help even one person then, I feel like I have come full circle. No two people are the same and none of us will truly experience life the same way. We all process love, happiness and traumatic events in our lives differently. And although one person's traumatic events may be more severe than another, we own our experiences. Don't ever deny that or let anyone trivialize what you have gone through. No matter how we seek to work on overcoming our traumatic events in life, whether we choose to do it on our own or seek professional help there is no wrong way. Be proud of every accomplishment you make in your own self recovery and survival. I have many more years of life and happiness to experience, so why waste it on being a victim of the past.

I firmly believe that God puts people in your life for a reason. God knew I needed an angel and a hero with so much love to give, so he gave me my mother, Soon Nam Lee.

I was blessed to have her with me for thirty-eight years, and I learned so much from her. As I continue to age, there isn't a day that goes by that I am not reminded of her in some way.

God brought Mike and me together to have beautiful children and to help me find my biological family. I thank God and my mother for the strength that I have and the woman that I am.

No matter how many times I almost drowned, I always managed to swim back to the surface. For which I am proud of myself. I made it through my traumatic experiences, and this is my story.

I am a survivor—and I am okay.

THANK YOU

Writing an autobiography about my childhood trauma, my adoption, love and loss, and my survival has been therapeutic in many ways.

Thank you for opening your hearts to reading and understanding the traumas that affected me.

None of us have a perfect life, but the life we have is perfect for us. Because that is the life we were meant to live. There is a purpose in each of our lives. We can learn from each other.

Never take your life for granted! No matter what tragedy or fortune you experience, embrace it and become a better, stronger version of yourself because of it.

www.ingramcontent.com/pod-product-compliance
Lightning Source LLC
Chambersburg PA
CBHW051507120626
46551CB00012B/807